W9-CHC-965

SHAKESPEARE
AND THE SUPERNATURAL

SHAKESPEARE

AND THE SUPERNATURAL

by

CUMBERLAND CLARK

*Shakespearean Lecturer, Vice-President of the Shakespeare Reading
Society, and Author of "Shakespeare and Science," "Shakespeare
and National Character," "A Study of 'Hamlet,'" "A Study
of 'Macbeth,'" "A Study of the 'Merchant of Venice,'"
"A Study of 'Julius Cæsar,'" "The Eternal
Shakespeare," etc., etc.*

HASKELL HOUSE PUBLISHERS Ltd.

Publishers of Scarce Scholarly Books

NEW YORK, N. Y. 10012

1971

First Published 1931

AAK 4893

HASKELL HOUSE PUBLISHERS Ltd.
Publishers of Scarce Scholarly Books
280 LAFAYETTE STREET
NEW YORK. N. Y. 10012

Library of Congress Catalog Card Number: 72-92957

Standard Book Number 8383-0966-6

Printed in the United States of America

CONTENTS

BIBLIOGRAPHY

A Literary History of the English People—J. J. Jusserand.

An Essay on the Writings and Genius of Shakespeare—Mrs. Montagu.

An Italian Psychologist's Studies in Shakespeare.

Characters of Shakespeare's Plays—W. Hazlitt.

Conduct and the Supernatural—L. S. Thornton.

Coleridge's Shakespearean Criticism—T. M. Raysor.

God in Shakespeare—Clelia.

Schlegel's "Werke"—E. Bocking.

Shakespeare—W. M. Alden.

Shakespeare—John Bailey.

Shakespeare—John Masefield.

Shakespeare and the Bible—Rev. T. R. Eaton.

Shakespeare: His Inner Life—J. A. Heraud.

Shakespeare and Holy Scripture—T. Carter.

Shakespeare and Music—Ed. W. Naylor.

Shakespeare, Puritan and Recusant—T. Carter.

Shakespeare Sermons—Rev. George Arbuthnot.

Shakespeare and Spiritual Life—John Masefield.

Shakespeare Studies—Edgar I. Fripp.

Shakespeare and the Supernatural—Margaret Lucy.

Shakespeare, Truth, and Tradition—J. Semple Smart.

Shakespeare's Books—H. R. D. Anders.

Shakespeare's England

    (a) Folk-lore and Superstition—H. Littledale.

    (b) Religion—Rev. Ronald Bayne.

Shakespeare's Haunts—Edgar I. Fripp.

Shakespeare's Knowledge and Use of the Bible—Bishop Wordsworth.

Shakespeare's Stratford—Edgar I. Fripp.

Shakespeare's Use of Song—Richmond Noble.

Shakespeare's Use of the Supernatural—Paul Gibson.

Studies in Shakespeare—Mary A. Woods.

The Elizabethan Fairies—Minor White Latham.

The English Drama in the Age of Shakespeare—W. Creizenach.

The Genuine in Shakespeare—J. M. Robertson.

The Higher Teaching of Shakespeare—L. H. Victory.

The Life and Poetry of W. Shakespeare—Rev. G. Gilfillan.

The Religion of Shakespeare—H. S. Bowden.

The Religion of Shakespeare—H. C. Beeching.

The Supernatural in Shakespeare—Helen Hinton Stewart.

The Wheel of Life—G. Wilson Knight.

They say miracles are past; and we have our philosophical persons, to make modern and familiar, things supernatural and causeless.

All's Well, II. 3.

This supernatural soliciting
Cannot be ill; cannot be good: if ill,
Why hath it given me earnest of success,
Commencing in a truth?

Macbeth, I. 3.

PREFACE

The Supernatural, as generally understood, includes all those phenomena which cannot be explained by the known and accepted laws of Natural Science. It is from supernatural "fictions and inventions," according to Mrs. Montagu,[1] that "Poetry derives its highest distinction, and from whence it first assumed its pretensions to divine inspiration, and appeared the associate of Religion." The ancient poet was permitted to assume a familiarity towards the pagan gods that would in these enlightened days of Christianity appear impious and sacrilegious. He would describe their natures, transmit their counsel, praise their virtues, and condemn their vices, without being thought presumptuous or profane. As religion became more sacred and revered, the poet found himself barred from freedom of expression on the creed and doctrine of the powerful and organized churches, and restricted to the world of tradition, folk-lore, and superstition. Towards religious supernaturalism he adopted an uncritical, conforming attitude, while towards superstition he retained his right to give free rein to his imagination, to criticize, repudiate, or confirm, as his artistic talent or literary expediency dictated.

This is exactly the position adopted by Shakespeare. He approaches the teachings of Christianity with an air of reverent acceptance. He repeats the very language of the Church. He never questions its tenets, and only reveals his individual religious thought in a remarkable tolerance towards all sects and creeds. This is all the more wonderful when we remember

[1] *An Essay on the Writings and Genius of Shakespeare*, p. 135.

that he lived in a time of fierce religious controversy. Yet so impartial did he remain amid all the bitterness and persecution that he has been claimed as Roman Catholic, Puritan, and orthodox Protestant in turn, by people who have failed to realize that his deep-seated humanity transcended all forms and dogma.

Coleridge called religion the poetry of all mankind, and said that we should not wonder that it had pleased Providence to reveal to us the divinest truths of religion in the form of poetry.[1] Religion and poetry, he declared, had a similar effect upon man, aiding his imagination, spurring him to self-improvement, and causing him to think less of self and more of his fellow-beings. He asserted that an undevout poet—that is, a true poet as opposed to a mere verse-maker —is insane; in fact, an impossibility. All that we know and feel about Shakespeare is a full endorsement of this dictum of Coleridge.

Shakespeare's thought on spiritual things must always be considered separately from that branch of the Supernatural that comes under the heading of vulgar superstition. The present book is therefore divided into two parts, which permit us to explore fully, firstly, the Poet's opinion on, and dramatic use of, the popular beliefs of his day, and secondly, his purely religious thought.

In studying the works of Shakespeare from the point of view of superstition, we find that his age commonly attributed to the agency of the spirit-world effects for which a reasonable and intelligible explanation has now been found. Particularly is this so in the field of astronomy, where the ignorance of the causes of

[1] See *Coleridge's Shakespearean Criticism* (T. M. Raysor), II. 147–148, 205.

eclipses, comets, meteors, and seeming disturbances in the heavens afforded the astrologers an opportunity to impose upon the credulous such theories as planetary influence.

There are to-day many who still believe in the interference of inimical supernatural powers with human existence. There is no doubt that men and women have experiences which cannot be explained by any known scientific process. These experiences are classed as supernatural, and will be so classed, until science has made further progress and discovery, particularly in the realm of the mind.

In Shakespeare's day superstitious supernaturalism took the form of witches, ghosts, fairies, demons, prophecy, divination, dreams, and astrology. Some of these beliefs still linger, although their disciples are comparatively few. No one, however, would dare to say that superstition is dead. The many meaningless habits still practised to appease the little god of ill-luck are proof that it is very much alive. It has only changed its form, because education and science have driven it from its old strongholds.

The Elizabethans were a generation particularly given to mysticism. A survey of their many extravagant beliefs occupies a chapter of its own in this study. Shakespeare was susceptible as a youth to the influences around him. When he had raised himself by observation, application, and learning above the common herd, many of his childhood's notions were exploded. As a popular dramatist, however, he found himself compelled to introduce into his plays numerous superstitions which to his own mind were nonsense. It was one of the sure canons of success. Few theatrical spectacles were more highly appreciated.

Most of the masques, which were interpolated into plays of the period to satisfy a love of pageantry, dealt with the Supernatural.

Sometimes Shakespeare was compelled against his will to incorporate something of a transcendental nature when writing a play for presentation at Court or elsewhere. More often he realized the immense dramatic value of ghosts, witches, fairies, and spirits, and used them with enthusiasm. But Shakespeare was not usually content to portray the creations of coarse superstition. He gave his immortals a meaning of their own, and invested them with a dignity and impressiveness of which lesser playwrights were incapable.

Shakespeare has something of metaphysical flavour in at least half of his plays; but there are four dramas that deal prominently with this fascinating subject. They are *Midsummer Night's Dream*, *Hamlet*, *Macbeth*, and *The Tempest*. These four plays were written when his approximate age was, respectively, 29, 37, 41, and 47. They reveal, therefore, the Poet's attitude towards the Supernatural at different points in his working career.

This attitude varied considerably. It began in his youth as one of light-hearted, amused tolerance, changed to one of serious meditation, darkened to pessimism and apprehension, and finally emerged into a renewed faith and confidence in good. This development is traced by a particular examination of the four above-mentioned pieces, which we may call, for our present convenience, the supernatural plays.

The active intervention of the Unseen World is not confined to these four dramas. We have already stated that half of Shakespeare's works contain some notice or other of the immortal and superhuman. Most prominent of these are *Julius Cæsar* and *Richard III*, which are reviewed in chapters of their own. The other plays, in which there is a brief and relatively unimportant mention of the Supernatural, are considered in chronological order in a final chapter in order to make the study as complete and useful as possible.

The study of Shakespeare and Religion (Part II of the book) commences with a review of the advance of Protestantism during the reign of Elizabeth. I have then proceeded to examine in detail all the evidence available that helps us to decide the much-disputed question as to which particular religious body Shakespeare himself belonged. It seemed to me essential to commence with a full investigation into the religion of his father, John Shakespeare, in order to discover the influences surrounding the Poet's boyhood. Following that, the three great divisions—Roman Catholicism, Puritanism, and orthodox Protestantism—with the Poet's attitude towards each as far as we can ascertain it, are fully set forth. His ready acceptance of Christian doctrine, his attitude towards church ritual and observances, and his extensive knowledge and use of the Bible, prove that his religion was something real and important to him, Nevertheless, it is obvious that creed and dogma, rite and ceremony, were not the things that held his loyalty. For this reason his own ethical philosophy is considered in a chapter of its own. Finally, a review of all the clerical characters of Shakespeare—the Cardinals and Bishops, Friars and Parish Priests—gives, I hope, an added interest and value to the book.

I append a list of authorities I have consulted and gratefully acknowledge the help derived therefrom. I have tried in all cases to give credit to the originator of new discoveries and points of criticism.

CUMBERLAND CLARK

PART I

SHAKESPEARE AND SUPERSTITION

I

ELIZABETHAN SUPERSTITION

WHAT may be termed the prestige of the Supernatural must be at its highest in an age as permeated with superstition as the Elizabethan. In Shakespeare's England the almost universal belief in the presence and power of the Unseen touched national life at every point. Customs were formed by it. Conduct was dictated by it. It was more powerful than sovereign or feudal lord to exact implicit obedience from the mass of the people. Nor was superstitious credulity limited to those who were ignorant and illiterate. All classes were beneath its spell from the nobles of the Court to the vagabonds.

Knowledge is generally recognized as the arch-enemy of superstition. The army of impossible and exploded beliefs is supposed to beat a hasty retreat before the advance of education. But in actual fact the battle is not nearly so one-sided as is commonly reported. Superstition dies hard. Indeed, it will never be wholly obliterated until science has left no mysteries to be explored. And "of that day and hour knoweth no man."

Thus it is that, even in these days which we are pleased to call enlightened, we have still our superstitions, and well-entrenched superstitions too, each with its band of simple and submissive disciples. Palmists flourish and coin money; and direct descendants of the astrologers and star-gazers of old have their deluded following. Séances, mediums, fortune-telling, divination, and other superstitious, and often unscrupulous, practices exist side by side with honest investigation into psychical phenomena. Rogues make fortunes out of a credulousness that seems properly to belong to the Dark Ages. People of all types and station carry mascots to bring them good fortune or to perform the protective office of the ancient witch-charms. In feats of daring, in sporting contests, even on the bonnet of the latest type of touring motor-cars, these ridiculous relics of superstition can be seen. Men and women, otherwise apparently in a state of mental sanity, have a horror of spilling salt, walking under ladders, sitting down thirteen at a table, or commencing a new enterprise on a Friday. There are superstitions connected with certain days of the year, with seasons and festivals, with birth, marriage, and death, with occupations and journeys, with names, colours, animals, birds—in short, with every activity and experience of human life.

If in these days of universal education, when the portals of the palace of knowledge are open wide to all comers, superstition can exercise so powerful an influence over thought and action, the extent of its hold upon the Elizabethans, when culture was reserved for the very few, can be imagined. It is hardly too much to say that it governed the people's lives down to the smallest details. Certain of the advanced religious reformers attempted to stamp out the grosser beliefs by explanation and instruction. But their campaign of suppression met with little success. Nor is it difficult to understand why, when we remember that those who enjoyed all the educational advantages that offered were themselves reluctant to shed the old fears and convictions.

Sceptics and doubters there were, for it was an age

which saw the beginnings of what are to-day established sciences. The Copernican school of astronomy
was questioning, though weakly, the rule of the
astrologers; and the pioneers of chemistry were
challenging the claims of the alchemists. Against
them, however, was ranged the stubborn conservatism
of many whom we should expect to know better. It
is surprising to find Queen Elizabeth consulting the
astrologers as to the most propitious date for her
coronation. It is astonishing to find Reginald Scot—
that sane, rational, and discerning writer, who attacked
the prevalent dread of witches, ghosts, and goblins
—opposed, and vehemently, by no less a person than
King James, himself a firm believer in demonology.
Even Oliver Cromwell, who could not be accused of
lack of progressive ideas, did not hesitate to employ
the astrologer, William Lilly, for the advancement
of his cause among the people. Aristocrats were as
much in the toils of beliefs of the nature of planetary
influence as were the plebeians. Few of the nobles of
Court circles omitted to have their horoscope read.
All were equally apprehensive as to the effects of
unusual phenomena in the heavens. The fruits of
scientific research made slow headway against this
mass of rock-like superstition.

A few progressive thinkers did, it is true, attempt to
sweep away theories which they had proved to have
no scientific foundation. Men like Reginald Scot
(already mentioned) were not afraid to assail cherished
beliefs. Bishop Hall is a typical example of those
Church reformers who attempted to free religion
from harmful superstition. Ben Jonson, again, exposed
the fraudulent practices of the alchemists, who existed
on foolish credulity alone. But some of the scientists

adopted an attitude of extreme tolerance towards ideas they knew to be nonsense. They did so for the sake of the investigations in which they were interested. Dry, scientific fact did not of itself win that support and help, without which progress was impossible. Colourful superstition, mystery, and occultism focused the necessary interest which made development practicable. Astronomy is the most striking example of this. Wonderful discoveries had been made in this field which revolutionized all previous knowledge. It was the age of Copernicus, Kepler, and Galileo. Yet these great men made no direct attempt to overthrow the astrologers; and Kepler himself gives the reason when he writes, "Astrology is the foolish daughter of a wise mother, and for one hundred years past this wise mother could not have lived without the help of her foolish daughter."

When the wealthy and educated were almost as much the slaves of superstition as the poor and illiterate, when scientists were compelled in the interests of their sciences to tolerate the most extravagant beliefs, when it required courage of the first order to strike a blow for reason and common sense, superstition found no difficulty in maintaining its position as the common interpreter of the experiences of life. Particularly was this so in the realm of natural phenomena. In my book, *Shakespeare and Science*, I have dealt fully with this aspect of Elizabethan thought. I have shown how the lives of men and women were supposed to be influenced by the star under which they were born; I have described with what terror any break in the celestial order was viewed, how comets were held to foretell the death of kings, and meteors and shooting-stars were thought to be the messengers of evil; I have related how eclipses of the sun and moon were regarded with awe and misgiving, frightening the wicked into repentance and sobering for a time the pleasures of a licentious age. It was believed that in all these phenomena supernatural agencies were at work, which were for the most part inimical to mankind's happiness and prosperity. Some scholars attribute the gloom and pessimism, in which the Supernatural is generally shrouded, to the enduring influence of the old Druidical worship and the despondence inherited from the Celtic bards.

The mass of folk-lore, which entwined itself around the lives of the Elizabethans like a prolific weed in an untended garden, is not properly within the scope of a study of "Shakespeare and the Supernatural" except in so far as it illustrates the undisputed reign of superstition. Natural history was in its toils; and there were popular beliefs to explain the habits and appearance of animals, birds, fishes, and planets. There were curious ideas about diseases, with weird directions for their cure. Old wives' tales, children's games, stories of giants and the like, contained much that was very ancient tradition. There were the strangest beliefs about courtship and marriage, the birth and rearing of children, old age, and death. All these superstitions, and many others like them, covering every phase of life, were handed down from generation to generation by word of mouth and implicitly believed by the country folk.

The extent to which the average mind was overshadowed by superstitious fears is described by Reginald Scot: "In our childhood our mothers maides have so terrified us with an oughlie divell having hornes on his head, fier in his mouth, and a taile in his breech, eies like a bason, fanges like a dog, clawes like a beare, a skin like a Niger, and a voice roaring like a lion, whereby we start and are afraid when we heare one cry Bough: and they have so fraied us with bull beggers, spirits, witches, urchens, elves, hags, fairies, satyrs, pans, faunes, sylens, kit with the cansticke, tritons, centaurs, dwarfes, giants, imps, calcars, conjurors, nymphes, changlings, Incubus, Robin goodfellowe, the spoorne, the mare, the man in the oke, the hellwaine, the fierdrake, the puckle, Tom thombe, hob gobblin, Tom tumbler, boneles, and such other bugs, that we are afraid of our own shadowes: in so much as some never feare the divell, but in a dark night; and then a polled sheepe is a perillous beast, and manie times is taken for our fathers soule, speciallie in a churchyard, where a right hardie man heretofore scant durst passe by night, but his haire would stand upright."

From this bold writer's protest against frightening the child mind with all these stupid tales of devils, witches, and goblins, we can pass profitably to the biting satire upon inveterate superstitious beliefs which Bishop Hall pens in his *Characters*: "Superstition is godlesse religion, devout impietie. The superstitious is fond in observation, servile in fear. . . . The man dares not stirre forth till his breast be crossed, and his face sprinkled: if but an hare crosse him the way, he returnes; or if his journey began unawares on the dismall (i.e. unlucky) day; or if he stumble at the threshold. If he see a snake unkilled, he feares a mischiefe; if the salt fall towards him, he lookes pale and red, and is not quiet till one of the waiters have powred wine on his lappe; and when he neezeth, thinks them not his friends that uncover not. In the

morning he listens whether the Crow crieth even or
odd, and by that token pressages of the weather. If
he heare but a Raven croke from the next roofe, he
makes his will, or if a Bittour flie over his head by
night: but if his troubled fancie shall second his
thoughts with the dreame of a fairie garden, or greene
rushes, or the salutation of a dead friend, he takes
leave of the world, and sayes he cannot live. He will
never set to sea but on a Sunday; neither ever goes
without an Erra Pater (i.e. an almanac marking the
lucky and unlucky days) in his pocket. Saint Paul's
day and Saint Swithune's with the Twelve, are his
Oracles; which he dares believe against the Al-
manacke. . . . Old wives and starres are his counsellors;
his night-spell is his guard, and charmes his Physicians.
He wears Paracelsian Characters for the toothach,
and a little hallowed waxe is his Antidote for all
evils. . . . Some wayes he will not goe, and some he
dares not; either there are bugges, or he faineth them;
every lantern is a ghost, and every noise is of chaines.
He knowes not why, but his custome is to goe a little
about, and to leave the Crosse still on the right hand."

Of all the forms which belief in the Supernatural
took in Elizabethan times, perhaps none is so strange
and so interesting to us to-day as witchcraft. Probably
the reason is that here we have a superstition which
is now dead. Unlike other beliefs which linger on in
strange forms, we have no modern equivalent of the
medieval witch.

Witchcraft appears to have been almost the ex-
clusive possession of the female sex. There were
wizards, it is true—some exorcists and some magicians
—who wielded supernatural powers; but those
demoniacal practices, which aroused the justifiable

wrath of all Christian people, were associated with old, withered, hideous, decrepit hags, the ministers of Satan upon Earth. These witches were real women, easily identified, like Mother Prat or Gillian of Brentford, whom Shakespeare mentions in the *Merry Wives of Windsor*. They were often seen, usually with a black cat as their familiar, and regarded with hate and fear in times of domestic tragedy, for which they were thought to be responsible. All kinds of strange powers were attributed to them. It was believed that they rode through the air, controlled the elements, raised storms, vanished at will, and rendered themselves insensible to pain. It was said that they fashioned little wax figures after the likeness of some human beings, and whatever cruelty or devilish design they practised on the figures was bound to happen to the unfortunate originals. Their power for mischief and their cleverness in coaxing the unwary to his fall caused them to be loathed and dreaded by all their potential victims.

All witches, however, were not bad. Some there were who had made themselves proficient in the healing arts, and some were able to render service in time of loss and danger. But the literature of the time suggests that the evil witches were in a great majority, or, at any rate, most in the minds of the anxious multitude.

There were also two kinds of evil witches. The most numerous and common were the old hags aforesaid, credited with occult powers by the general superstitious public. Among such the dramatist of 1 *Henry VI* included Joan of Arc. In addition to these witches of flesh and bone were those supernatural beings who interfered with the affairs of this world but were not of it. Such were the Weird Sisters of *Macbeth*.

Few doubted the reality and power of witchcraft. The enlightened Reginald Scot published his *Discovery of Witchcraft* in 1584, in which book he exposed the foolishness of widespread superstition. But his book was ordered to be burnt by King James, who himself replied to Scot in his *Demonology*. The King was energetic in his efforts to stamp out the "impious and damnable magic" and inspired the activities of his witch-finders, which were carried to extremes of horror and cruelty.

As an example of the firm hold which this superstition had even upon so cultured a man as the king, Sir John Harington's description of his interview with His Majesty in 1604 is instructive. "His Majesty," he writes,[1] "did much press for my opinion touching the power of Satane in matter of witchcraft; and askede me, with much gravitie, if I did trulie understande why the Devil did worke more with ancient women than others? . . . His Highness told me (the Queene his mother's death) was visible in Scotlande before it did really happen, being, as he said, spoken of in secrete by those whose power of sight presentede to them a bloodie head dancing in the aire. He then did remarke muche on this gifte, and saide he had soughte out of certaine bookes a sure waie to attaine knowledge of future chances."

The campaign against the witch was waged with unrelaxed intensity. The trials of accused wretches were numerous and revolting. Torture was frequently resorted to. Suspected females were sometimes tied to stools in such a way as to stop the circulation of the blood. There were they kept, suffering great pain, for twenty-four hours, until they confessed to dealings

[1] *Nugæ Antiq.*, ed. 1779, II. 116.

with the Evil One. Other unfortunates had their thumbs tied crosswise to their big toes, and, so bound, were hurled into water. If they floated, it was a proof of guilt. A common test was to prod a woman with a sharp instrument in different parts of her body to find if there were any that were insensible to pain. Witches were often shaved because the familiar spirit was believed to cling to the hair. Others were weighed against the Bible. Others again were required to repeat the Lord's Prayer, and if unable to do so were hurried to the stake, where many a poor innocent was burnt to death. Zeal on the part of the witch-finder generally brought a handsome reward, but to be too successful was to incur a suspicion of witchcraft oneself. Matthew Hopkins, one of the most assiduous persecutors of witches, ended by being hanged for the same offence.

One of the strangest circumstances in the whole history of witchcraft was the frequency with which the witches themselves confessed to associations with the Devil. No weight, of course, should be attached to those confessions wrung from the victim under torture. Extreme physical agony can extort anything. Many women, however, without being submitted to undue pressure, and with a full knowledge of the terrible consequences of their avowal, admitted they were guilty of the charges against them. By so doing they justified their accusers, and by their own showing deserved the terrible punishment which the law inflicted upon them. There were certainly cases where these women were mad. But there is no doubt that there were witches who realized they had exceptional powers, could exercise them, and believed they derived them from witchcraft. Such powers we should call to-day by such words as hypnotism, telepathy, and auto-suggestion; but these ignorant, unhappy creatures were honestly convinced that Satan had conquered them, and willingly faced the excruciating ordeal of the stake for the salvation of their souls.

Compared with witches, wizards appear to have exercised a very minor influence. They did not inspire the terror of their sisters in magic and consequently were less respected. As in the case of witches, wizards were good and bad. Many scholars and physicians and even priests of the church were reputed to deal with the Evil One. They were known as exorcists; and the exorcist's intentions were generally noble.[1] His greatest service to mankind was the invocation of divine authority to expel devils which had taken possession of unfortunate mortals. He was also a great protection to those who were assailed by demons and their evil influence.

Unlike the exorcist, the magician was a wizard of a different kind. His purpose and actions were wicked. He summoned devils to his aid, and in return for their assistance in furthering his designs—usually gratification of his senses—sold his soul to Satan. Marlowe's Doctor Faustus is the classic example of the Elizabethan magician; and when we come to consider *The Tempest* we shall see how original and wonderful is Shakespeare's higher conception in the person of Prospero.

One of the most abhorred features of witchcraft was the Evil Eye. The power of certain uncanny individuals to harm, cast a spell, and even cause death by a mere glance was commonly credited in Elizabethan times. Where such a power was maliciously

[1] See *Comedy of Errors*, IV. 4, 57–60.

and consciously employed, its effects can now be explained by hypnotism. But some unhappy people were convinced that they were involuntary channels of evil and would willingly have renounced, if they could, their mysterious gift.

The less harmful type of witch was often consulted, as a palmist is consulted to-day, by those seeking advice in present difficulties, or filled with either anxious foreboding or insatiable curiosity regarding the future. Just as astrologers read coming events from the stars, so the witches resorted to divination to satisfy their clients. Not only did they peer into the future, but they could give valuable information about the present, particularly as to the whereabouts of lost possessions. Many were the means employed by these withered old women. Some read secrets in water, others in air, others in fire and smoke. Some consulted the souls of the dead, others could interpret the crowing of cocks. Incense, palmistry, ventriloquism, and numerous other tricks were used to impress the credulous. The interpretation of dreams and the provision of love potions and charms for protection against evil were other services rendered by the less harmful witches. The higher grade of witch, who existed simply to work mischief and carry out the behests of Satan, was shunned with horror.

Devils were the relics of old mythological beliefs, and their connection with the pagan gods gave them a character that was wholly wicked. Fiends were supposed to hold sway over people, a condition we shall find mentioned in *King Lear*. People who were mad were said to be possessed of a devil in the sense we find in the New Testament. These unfortunates were often submitted to the cruellest treatment, while the exorcist was beseeched to use his power to cast out the demon with Divine aid.

The Church taught that beside every individual was his guardian angel, whose constant call to repentance and salvation was a protection to the soul. In opposition to the good voices were the alluring temptations of the devils, whose purpose was to win the distracted creature for Hell. Such was the medieval explanation of the battle between evil and good suggestions which is continually being fought in human consciousness.

One of the forms of the Supernatural of which Shakespeare was very fond was the ghostly apparition. The frequency with which he introduces such spectres into his plays is proof of the widespread belief in their reality. Their existence was nowhere seriously questioned. Men only differed over the explanation. The uneducated saw them as departed spirits of those who had once lived in the flesh, returned to Earth for some special reason, such as revenge, retribution, warning, or the guidance of those still living. The scholars were rather prone to regard the ghosts as the manifestation of some evil influence not properly understood—in other words, devils of the underworld in visible form.

Shakespeare shows us two kinds of ghost—the objective and the subjective. The objective ghost was supposed to be actually present and apparent to several people at the same time. To this class belongs the Ghost in *Hamlet*. The subjective ghost was recognized to be the product of the mind of the person who sees it, an hallucination or fiction of the imagination. Such is the Ghost of Banquo in *Macbeth* and Cæsar's Ghost in *Julius Cæsar*. On occasions ghosts appeared in dreams, as did the apparitions to Richard III before

the battle of Bosworth and to Posthumus in *Cymbeline*.
From *Hamlet* we gather much information about
popular superstition on the subject of Ghosts. The
dramatist included all the generally accepted ideas
in order to arrest and convince his audience. He introduces his spectre in eerie circumstances, on a cold,
dark, silent night. He emphasizes its silence and
inability to speak unless spoken to. He explains how
its return to its earthly environment is dictated by a
solemn purpose. He makes it reticent about its life
in the underworld, but hints at torture and cruel
flames. He shows how its appearance inspires terror
in the hearts of those who see it, and how the spirit
itself is terrified by the cock-crow and the approach
of daylight. All these were current ghostly superstitions, and clever dramatic use was made of them
by the Poet. We shall examine the *Hamlet* Ghost more
closely in a subsequent chapter. Here it is sufficient
to say that it was true to type, a ghost in which the
audience of the day had no difficulty in believing.

Most of the forms of the Supernatural, in which the
Elizabethans had faith, were awe-inspiring, terrifying,
uncanny, gloomy, and depressing. It is a relief to turn
to one which was contemplated in lighter vein—
namely, the fairies.

Shakespeare shows us the fairies as little people,
joyous, beautiful, immortal, and harbouring good
thoughts towards man. They meddled in human
affairs, it is true, played many a mischievous prank,
and awarded minor punishments for minor sins.
But in the main they were friendly, helpful, childlike,
and harmless. They did not awaken thoughts of terror
or anxious foreboding, nor were they the channels of
insidious evil. One could believe in them, submit to

them, associate with them, and be joyous and carefree as they were.

There was a wide gulf, however, between the Shake-spearean fairies and the fairies of rustic belief.[1] The very diminutive beings of *Midsummer Night's Dream*, with their acorn cups, their fans of butterfly wings, and torches of the thighs of humble bees, were wholly the creation of Shakespeare. The folk-fairies differed widely from them, particularly in size and disposition. The fairies of popular superstition were equal in stature to the smaller size of men, and so far from being helpful, friendly, and happy, were wicked and dreaded spirits, who were associated with witches, abducted mortals, dealt in changelings, smote humans with disease, blasted crops, stole cattle, and punished with pinchings and nippings unchastity, uncleanliness, and any invasion of their fairy privacy. It is eloquent of the supreme genius of Shakespeare that his original creation of the subjects of Oberon and Titania proved so beautiful, poetic, and fascinating, that the unlovely folk-fairies disappeared entirely from literature, and the Shakespearean conception usurped and retained their place in the popular mind.

Although the reign of Elizabeth witnessed the beginnings of some of the great sciences of to-day, yet knowledge of the truths of nature had not advanced far enough to offer any serious threat to the old super-stitions. Men still believed in witches, the exorcists, the astrologers, the fairies, the evil eye, spells, charms, dreams, and divination. This universal faith in, and fear of, the Supernatural forced a popular dramatist to adopt the current beliefs, though he himself might be the most hardened sceptic.

[1] *The Elizabethan Fairies* (M. W. Latham) deals fully with this question.

II

SHAKESPEARE AND POPULAR BELIEF

EVERY man, woman, and child is influenced by the current beliefs of the age into which they are born; and few superstitions have greater power to affect them profoundly than those admitting the drastic interference of supernatural agencies. Shakespeare was no exception to this rule. In fact, knowing what an imaginative and impressionable boy he must have been, he was probably governed to a greater degree than his fellows by the peculiar spiritual and mental forces of his time and environment.

The English have always been susceptible to belief in the Supernatural. The Unseen seems to have a special attraction and interest for them. Perhaps more than other peoples they have been prompted to question and theorize on matters beyond the range of mortal vision. Shakespeare was a true son of his race. He had the inquiring mind, which refused to be enclosed in a prison bounded by the limitations of matter. He had that gift of penetrating insight which could see beyond finite forms to mental causes, beyond the fleshly form to the human heart behind.

To the influence of race must be added that of environment. Although biographical details of the Poet's youth are meagre, we can form a fairly accurate picture of his boyhood from the surroundings in which we know it was spent. We can guess, with considerable confidence in being right, at the various ways in which he passed his days. We can picture him as the son of a well-to-do citizen of a small but prosperous market town in the heart of England. We can imagine him going to his lessons at the Grammar School and filling his many hours of recreation by strolling through the lanes and fields, into the woods, along the banks of Avon, playing with other children, gossiping with the rustics, taking an interest in the hundred and one activities of farming and agriculture, attending the fairs and the festivals of sheep-shearing, and entering fully into every phase of the country life around him. Remembering Shakespeare's faculty for absorbing knowledge, whether it came by hearsay or personal observation, and remembering also how the lives of the country folk were practically guided and controlled by superstition, we should expect to find him repeating the quaint ideas which had been deep-planted in rural England for generations. Nor does he disappoint us. His poetry is so thickly sprinkled with folk-lore that its study has engaged the attention of great scholars, who have written many volumes on this aspect of his work alone.

It would be impossible, even if it came within the limits of our present study, to list the numberless superstitions which the Poet gathered from his Stratford neighbours. His own observations of the habits of birds, animals, plants, fish, were supplemented by stories and explanation from folk-lore which were more picturesque than true. The experiences of changing weather and season had also their superstitious trappings. The sad phases of life, sickness and death, like the happy ones of prosperity and marriage, were woven with the quaintest fears and faiths, and attended by the most curious customs to ensure good luck and guard against evil. Space forbids the giving of many examples, but a few typical and representative

quotations can usefully be made from the rich mine
of material which he has bequeathed us.

The supposed ability of dying men to see into the
future is used by Shakespeare at the death of John of
Gaunt in *Richard II* (II. I. 31), and of Harry Hotspur
in *1 Henry IV* (V. 4. 83). In *As You Like It* Touchstone
mentions (II. 4. 52) the custom known as peascod
wooing. The lover plucked a peascod and crushed it.
If the peas remained in the pod, it was a good omen,
and was then presented to the lady. A fragment of
bird-lore is spoken by Portia as Bassanio is about to
make his choice of the caskets (*Merchant of Venice*,
III. 2. 43–45):

> Let music sound while he doth make his choice;
> Then, if he lose, he makes a swan-like end,
> Fading in music.

Another instance occurs in *3 Henry VI* (II. I. 91–92):

> Nay, if thou be that princely eagle's bird,
> Show thy descent by gazing 'gainst the sun.

(The eagle was supposed to make her offspring gaze
at the sun, and if they blinked to cast them from the
eyrie.)

Plant-lore supplied the Poet with many an idea.
In *1 Henry IV* (II. I. 96) Gadshill refers to the old
superstition that fern seeds were invisible, and that
anyone who could gather them had the power to
make himself invisible. The dislike of the yew, because
it was generally planted in churchyards, is noted in
the words "the dismal yew" in *Titus Andronicus*
(II. 3. 107). Hamlet is also probably referring to the
tree when he speaks of "cursed hebenon" (I. 5. 62).
The world of creeping things also had its impossible

tales. We learn from *Richard II* (III. 2. 14) that spiders suck their poison up from the earth. There is also the well-known mention of the toadstone in *As You Like It*" (II. 1. 12–14):

> Sweet are the uses of adversity;
> Which, like the toad, ugly and venomous,
> Wears yet a precious jewel in its head.

Such examples could be quoted to cover all the departments of life touched by superstition—and no department was untouched when life was lived in the heart of medieval England.

This ready, uncritical acceptance of the folk-lore of the countryside was typical of the attitude of the young Shakespeare towards life in general. He was happy, confident, trustful, optimistic. That doubt and gloom which settled on him in later years had not yet showed signs of its coming. In this spirit of light-heartedness and hope he wrote his early plays; and we shall see that his first dramatic use of the Super-natural was in the comparatively harmless and amusing form of Fairies.

Shakespeare's gay enthusiasm and assurance did not last. When he left Stratford and migrated to London, he entered a new environment. He came into contact with influences which did not reach out-of-the-way market towns in Warwickshire. He mixed with scholars and enlightened men, products of the Reformation, who had discarded medieval conceptions and threw doubts upon the most cherished beliefs. Shakespeare was quick to appreciate the progressive thought and welcome it. Many of his old ideas, ideas firmly held since childhood, were shattered. He let them go. He had risen above them. But his questionings were not limited to idle stories of the countryside. They covered religion and the very meaning of life itself. And as he developed as a thinker and philosopher, so he lost that cheerfulness, that joy of being alive, which are so apparent in his early work. It was a gradual process. His earlier plays, some of them written when he had resided in London for several years, retain much of the old spontaneous gaiety. But the passage of years and progress in letters replaced it with the seriousness and gravity which we find in *Hamlet*, to be followed in turn by that phase of dark, unrelieved pessimism which is revealed by *Macbeth*. Shakespeare, however, did not end his days in this atmosphere of mental gloom. When he had retired once more to the peace and quiet of Stratford, when he had realized his ambition to be a respected country gentleman, was rich, famous, and a man of substance and property, then there is a return to the enthusiasm and hopefulness of his youth, though they are tempered by a life's experience and rest now upon more enduring foundations. This last state we find reflected in his final play, written in retirement, *The Tempest*.

Although thinkers dissented from the old beliefs, and new ideas and scientific discoveries were being discussed and debated by an ever-widening scholastic circle, the superstitions of the people at large remained untouched. There was no serious attempt to overthrow them. Isolated writers assailed the ignorance of the masses, but the common people were still in the grip of the old habits of thinking. It was not as if the whole cultured class accepted the enlightened views. Only a minority did so; and we have seen how King James himself ordered Scot's exposure of witchcraft to be suppressed. With astrologers honoured at the Court, with a campaign against witchcraft prosecuted under royal favour, with the nobles as simple and credulous as ever in most of their practices, it is little wonder that the mass of the people still clung to the old fears and superstitions.

Shakespeare, whatever his private opinion and prejudices, was compelled as a working dramatist to adopt the views of the majority. That he often dissented from them is known from many a flash that reveals the true Shakespeare. For example, he makes Cassius say, *Julius Cæsar* (I. 2. 140–141):

> The fault, dear Brutus, is not in our stars,
> But in ourselves, that we are underlings.

Again, Helena, in *All's Well that Ends Well* (I. I. 231–234), declares:

> Our remedies oft in ourselves do lie,
> Which we ascribe to heaven: the fated sky
> Gives us free scope; only doth backward pull
> Our slow designs when we ourselves are dull.

In the same play the old lord, Lafeu, calls attention to the growing popularity of the new philosophy which discredits the marvellous (II. 3. 1–6):

They say miracles are past; and we have our philosophical persons, to make modern and familiar, things supernatural and causeless. Hence is it, that we make trifles of terrors; ensconcing ourselves into seeming knowledge, when we should submit ourselves to an unknown fear.

In *King Lear* we find the firm belief of the superstitious Gloucester in the baneful effect of eclipses contrasted with the frank confession of Edmund that he considers all such superstition humbug, even hypocritical (I. 2. 128–239):

This is the excellent foppery of the world, that when we are sick in fortune—often the surfeit of our own behaviour—we make guilty of our disasters the sun, the moon, and the stars: as if we were villains by necessity; fools, by heavenly compulsion; knaves, thieves, and treachers, by spherical predominance; drunkards, liars, and adulterers, by an enforced obedience of planetary influence; and all that we are evil in, by a divine thrusting on: an admirable evasion of whoremaster man, to lay his goatish disposition to the charge of a star!

Iago, also, delivers himself as follows (*Othello*, I. 3. 322–330):

Virtue! A fig! 'tis in ourselves that we are thus, or thus. Our bodies are gardens; to the which, our wills are gardeners: so that if we will plant nettles or sow lettuce, set hyssop and weed up thyme, supply it with one gender of herbs or distract it with many, either to have it sterile with idleness or manured with industry, why, the power and corrigible authority of this lies in our wills.

But the people who crowded the theatres and made the playwright's fortune would not have thanked him for too much dry, philosophic discourse, which was far above their heads. They demanded fairies, ghosts, and witches, and all the commonly held beliefs regarding them; and Shakespeare continually made concessions to this demand and packed his plays with popular opinions on the Supernatural. Perhaps this is the explanation of the striking fact that it is the bad characters like Edmund and Iago, the men who pursue their own advantage and shrink from no steps to attain their end, who pronounce the more reasonable, sane, and scientific opinions. Even

the sceptical Cassius is made to confess before he dies:
"Now I change my mind, And partly credit things
that do presage" (*Julius Cæsar*, v. i. 78–79). Shakespeare seems to justify superstition by following
dreams and unusual meteorological phenomena with
tragedy and disaster; and doubtless he realized that
a popular play was not the place to allow philosophical doubts too much prominence.

Shakespeare, however, was too great a man merely
to pander to the vulgar taste. There are signs that
intolerable pressure was sometimes brought to bear
upon him to interpolate a masque, spectacle, or
special piece of pageantry, which he felt was out of
keeping with his theme. Sometimes this pressure
emanated apparently from Court circles, where we
might have expected a higher appreciation of true
art to exist. Doubtless he often protested; and we can
imagine him giving way with a bad grace. But he
rarely allowed his concessions to mar his own conception of how the Supernatural should be used
dramatically. His original fancy was most often
preserved intact.

As a poet Shakespeare felt fully entitled to make all
the use he could of current superstition. He saw how
valuable mythological belief had been to the poets of
Greece and Rome, what a fund of picturesque simile
and metaphor it had provided, and how helpful it had
proved, not only in the coinage of original phrasing,
but as a means of conveying the poet's meaning.
Medieval superstition was the successor of classical
mythology; and even poets handling a historical or
philosophic theme could not resist so obvious a means
of enriching their language. The material was ready
to hand and had the inestimable advantage of being

understood and appreciated by all classes of readers and hearers.

To understand how far Shakespeare exceeded his contemporaries, a comparison of their supernatural characters with those of the master is illuminating. In other plays the ghosts, witches, and devils are merely the product of coarse superstition. In Shakespeare the characters are real; and while they are evil and terrifying, and embody most of the current superstitions, they never fail to be impressive and dignified. Dramatists like Greene, Dekker, Middleton, and even Marlowe, all of whom handled the Supernatural, were unable to invest their beings with those qualities which distinguish Shakespeare's creations.

Another point which emphasizes the genius of Shakespeare is his refusal to use the Supernatural for its own sake and not for the purposes of his plot. Lesser playwrights were tempted by the hope of popular applause to introduce a supernatural element which had no connection with the theme and was often out of harmony with it. Shakespeare does not do this. The witches of *Macbeth* are not mere specimens of popular witch-lore introduced at random. They are material to the plot—a most important factor in it, and the motive power of the drama. The Ghost in *Hamlet* is not a meaningless apparition, though he acts and talks as ghosts were supposed to act and talk. The Ghost starts the train of contradictory thoughts in Hamlet's brain which makes the whole play. Sometimes, as in *The Tempest* and *Cymbeline*, there are, it must be admitted, supernatural scenes that could be omitted; these, in all probability, are the instances in which the dramatist was compelled to interpolate matter against his inclination to meet the shallow tastes of the Court. In all such cases the suspected interpolations can be omitted without spoiling the drama or even leaving traces of their existence.

A further point to be noted in Shakespeare's skilful handling of the Supernatural is the absence of senseless repetition. He never allows it to appear forced. He knew that familiarity breeds contempt, that terrifying beings lose their power to terrify the more they are seen. The Weird Sisters in *Macbeth* were given two appearances only by Shakespeare— one at the beginning of each half of the drama. (The extra witch scenes are now generally accepted as interpolations). Although they only appear once on the heath and once in their cavern, their presence is felt by the audience throughout the play, and the real aim of the dramatic use of the Supernatural is achieved. But only a genius could do it.

To summarize Shakespeare's attitude towards the superstitions of his age, we can surmise that as a young man he imbibed and believed in all the folk-lore poured into his ears by the country people among whom he lived. When he came to London and mixed with men of advanced thought, he dropped many of his old ideas and ranged himself with the philosophers and scientists. As a dramatist, however, he still handled and portrayed the old beliefs, but always with some higher dramatic purpose in mind than a desire to delight the shallow and ignorant audience. By the success he attained in the task he set himself, he gave one of the highest proofs of his unequalled gifts.

III

"MIDSUMMER NIGHT'S DREAM"

Midsummer Night's Dream is not the most important of the Shakespearean plays in which the Supernatural plays a prominent part—that distinction belongs to *Macbeth*—but it is necessary to consider it first because it was earliest in point of writing. The fantasy belongs to the initial period of the poet's career as a dramatist. There are scholars and critics who believe that he first began to think of *Midsummer Night's Dream* as early as 1592; that is to say, when he was still in his twenties. The text shows abundant signs of considerable revision; and the finished article is usually assigned to the year 1595, although the possibility of subsequent polishing cannot be ruled out.

Shakespeare's first important use of the Supernatural occurred, then, when he was still a young man, when the beliefs and prejudices of his childhood had not been clouded by contact with the grim realities of life. His youthful fancies and the untamed flights of his native imagination had not yet been moderated by the grave and sobering influence of the New Learning. He still had the spontaneous gaiety and optimism of early manhood—was not yet oppressed by the sorrow, sin, and suffering in the world. He was content to enjoy life rather than to inquire meditatively into its meaning.

Shakespeare's genius is so transcendent that we are apt to think of it as ready-made, something that he always possessed. We forget that he had to grow and develop like other men, that he only attained

_wer after years of hard work in an
chool. As happens in nearly every human
iews changed as he grew older, his opinions
altered, ld beliefs and superstitions were shed, new
philosophical ideas were embraced, until his whole
outlook was transformed like a summer afternoon
overcast by a thunderstorm. It is true that the
storm passed, and the cool and peace of a still
evening followed, but years elapsed before the
skies cleared and the discordant rumblings were
hushed.

A study of Shakespeare and the Supernatural
follows the Poet through his changing moods, and
throws a new light upon the process of his development
which enables us to understand him better. In
Midsummer Night's Dream we deal with the Shakespeare
of the first period—the period of the early comedies
and the Chronicle Plays. He is young enough still to
retain more than glimpses of that light-hearted,
observant, and interested boy who walked the lanes
and fields of Stratford. He has not been in London
so long, he has not become so engrossed in erudite
scholarship, that the woodland notes and the song of
the river are not still clearly audible to him. A happy
optimism remains the trend of his active mind. This
coloured everything he handled and is nowhere more
evident than in his first dramatic use of the Supernatural.

The form of the Supernatural employed by the
Poet in *Midsummer Night's Dream* is fairies. Fairies
gave him a full opportunity to follow his bent and
allow free rein to his imagination. He revels in
imagery. He reveals himself in the following lines
(V. I. 12–17):

The poet's eye, in a fine frenzy rolling,
Doth glance from heaven to earth, from earth to heaven;
And, as imagination bodies forth
The forms of things unknown, the poet's pen
Turns them to shapes, and gives to airy nothing
A local habitation and a name.

Shakespeare's choice of Fairies was, however, not dictated solely by his own feelings and preference as a poet. Obviously he welcomed the suggestion and was thoroughly happy in working it out, but most probably it had another origin than his own fertile brain. *Midsummer Night's Dream* was written to be performed at a wedding. There cannot be much doubt about that. The plot itself makes it quite clear. As to whose wedding Shakespeare intended to honour there is less certainty. Several have been put forward and supported by ingenious argument; but the occasion that appeals to us most is the marriage of the Poet's patron, the Earl of Southampton, to Mistress Elizabeth Vernon. The objection is that this happy event did not take place until 1598, while it is beyond doubt that he was at work on the play before this. *A* wedding rather than *whose* wedding is the point that concerns us at the moment; for the Elizabethans associated Fairies very intimately with these functions, and so naturally determined the dramatist's choice of this form of the Supernatural.

None was more qualified to handle a fairy theme successfully than the young poet of the Warwickshire countryside, who knew all the rustic beliefs about these little people and was once upon a time a firm believer himself in their existence. The scholastic product of the university, steeped in classical lore and hedged in by science and philosophy, could not easily escape into the fantastic realm of fairyland and give a convincing picture of its life and people. For Shakespeare this presented no difficulties.

Those who deny the poet the ability to originate a plot, and take a delight in tracing every incident of his stories to some source or other, are in difficulties with *Midsummer Night's Dream*. Apart from current fairy-lore, with which he became familiar enough in his childhood, the play seems to be almost wholly the creation of the Poet's own fancy. In the other fairy play, *The Tempest*, the critics are again compelled to give Shakespeare the credit for thinking out the plot for himself; while in *Macbeth*, though he obtained a hint for the Weird Sisters from Holinshed, the whole conception of the witch character is entirely unlike that of any other man. In the Supernatural, therefore, we find the Poet's creative faculty at its busiest.

Shakespeare's use of the Fairies is original and clever. He avoids anything heavy. He deserts the unattractive fancies of folk-lore for delightful beings of his own creation. He does not employ the Supernatural in this early play with any special dramatic purpose beyond the desire to entertain. He does not attach any particular meaning or significance to his Little People, nor does he endow them with any great powers or control over mortals. Undoubtedly he shows considerable ingenuity in his dramatic construction by deftly interweaving the three themes —the quarrels of the lovers, the fooling of Bottom and the clowns, and the meddling interference of the Fairies. As a whole, though, he writes in happy, carefree vein, drawing prodigally on his imagination, and adopting the attitude of one who has made startling discoveries of the truth about fairies and has decided to pass his knowledge on to his fellows.

There is the spontaneity of effortless creation in Shakespeare's handling of the Fairies of the *Dream*. He does not keep his light and aery beings separate from his mortal characters, as the Weird Sisters are kept separate in *Macbeth*. The Fairies mix freely with the very worldly men and women of the Court of Theseus; and, be it noted, in these scenes it is the human element that is dominant, whereas the enchanted forest is the kingdom where the Fairies have their own way without effective opposition. The Poet, however, does not in this early incursion into the realm of the Supernatural endow his immortals with any real influence over the human soul. Certainly they are guilty of much mischievous interference, which causes a good deal of temporary annoyance, but there is no evidence of any power to tempt, to deceive with malice, or to destroy.

When Shakespeare resolved to enter fairyland, he was not content with any half-way house. He reached the very heart of Oberon and Titania's kingdom. He clothed his Fairies in many of the common superstitions which he had gathered from years of sojourn amongst convinced believers. Few of the rustics of the Stratford country would care to deny the existence of the Little People. They were too frightened of being paid out for their disloyalty by some mischievous prank on the part of a local fay. But Shakespeare's Fairies differed greatly from the products of rustic belief. Mr. Harry Furness writes: "The fairies of folk-lore were rough and repulsive, taking their style from the hempen homespuns who invented them." In *The Elizabethan Fairies* Mr. M. W. Latham explains at length how utterly unlike the troublesome folk-fairies were the delightful beings of Shakespeare. Titania, Oberon, and their trains, are fairies of "another sort"; and Shakespeare undoubtedly owed a great deal in their conception to the old Greek writers. We can recognize in them "the nymphs and fauns, the naiads and dryads of Greece."[1] There he found the grace and beauty of his Titania and her subjects. But, as usual, he was not content to copy. He did not merely reproduce the Nymphs, Fauns, and Satyrs of mythology. He draped their forms artistically in current superstitions, softening their classical character, and making them thoroughly English and modern.

The little band of *Midsummer Night's Dream* are to be understood as diminutive in size, for we learn that, while Titania and Oberon are quarrelling over the changeling boy, their subject-elves "for fear Creep into acorn cups and hide them there" (II. I. 30–31). Again, we have Titania's commands to her subjects at the beginning of II. 2:

> Come, now a roundel and a fairy song;
> Then, for the third part of a minute, hence;
> Some to kill cankers in the musk-rose buds;
> Some war with rere-mice for their leathern wings
> To make my small elves coats; and some keep back
> The clamorous owl, that nightly hoots and wonders
> At our quaint spirits.

The matter of size was one of Shakespeare's principal departures from popular ideas, which pictured the folk-fairies as equal in stature to smally made mortals.

The immortality of the Fairies is made clear from

---

[1] *The Supernatural in Shakespeare*, Helen H. Stewart, p. 97.

D

several passages. Puck remarks contemptuously of the humans, "Lord, what fools these mortals be!" (III. 2. 115); and Titania, speaking of the mother of her Indian protégé, says (II. 1. 135–137):

> But she, being mortal, of that boy did die;
> And for her sake do I rear up her boy;
> And for her sake I will not part with him.

When waking beneath Oberon's spell Titania falls instantly in love with the ass-pated Bottom, addresses him as "gentle mortal," and promises: "I will purge thy mortal grossness" (III. 1. 163). When she is released from her spell by the Fairy King, she inquires of him how it came about that she was found sleeping with mortals on the ground (IV. 1. 104–107).

Further evidence of immortality lies in the strange powers which the Fairies are shown to possess. These powers were all drawn from popular superstition. Firstly, there is the ability to make themselves invisible. Oberon finds this useful when Demetrius appears in the wood with Helena following him. He says (II. 1. 186–187):

> But who comes here? I am invisible;
> And I will overhear their conference.

Puck takes full advantage of his invisibility when he plays his cruel joke on Bottom; and he and Oberon are able to listen-in to the confusion amongst the lovers without risk of detection.

Not only were fairies thought to be able to vanish at will, but they enjoyed great powers of metamorphosis and could assume almost any shape they pleased. Puck glories in the opportunities for mischief which this gives him. He says to the Fairy (II. 1. 43–48):

I am that merry wanderer of the night.
I jest to Oberon, and make him smile,
When I a fat and bean-fed horse beguile,
Neighing in likeness of a filly foal:
And sometime lurk I in a gossip's bowl,
In very likeness of a roasted crab.

Again, he calls after Quince and his friends (III. 1.
109–114):

I'll follow you, I'll lead you about a round,
Through bog, through bush, through brake, through brier:
Sometime a horse I'll be, sometime a hound,
A hog, a headless bear, sometime a fire;
And neigh, and bark, and grunt, and roar, and burn,
Like horse, hound, hog, bear, fire, at every turn.

The speed with which the Fairies move shows that
they are not fettered by mortal limitations of time
and space. Puck says that he goes "swifter than arrow
from the Tarter's bow" (III. 2. 101) and boasts that
he can "put a girdle round about the earth in forty
minutes" (II. 1. 175-176). One of Titania's fairies tells
Puck (II. 1. 6–7):

I do wander everywhere,
Swifter than the moon's sphere.

Fairie exercised considerable influence over weather
conditions and in a measure were able to control
them. Titania tells Oberon that the quarrel between
them has had most disastrous climatic results:

. . . the winds . . .
. . . have suck'd up from the sea
Contagious fogs; which, falling in the land,
Have every pelting river made so proud,
That they have overborne their continents.

(II. 1. 88–92.)

After listing a number of other disasters, she continues (*ibid.*, 107–117):

> The seasons alter: hoary-headed frosts
> Fall in the fresh lap of the crimson rose;
> And on old Hiem's thin and icy crown
> An odorous chaplet of sweet summer buds
> Is, as in mockery, set: the spring, the summer,
> The chiding autumn, angry winter, change
> Their wonted liveries, and the mazed world,
> By their increase, now knows not which is which:
> And this same progeny of evils comes
> From our debate, from our dissension;
> We are their parents and original.

In the above exquisite lines the Poet suggests that chaotic conditions must follow quarrels among the Fairies, whose duty it is to order them. Oberon's power over the elements is illustrated in III. 2, when, seeing that Lysander and Demetrius are bent on a fight, he commands Puck (355–359):

> Hie, therefore, Robin, overcast the night;
> The starry welkin cover thou anon
> With drooping fog, as black as Acheron;
> And lead these testy rivals so astray,
> As one comes not within another's way.

Fancy gave the Fairies the most beautiful dwelling-places:

> . . . in dale, forest, or mead,
> By paved fountain or by rushy brook,
> Or in the beached margent of the sea.
>
> (II. 1. 83–85.)

And what could be more lovely than Titania's couch?

> . . . a bank where the wild thyme blows,
> Where oxlips and the nodding violet grows;
> Quite over-canopied with luscious woodbine,
> With sweet musk-roses, and with eglantine.
>
> (II. 1. 249–252.)

The soft, scented summer night, under the gentle light of the argent moon, was the time the Fairies chose for their fun and frolic. Says Theseus in the last scene of the play, "The iron tongue of midnight hath told twelve: . . . 'tis almost fairy time" (v. 1. 370–371). By the time dawn broke fairies should be safe in their haunts. When Oberon explains to Puck all he means to do to straighten out the tangles, which are mostly of the imp's making, he receives the answer (III. 2. 378–380):

> My fairy lord, this must be done with haste,
> For night's swift dragons cut the clouds full fast,
> And yonder shines Aurora's harbinger.

Puck is a conventional sprite in so far that he thinks it improper, even dangerous, for any of his tribe to be abroad in daylight. Oberon boasts that he has lingered in the forest until the sun has actually risen. But he seems to regard these occasions as exceptionally daring, and tells Puck that, if they do not delay, "We may effect this business yet ere day" (III. 2. 394). As the title of the play suggests, it is the warm nights of June that the Fairies enjoy. Titania says, "The summer still doth tend upon my state" (III. 1. 158). When winter comes, they migrate like the swallows to warmer lands, such as "the spiced Indian air" (II. 1. 124).

Immortal though they may be, the Fairies partake of mortal pleasures. They eat, drink, and make merry, and are particularly fond of music and dancing. Titania complains bitterly to Oberon that his brawls have disturbed their sport when they have met to dance their ringlets to the whistling wind (II. 1. 86–87). The "ringlets" are a reference to those circles of bright-green grass, which were then supposed to be made by the Fairies, but which science has now coldly explained to be a growth of fungi. Another mention of the fairy rings occurs in II. 1. 8–9, where the Fairy tells Puck:

> And I serve the fairy queen,
> To dew her orbs upon the green.

The main characteristic of the Fairies of *Midsummer Night's Dream* is their penchant for mischief. They are always meddling and interfering in other people's affairs, especially Puck, who is the very embodiment of rascality. There is, however, no malice in their fun. They are just naughty children, naturally happy, laughing and skipping about, easily frightened, and repentant when scolded. They do not hate. When a joke has gone too far, they are ready and willing to put matters right again. Oberon clears up the muddle which Puck has made in anointing Lysander, and not Demetrius, with the love-potion, and releases Titania from her infatuation for Bottom. Goodwill is expressed in Puck's speech at the end of Act III, when curing Lysander:

> Jack shall have Jill;
> Nought shall go ill;
> The man shall have his mare again, and all shall be well.

And again, at the end of the play:

> Give me your hands, if we be friends,
> And Robin shall restore amends.

Original though his own conception of the Fairies is, Shakespeare packs *Midsummer Night's Dream* with folk-lore and popular fairy beliefs. To the many already noted we must add the changeling boy. Abduction of human beings was among the Fairies' chief activities, though the motive is obscure. Shakespeare's more refined conception improves upon the general version. Titania has robbed no human cradle, but has brought up the child for the sake of friendship with the mother, who, "being mortal, of that boy did die" (II. 1.135). Changelings, as a rule, caused much heartache and anxiety.

An important and delightful feature of the fantasy is the fairy music which is interspersed throughout. It is an instructive instance—we shall encounter many others in the course of our study—of Shakespeare's dramatic use of music in the portrayal of the Supernatural.

At the end of Elizabeth's reign the English could be described with some justice as a musical nation. Music held an important place in the school curriculum; and those who could not read a part at sight, or play some instrument like the lute or viol, were thought to have gravely neglected an essential side of their education. Commentators have established the truth that Shakespeare was not only extremely fond of music, but also had a sound technical knowledge of it. Certainly he was fully aware of its effect and influence on theatre audiences. He used music freely when presenting the mysterious and ethereal. It was closely associated in his mind with the preternatural. As a poet he accepted the Pythagorean notion of the music of the spheres, and in the famous lines on music in *The Merchant of Venice* makes Lorenzo declare (v. 1. 63–65):

> Such harmony is in immortal souls;
> But while this muddy vesture of decay
> Doth grossly close it in, we cannot hear it.

In *Midsummer Night's Dream* music materially assists

Shakespeare in creating that fairy atmosphere which is so enchanting, visionary, and idealistic.

Titania, we have seen, early reveals herself as 'a music-lover by her protest to Oberon that his brawls have disturbed the fairy dances to the piping winds (II. 1. 86–87). In the following scene she calls to her attendants, "Come, now a roundel and a fairy song" (II. 2. 1), and later says. "Sing me now to sleep . . . and let me rest" (8). She dozes off as the first Fairy sings the dainty song, "You spotted snakes", and all the other little voices join in the soothing lullaby chorus. When releasing Titania from his charm, Oberon bids her "music call"; and Titania responds with "Music, ho! music such as charmeth sleep" (IV. 1. 88). The king and queen then dance together to a lilting strain while the effect of the magic spell passes from the entangled lovers, Lysander, Demetrius, Hermia, and Helena. At the end of the play, when the happily married couples have retired, Oberon, Titania, and their fairy train, led by Puck, creep in by the "glimmering light" of the "drowsy fire," and skipping through the sleeping house, with song and dance pour out a blessing on the newly wed. Though not marked in the Stage Directions, the final passage (from line 398) is usually sung, the lines commencing "Now, until the break of day" being one of the few Shakespearean dance-songs. Similarly, the Fairy's speech, "Over hill, over dale" (II. 1. 2–13), is treated as a song; while "I know a bank where the wild thyme blows" (II. 1. 249 *et seq.*) is frequently made into a solo for Oberon. Apart from Bottom's outburst into a frankly rural ditty, the music of *Midsummer Night's Dream* is in keeping with the immortal and fantastic theme, and gives that airy, gossamer-like effect, which was wonderfully recaptured by the genius of Mendelssohn.

Puck, the sprightly messenger of Oberon and Titania, embodies practically everthing that tradition said about the fairy love of mischief-making. Puck is strictly speaking the title for a class of malicious, teasing sprites; and the name of Oberon's court jester is more properly Robin Goodfellow, the popular practical joker of folk-lore. The Fairies hardly regarded Puck as one of themselves, for he was bigger than they and was more of the brownie.[1] The dialogue between him and the Fairy, which opens Act II, gives the keynote of the whole play. First the fairy describes her night's duties as a subject of Titania, and then Puck speaks of Oberon's revels and warns the Fairy of his master's resentment against her mistress over her refusal to let him have the Indian boy as a page. The Fairy then recognizes the brownie (II. I. 32–34):

> Either I mistake your shape and making quite,
> Or else you are that shrewd and knavish sprite
> Call'd Robin Goodfellow: are not you he
> That frights the maidens of the villagery;
> Skim milk, and sometimes labour in the quern,
> And bootless make the breathless housewife churn;
> And sometime make the drink to bear no barm;
> Mislead night-wanderers, laughing at their harm?
> Those that Hobgoblin call you, and sweet Puck,
> You do their work, and they shall have good luck:
> Are not you he?

Puck confesses, "I am that merry wanderer of the night," and proceeds to tell the Fairy of his jests and practical jokes. Further on in the play he admits

[1] H. Littledale in *Shakespeare's England*, I. 539.

again, "Those things do best please me, that befall preposterously" (III. 2. 120–121).

As H. Littledale writes in *Shakespeare's England*,[1] Puck has "nearly as many aliases as he has transformations." The names already mentioned, Robin Goodfellow and Hobgoblin, seem to be the same, for "Hob" was merely a variation for "Robert" or "Robin."[2] Another of his characters was Lob-lie-by-the-fire, a house-elf, who entered the homesteads and did menial service. He is addressed by the Fairy as "Thou lob (i.e. clown) of Spirits" (II. 1. 16). When he "misled night-wanderers," he was Will-o'-the-wisp, Jack-o'-lantern, or Kit-with-the-canstick, the folk-lore explanation of that phenomenon known as "ignis fatuus." He is thoroughly English in character, and is used to portray all the roguishness and rascality of the Fairies in their most mischievous mood.

Oberon, the King of the Fairies, rules a band of subjects who are the joint creations of folk-lore and mythology. His dwelling is the forest, where he indulges in feasts and revellings with a splendid court, and uses his supernatural powers for no higher end than his own amusement. He plans most of the mischief which Puck carries out, though the imp, both carelessly and intentionally, improves upon his instructions. There is no malice in Oberon, quarrelsome though he may be. He straightens out the lovers' tangle, makes it up with Titania, and gives his blessing to Theseus and his court when the triple wedding is celebrated.

An Oberon appeared on the stage before Shake-

[1] I. 539.
[2] M. W. Latham in *The Elizabethan Fairies* suggests that Hobgoblin was a separate spirit.

speare's immortal in Greene's *James IV*, where he is called "Oboram, King of the Fayeries." The name seems to have come originally from the Charlemagne romance, *Huon of Bordeaux*, which was translated from the French by Lord Berners about 1534. This Auberon, as the name was there spelt, was reputed to be the son of Julius Cæsar and the sister of the British King Arthur, Morgan le Fay. He may be identified with the dwarf Alberich in the German epic, *Nibelungen Lied*, who dwelt with his fairy-subjects in a forest on the way to Babylon. All that part of the world was loosely known to Shakespeare's contemporaries as "India." Hence, Oberon has come to the wood near Athens "from the farthest steppe of India" (II. I. 69); and it is an Indian boy over whom he quarrels with Titania. Titania clings to the changeling for love of the dead mother, who was her bosom companion "in the spiced Indian air" (II. I. 124). Oberon of *Midsummer Night's Dream* is, however, entirely different to Auberon of *Huon of Bordeaux*. He is a wholly Shakespearean creation and composed of the elements of classical tradition mixed with the country superstitions which the Warwickshire Poet knew and loved.

The name Titania means "a daughter of the Titans." The Titans were the rulers of heaven and earth until overthrown by Zeus, or Jupiter, who made himself Lord of Olympus. "Titania," then, presumed a very long pedigree indeed; and the name was applied by Ovid in his *Metamorphoses* to the goddess Diana. There Shakespeare found it, and in the original Latin, too. Golding in his English translation of the *Metamorphoses* does not write the word "Titania" at all, but uses other expressions in its place. It would seem from this that Shakespeare's Latin was not so "small" as Ben Jonson would have us believe.

The grace and dignity of the classical Diana are retained in Shakespeare's Titania, though the character as a whole is a lighter and more beautiful conception. But the Poet kept the goddess in mind, for it was generally believed at the time that the nymphs who attended her were identical with the medieval Fairies. Titania queens it in a moonlit, woodland kingdom; and though she has traces of mischievousness, she is not that player of vexatious pranks who was known among country folk as Queen Mab.[1] For the quarrel between Titania and Oberon, it is probable that Shakespeare remembered Chaucer's *Merchant's Tale* and gathered a hint or two from it.

The little Fairies, Peaseblossom, Cobweb, Moth, and Mustard-seed, who are instructed by Titania to be "kind and courteous" to Bottom, are apparently the product of Shakespeare's fancy alone. Their names suggest beauties of Nature personified, and their presence gives an excuse for introducing many of the quaint ideas of the countryside. Hear Titania's instructions to them (III. 1. 167–177):

> Be kind and courteous to this gentleman;
> Hop in his walks, and gambol in his eyes;
> Feed him with apricocks and dewberries,
> With purple grapes, green figs, and mulberries;
> The honey-bags steal from the humble bees,
> And, for night-tapers, crop their waxen thighs,
> And light them at the fiery glow-worm's eyes,
> To have my love to bed, and to arise;
> And pluck the wings from painted butterflies,
> To fan the moonbeams from his sleeping eyes:
> Nod to him, elves, and do him courtesies.

[1] For Shakespeare's description of Queen Mab, see the lines in *Romeo and Juliet*, I. 4. 55–69.

Shakespeare makes no attempt in *Midsummer Night's Dream* at a serious discussion on the real existence of fairies. Whether his audience believes or disbelieves is no concern of his. For the purposes of his fantasy he writes as if there were no doubt upon the matter, but he does not compel us to agree with him. At the opening of the last Act he does, indeed, present Theseus as a sceptic. When Hippolyta remarks upon the strangeness of the lovers' accounts of their experience, he answers (v. 1. 2–6):

> More strange than true: I never may believe
> These antique fables, nor these fairy toys.
> Lovers and madmen have such seething brains,
> Such shaping fantasies, that apprehend
> More than cool reason ever comprehends.

But this practical, common-sense view is not accepted by Hippolyta; and she frowns on Theseus' scepticism (23–27):

> But all the story of the night told over,
> And all their minds transfigured so together,
> More witnesseth than fancy's images,
> And grows to something of great constancy;
> But, howsoever, strange and admirable.

Shakespeare's first dramatic use of the Supernatural is happy, gay, and sprightly. The only hint in this play of the darker, gloomier thought that was soon to supplant his youthful optimism is found in those cold, clammy lines about ghosts (III. 2. 380–387):

> . . . Yonder shines Aurora's harbinger;
> At whose approach, ghosts, wandering here and there,
> Troop home to churchyards: damned spirits all,
> That in crossways and floods have burial,
> Already to their wormy beds are gone;
> For fear lest day should look their shames upon,
> They wilfully themselves exile from light,
> And must for aye consort with black-brow'd night.

Here, it would seem, Shakespeare's thought wandered back to the malicious, inimical fairies of folk-lore, who were held by some to be the departed spirits of men and women, and for this reason were often confused with ghosts. We shall find a great deal in this strain in *Hamlet*, and still more in *Macbeth*, but it is not allowed to intrude into *Midsummer Night's Dream*. Oberon immediately dismisses this shadow on their careless joy with, "But we are spirits of another sort" (388).

While the Fairies intermingle with the humans in this first supernatural play, Shakespeare never allows us to forget the gulf between them—that they live in different worlds governed by different laws. This point is strongly emphasized in his later handling of the Supernatural, when his object has ceased to be light diversion and easy laughter, and has become the portrayal of tragedy in its most awe-inspiring and terrifying mood.

Although Shakespeare handles the Supernatural in *Midsummer Night's Dream* in such a jocular and irresponsible spirit, yet the comedy had a more profound influence on well-established superstition than any other play ever written. The Poet's original conception of fairies as tiny, benevolent, aery beings influenced all subsequent literature on the subject and finally dispelled the old ideas of malicious, evil, awful creatures who had to be obeyed and propitiated. The picture conjured up in our minds to-day by the word "fairy" is as different as could be to the repulsive fairy of the Elizabethans; and the change can be traced to Shakespeare and *Midsummer Night's Dream*."[1]

[1] See *The Elizabethan Fairies* (Latham).

IV

"HAMLET"

AT least six or seven years pass after the writing of *Midsummer Night's Dream* before we find Shakespeare engaged on *Hamlet,* the second of the great plays with an important Supernatural element, and, in the opinion of many, the greatest tragedy ever penned. What a profound change has come over his attitude towards the Unseen! No longer does he handle it in that cheerful, jocular, irresponsible spirit in which he showed us the adventures of Puck, Oberon, and Titania. He is now in deadly earnest and foreshadows the gloom of *Macbeth.*

The Poet was in the late thirties when *Hamlet* was written. He had been an established dramatist for ten years, and the happy boyhood days at Stratford seemed very far away. No longer did he enjoy the optimism and high spirits associated with youth. He looked out upon life with a cynical eye. His old faith was shaken, and his mind darkened by doubts, misgivings, and questionings. Much of *Hamlet* is agreed to be autobiographical; and passages like the following (III. 1. 78–82) reveal the mental uneasiness of the Poet as surely as that of the Danish Prince:

> . . . the dread of something after death,
> The undiscover'd country from whose bourn
> No traveller returns, puzzles the will,
> And makes us rather bear those ills we have
> Than fly to others that we know not of.

Shakespeare is depressed. The wickedness of the world

and the burdensome memory of his own lapses have cast their shadows over him. He makes Hamlet say to Polonius, "To be honest, as this world goes, is to be one man picked out of ten thousand" (II. 2. 178–179). He feels that there is a destiny controlling the life of man, bending him to its will and punishing him for his rebellion:

> There's a divinity that shapes our ends,
> Rough-hew them how we will.
>
> (V. 2. 10–11.)

Shakespeare's attitude towards the Supernatural coincides, as we should expect, with his general view of life. He is in no mood now to deal with the empty, frivolous, meaningless little fairies. The form of the Supernatural, which he adopts at this stage, is the eerie, horrible, terrifying ghost. We had a brief foretaste of it in the very midst of the happy revels and practical joking of Oberon and Puck.[1] But the subject was then dismissed almost as soon as it was mentioned, for it was quite foreign to the atmosphere of that pleasant fantasy. The reference shows, however, that as early as 1595, Shakespeare's mind had begun to run on this grimmer form of supernatural manifestation. He had, indeed, used it in *Richard III*; but not till *Hamlet* did he develop it fully and demonstrate the dramatic use of the ghost-belief in its most powerful and impressive form.

Once Shakespeare had decided to introduce a ghost into *Hamlet*—or rather, to retain the ghost he found in the old play upon which he worked—he set about endowing it with the dignity and convincingness which distinguished all his supernatural

[1] *Midsummer Night's Dream*, III. 2, 380–387.

characters. As a dramatist he knew the need of clothing his spectre in all the current ghostly superstitions. His aim was not merely to entertain the less intelligent portion of his audience, important as he realized that to be; but, in the interests of his plot, to make the ghost appear real and possible to all. He meant to persuade even the most sceptical of the actual existence of ghosts, and presented his proofs with such assurance that most readers of the play cannot escape the feeling that the Poet was himself a firm believer in the visits of these eerie creatures to our Earth.

The *Hamlet* Ghost fulfils all the demands of popular superstition. In the first place it comes in strange and creepy circumstances, at dead of night, when it is cold and still and lonely.

> 'Tis now the very witching time of night,
> When churchyards yawn, and hell itself breathes out
> Contagion to this world.
>
> (III. 2. 405–407.)

It appears clad in the garments worn in mortal life. Horatio, describing it to Hamlet, says, "A figure like your father, armed at point exactly, *cap-à-pé*" (i.e. from head to foot) (I. 2. 199–200). Its appearance arouses the terror of the sentries on the platform before the castle at Elsinore. It cannot speak unless spoken to. This last was a very important point in Elizabethan ghost-lore. Not only were apparitions silent until addressed, but it needed an educated man to make them talk. All exorcists were supposed to be learned and fluent in the Latin tongue. Herein is the explanation of Marcellus's remark, "Thou art a scholar; speak to it, Horatio" (I. 1. 42). When

persuaded to speak, the ghostly visitors confine themselves to their mission and its immediate purpose.
Of life beyond the grave they are stubbornly reticent.
When they do lift the curtain, it is a peep at hell
they give us, not a peep at heaven. The *Hamlet* Ghost
says (I. 5. 2–4, 9–13):

> My hour is almost come,
> When I to sulphurous and tormenting flames
> Must render up myself . . .
>
> .   .   .   .   .
>
> I am thy father's spirit;
> Doom'd for a certain term to walk the night,
> And for the day confined to fast in fires,
> Till the foul crimes done in my days of nature
> Are burnt and purged away.

Ghosts were thought to appear before some great
crisis in human affairs, to exact justice, to revenge
a foul deed, to give a warning, to reveal hidden
treasure, or otherwise perform the commands of the
supernatural powers. After the first visit of the *Hamlet*
spectre, Horatio and the soldiers try to determine
its cause, and agree that the threat of war with
Norway must be the explanation. This dialogue
engages our attention and hints at the importance
of the apparition. It enables us to believe in it, and
assures us that the appearance is not frivolous and
meaningless. When the Ghost meets Hamlet himself,
we learn the true reason—"to revenge his foul and
most unnatural murder" (I. 5. 25).

On first seeing it, Horatio is prepared to face all
risks—"I'll cross it, though it blast me" (I. 1. 127)—
and pluckily tries to make the spirit reveal the
message it comes to deliver. Before he breaks its
silence, however, the cock crows, and it is gone.

Ber. It was about to speak, when the cock crew.
Hor. And then it started like a guilty thing
    Upon a fearful summons. I have heard,
    The cock, that is the trumpet to the morn,
    Doth with his lofty and shrill-sounding throat
    Awake the god of day, and at his warning,
    Whether in sea or fire, in earth or air,
    The extravagant and erring spirit hies
    To his confine: . . .

(I. I. 147–155.)

On learning from Horatio and the Watch of this strange manifestation, Hamlet himself agrees to join the little group on the platform. Again "in the dead vast and middle of the night" (I. 2. 198), when there is a "nipping and an eager air" (I. 4. 2), the terrible unearthly visitant glides through the darkness, while the men, "distill'd almost to jelly with the act of fear, stand dumb" (I. 2. 204–206). Up to this point Hamlet has been incredulous, but all his doubts vanish on the instant. He exclaims, "Angels and ministers of grace defend us!" (I. 4. 39). With Hamlet's conversion we find our own tendency to reject the spectre leaving us. It is now easier to believe in its reality.

Hamlet addresses the spirit, which beckons him to follow it. Horatio tries to dissuade the willing Prince, for ghosts were credited with the vile intention of enticing men to their self-destruction (I. 4. 69–74):

    What if it tempt you toward the flood, my lord,
    Or to the dreadful summit of the cliff
    That beetles o'er his base into the sea,
    And there assume some other horrible form,
    Which might deprive your sovereignty of reason
    And draw you into madness?

Hamlet disregards his friend's plea and follows to hear the ghastly tale of his father's murder and his mother's infidelity. The duty of revenge is laid upon his incapable shoulders before

> The glow-worm shows the matin to be near,
> And 'gins to pale his uneffectual fire
>
> (I. 5. 89–90)

and the Ghost bids him a hasty adieu.

There were two opinions commonly held in regard to ghosts. The first, and that in which the more educated people concurred, maintained that their origin was evil, that they were devils from hell, charged with a special mission to earth which could only be conveyed by supernatural means, and that they adopted for their purpose the form, figure, and characteristics of a deceased person. The second opinion interpreted ghosts as the actual spirits of departed men and women, who rose from the grave and appeared in a form recognizable to those still living, in order to impart information of the first consequence. Horatio, the scholar, takes the first view of the *Hamlet* Ghost (I. 1. 46–49):

> What art thou, that usurp'st this time of night,
> Together with that fair and warlike form
> In which the majesty of buried Denmark
> Did sometimes march?

He will cross it, though it blast him. He addresses it as "illusion," and believes it is some spirit that has the power to assume the shape and form of the late King of Denmark. The cultured Hamlet also believes it to be some devil masquerading as his father. When he decides to watch with the sentry, he says, "I'll speak to it, though hell itself should gape and bid

me hold my peace" (i. 2. 245–246). When he sees
the Ghost for the first time, he cries (i. 4. 40–45):

> Be thou a spirit of health, or goblin damn'd,
> Bring with thee airs from heaven or blasts from hell,
> Be thy intents wicked or charitable,
> Thou com'st in such a questionable shape
> That I will speak with thee: I'll call thee, Hamlet,
> King, father, royal Dane.

Hamlet obeys the Ghost's command to follow him,
ignoring the protest of Horatio, who is much relieved,
on coming up with him later, to find him safe.
Despite his long conversation with the Ghost and
the justification of his own feelings of depression,
Hamlet cannot shake off his old beliefs and feel
convinced that the apparition was in very truth his
father returned from the dead. The call to revenge
falls on doubting ears and results in hesitancy and
inaction. In his long soliloquy at the end of Act II,
the Prince says (ii. 2. 627–632):

> The spirit that I have seen
> May be the devil; and the devil hath power
> To assume a pleasing shape; yea, and perhaps
> Out of my weakness and my melancholy,
> As he is very potent with such spirits,
> Abuses me to damn me.

Therefore he decides to stage the interlude in order
to make the king himself betray his guilt. Only when
this trick succeeds, does he say to Horatio, "I'll take
the ghost's word" (iii. 2. 298) and really believes
at last that his father has communicated with him.
On the later appearance of the Ghost in Gertrude's
closet he admits the relationship and asks, "Do you
not come your tardy son to chide?" (iii. 4. 106).
In *Hamlet*, then, Shakespeare gives us a ghost that

is true to type, a ghost that makes every important concession to prevalent superstition, even adopting the more popular notion as to its origin, after toying with and rejecting the more scholarly construction of an emanation from the Evil One.

Nothing could be more masterly than Shakespeare's treatment of the *Hamlet* Ghost. Such is his skill that he makes the impossible appear real and convincing. He leaves the impression that he himself believed that such a manifestation of the Unseen was not beyond the bounds of probability. Modern audiences, comparatively free of the shackles of Elizabethan superstition, are still thrilled by the Ghost and do not regard it as ridiculous. This is an achievement beyond the power of any dramatist who is not a genius.

The popularity of the Supernatural on the Shakespearean stage was so great that, as we have seen, some playwrights were tempted to introduce ghosts and witches even when quite extraneous to their plots. Shakespeare was never guilty of this artistic blunder, although there is evidence that he was pressed at times to introduce pieces of pageantry, which could quite easily, and perhaps with advantage, have been omitted. Contemporary dramatists treated the Supernatural with much less dignity and respect than Shakespeare. They were far less restrained. They brought their immortals on to the stage at random and allowed them to mix casually with their human characters. Shakespeare knew the error of this—knew that by so doing the illusion was entirely destroyed.

Shakespeare's superiority over his fellows, good dramatists though many of them were, is revealed in nearly every branch of the playwright's art. There is no department, however, in which it is more obvious than in the treatment of the Supernatural. Note how carefully he arranges the unusual circumstances of every spectral appearance, and the gulf he places and retains between his human and supernatural beings. The Ghost in *Hamlet* is a typical example of Shakespeare's peculiar talent.

The opening scene of the play sketches with an amazing economy of language the surroundings and atmosphere particularly favourable to some eerie, unearthly experience (1–11):

Ber. Who's there?
Fran. Nay, answer me: stand, and unfold yourself
Ber. Long live the king!
Fran. Bernardo?
Ber. He.
Fran. You come most carefully upon your hour.
Ber. 'Tis now struck twelve; get thee to bed, Francisco.
Fran. For this relief much thanks: 'tis bitter cold,
   And I am sick at heart.
Ber. Have you had a quiet guard?
Fran. Not a mouse stirring.
Ber. Well, good night.

Bernardo also retails to the sceptical Horatio the circumstances of the two appearances of the Ghost to the Watch, which have occurred before the opening of the play (I. I. 30–39):

Ber.   Sit down awhile,
   And let us once again assail your ears,
   That are so fortified against our story,
   What we have two nights seen.
Hor.   Well, sit we down,
   And let us hear Bernado speak of this.
Ber. Last night of all,
   When yond same star that's westward from the pole,

Had made his course to illume that part of heaven
Where now it burns, Marcellus and myself,
The bell then beating one—

Bernardo breaks off suddenly as the Ghost appears. As Mrs. Montagu writes,[1] "There is something solemn and sublime in thus regulating the walking of the Spirit by the course of the Star: It intimates a connection and correspondence between things beyond our ken, and above the visible diurnal sphere."

Similarly uncanny conditions recur on the second appearance (in the play) of the Ghost, when Hamlet is with the watchers on the platform (1. 4. 1–6):

Ham. The air bites shrewdly; it is very cold.
Hor. It is a nipping and an eager air.
Ham.   What hour now?
Hor.   I think it lacks of twelve.
Mar.   No, it is struck.
Hor.   Indeed? I heard it not: it then draws near the season
      Wherein the spirit held his wont to walk.

Coleridge has called attention to Shakespeare's exquisite judgment in the writing of the dialogue of this scene.[2] It is natural for men when facing a strange and terrifying ordeal to try to distract their anxious minds by remarking on the trivial and familiar. Thus Hamlet and the soldiers speak of the weather and the hour of night, observations which have the added dramatic importance of describing the circumstances of the Ghost's visit. Hamlet then proceeds to discuss the custom of wassailing; and his criticisms so engross the attention of the audience

[1] *An Essay on the Writing and Genius of Shakespeare*, p. 166.
[2] See *Coleridge's Shakespearean Criticism* (T. M. Raysor), II. 274–275.

that when the Ghost suddenly interrupts the discourse, they are as much surprised as the actors pretend to be.

Characteristic of Shakespeare's treatment is the aloofness of *Hamlet* Ghost. It appears to ignore the existence of the soldiers. Even when the scholarly Horatio addresses it, it declines to answer until it delays too long and the cock crows. When it refuses to obey the order to halt and the sentries strike at it with their halberds, it eludes them easily and vanishes. On its next appearance, it refuses to speak to Hamlet while he is with his companions. Only when it has beckoned him to a place apart does it deliver its vital message. In the later appearance, in Gertrude's chamber, it is more distant still, and the fleshly minded queen cannot see it at all.

The importance of the Ghost in the unfolding of the plot of *Hamlet* will be apparent to all students of drama. Its revelations summarize briefly the previous history of Denmark and put the audience in possession of facts which it is essential they should know. As the play proceeds, we find the Ghost's story gradually confirmed and see the evil results of adultery and murder. Here we may note a contrast with the tragedy of *Macbeth*. In *Hamlet* the Super-natural reveals the *past* and is corroborated: in *Macbeth* it reveals the *future*, and its prophecies are fulfilled. There is a further difference of first impor-tance. In the Scottish tragedy the Weird Sisters succeed in persuading Macbeth to carry out their designs: in *Hamlet* the Ghost really fails in his mission, for the Prince hesitates, doubts, and delays, and finally is moved to kill the murderer by other causes altogether. The Weird Sisters do not return to Macbeth to lead him further into the mire. They are apparently satisfied with the mischief they have already done. It is only when Macbeth comes of his own free will to consult them that they continue their game of treacherous, misleading prophecy. The Ghost in *Hamlet*, however, is forced to return to whet his son's "almost blunted purpose" (III. 4. 111).

An important question arises here as to the extent of the power of the Supernatural over mortal men and women. A study of the two plays *Hamlet* and *Macbeth* suggests that its influence is only limited. Man is ever his own master, always able to exercise his sovereign free-will. Ghosts and witches can only suggest, tempt, persuade, and appeal; they cannot command, nor compel. When Horatio tries to dissuade Hamlet from following the Ghost, the Prince replies (I. 4. 64–67):

> Why, what should be the fear?
> I do not set my life at a pin's fee;
> And, for my soul, what can it do to that,
> Being a thing immortal as itself?

The most the Shakespearean Fairies could do was to annoy mortals with some childish prank. Ghosts have more power than that. It is, however, the power that comes from greater knowledge and experience. According to the beliefs most widely held, ghosts were the spirits of those who had once lived in the flesh themselves. Any influence they wielded over human kind was due to their acquaintance with life beyond the grave. But mortals were free to reject this claim of influence and assert their independence.

How circumscribed was the power of ghosts is clearly shown in *Hamlet*. They return to Earth with a special duty to perform, but they cannot accomplish this duty by their own efforts alone. They are compelled to work through a human personality. The Ghost had no power to float into the Castle at Elsinore and slay Claudius with its own hands. It must choose the living Hamlet as an instrument; and even then, it could not insist on his carrying out the task of revenge. It could only spur him on in the hope that the deed would be done.

The course pursued by supernatural agents in persuading mortals to act as they wish is depicted in the two tragedies of Shakespeare's great but gloomy period, when the Unseen had assumed for him so terrible an aspect. The method was to connect with ideas latent in the human mind and to strengthen and influence them until they ripened into deeds that suited them. The Weird Sisters would have had no hold upon Macbeth at all if they had not played upon his secret ambitions. Likewise the Ghost would not have obtained the ear of Hamlet if he had not been depressed by the loss of his father, the hasty remarriage of his mother, his own exclusion from the throne, and the unworthiness of his uncle. Shakespeare prepares the soil for the seeds to be planted by the Ghost. Before Hamlet sees or even hears of the apparition, he unburdens his soul in soliloquy (I. 2. 137–145, 156, 158):

> That it should come to this!
> But two months dead! Nay, not so much, not two:
> So excellent a king; that was, to this,
> Hyperion to a satyr: so loving to my mother,
> That he might not beteem the winds of heaven

> Visit her face too roughly. Heaven and earth!
> Must I remember? why, she would hang on him,
> As if increase of appetite had grown
> By what it fed on: and yet, within a month . . .
> She married . . .
> It is not, nor it cannot come to, good.

When the Ghost reveals the truth to Hamlet and shows him the real cause of all his melancholy, he cries out, "O my prophetic soul!" The Ghost, now that he has connected with the secret thoughts whirling in Hamlet's mind, gives a full and detailed account of the whole ugly chapter of vice and crime in the hope that it will incite him to take a just, swift, and fearful revenge. And Hamlet's outburst of fury and indignation is such that the Ghost might well congratulate himself on the successful accomplishment of his mission.

But the Ghost fails. He is defeated by the character and temperament of Hamlet. The Prince is totally unfitted for the task of killing. His sensitive soul shrinks from the crime of murder. The Ghost has scarcely disappeared, when his whole soul revolts against the duty laid upon him (I. 5. 189-190):

> The time is out of joint: O cursèd spite,
> That ever I was born to set it right!

Hamlet's very learning and culture were inimical to the Ghost's purpose. If he had been one of the ignorant multitude, he would have regarded ghosts as the spirits of the departed and had no doubt that it was really his father who spoke to him. But Hamlet subscribed to the more educated belief that ghosts were instruments of the devil. He began by doubting its existence and insisted on seeing it himself. When

he did see it, he was not convinced that it was not
the product of his own imagination.[1]

• Hamlet does not credit the Ghost's story sufficiently
to act upon it without further proof: "I'll have
grounds more relative than this" (II. 2. 632–633).
Indeed, if his other tests of the King's guilt fail, he
is ready to discard the Ghost's testimony altogether
(III. 2. 85–89):

> If his occulted guilt
> Do not itself unkennel in one speech,
> It is a damned ghost that we have seen;
> And my imaginations are as foul
> As Vulcan's stithy.

How unfortunate is the Ghost in the choice of its
human instrument is shown when Hamlet, even after
the interlude has left no doubts as to the King's
guilt, lets pass an opportunity to kill him because
he happens to be at prayer. After this failure comes
another appearance of the Ghost, who realizes that
its first visit has proved abortive and resolves to try
again. It is no more successful. Hamlet allows himself to be sent away to England without making any
attempt at all to carry out the "dread command."
In the last scene of the play, when Hamlet sees his
mother drink the poison and learns that his own
death is near through the vile treachery of the King,
he leaps upon him on the impulse and wounds him
mortally. But no credit remains with the Ghost for
this *dénouement*. The Supernatural has failed.

• Shakespeare uses two kinds of ghosts in his dramas,
the objective and the subjective. The objective ghost
is intended to be really present and is seen by several

[1] See II. 2, 627–632, quoted on p. 69.

people at once. Hamlet's Ghost is objective, for it
manifests itself to all those who happen to be on
the platform at the moment. Bernardo and Marcellus,
and the men under them, are matter-of-fact soldiers,
not at all the type liable to psychical experiences.
They are upset when the sceptical Horatio makes
light of their story and taxes them with imagining
things. Marcellus observes (I. I. 23–25):

> Horatio says 'tis but our fantasy;
> And will not let belief take hold of him,
> Touching this dreaded sight, twice seen of us.

Therefore they bring him along to the platform so
that he may see for himself and change his opinion
of them. The Ghost obligingly reappears, and the
unbeliever is convinced by the testimony of his own
senses (56–58):

> I might not this believe
> Without the sensible and true avouch
> Of mine own eyes.

By these means the reality of the *Hamlet* Ghost is
attested. Shakespeare means us to accept it as an
actual manifestation. It is an objective ghost,
not a trick of the imagination caused by terror,
worry, or madness, nor the unsubstantial product
of a dream. These last were the common conditions in which subjective ghosts were seen, such
a ghost being visible only to the person whom it
closely concerned. It was when Macbeth was in the
grip of guilty fear that he saw the Ghost of Banquo.
It was during his troubled sleep on the eve of Bosworth that Richard III was visited by the spirits of
his slain. It was when Brutus was obsessed with a

premonition of his own death that he saw the shade of Cæsar. Shakespeare, indeed, made more use of the subjective than the objective ghost. It would seem that the *Hamlet* Ghost itself becomes subjective on its appearance in Gertrude's closet, for while Hamlet talks with it, the Queen can see nothing. She accepts the common explanation of Hamlet's behaviour and believes (III. 4. 137-139):

> This is the very coinage of your brain:
> This bodiless creation ecstasy
> Is very cunning in.

But Hamlet, though earlier he has himself wondered if his senses are playing him false, now indignantly repudiates the subjective explanation (139-146):

> Ecstasy! [i.e. madness]
> My pulse, as yours, doth temperately keep time,
> And makes as healthful music: it is not madness
> That I have utter'd: bring me to the test,
> And I the matter will re-word, which madness
> Would gambol from. Mother, for love of grace,
> Lay not that flattering unction to your soul,
> That not your trespass but my madness speaks.

In Belleforest's French translation of the story of Hamlet from the Latin of the Danish historian, Saxo Grammaticus, no mention of a ghost occurs. There is no doubt, however, that there was an older tragedy of *Hamlet*, probably written by Kyd, upon which the Shakespearean play was based, and this earlier piece apparently contained a ghost. The chief piece of contemporary evidence in support of this ghost is found in *Wit's Miserie, and the World's Madness* by Lodge, published in 1596, half a dozen years before Shakespeare's *Hamlet*. Lodge writes: "Hate-Vertue is a foul lubber, and looks as pale as the Vizard of ye Ghost, which cried so miserally at ye Theator like an oister wife, 'Hamlet, revenge.' ".

There seems little doubt that Shakespeare took the appearance of the Ghost in Act I of *Hamlet* from Kyd's play. The long speeches in Scene V with their invective and moralization are not at all characteristic of the Shakespearean ghosts, who are usually the most reticent of beings. Shakespeare in this part of the play was probably rewriting Kyd. The second appearance of the *Hamlet* Ghost presents an extraordinary contrast with the first. On this occasion (III. 4) the Ghost limits itself to half a dozen lines, four of which refer to the Queen and have little to do with the purpose of its reappearance. This is more typical of Shakespeare's use of this particular form of the Supernatural. We draw the conclusion, then, that while Kyd furnished the groundwork for the first visit of the spectre, the second visit was Shakespeare's own invention. (The underground ghost of I. 5—the old mole—looks like a theatrical interpolation.)

How valuable ghosts were to Shakespeare in his work of providing plays for the multitude we shall appreciate more fully when we have added to our study of the shade of *Hamlet* that of the ghosts of Banquo, Julius Cæsar, and the victims of Richard III. We cannot fail to be impressed by his sparing use of the Supernatural and his refusal to be tempted to introduce so sensational a feature without real dramatic purpose. He was always careful to give his ghosts an essential part to play and never introduced them as meaningless supernumeraries. The *Hamlet* Ghost, like the Weird Sisters of *Macbeth* and the spirit of *Julius Cæsar*, dominates the whole action, and controls the fortunes and characters of all who come beneath its influence. Hamlet is a changed man after his eerie experience; and his own violent death, as well as the tragedies of Polonius, Ophelia, Gertrude, Laertes, and Claudius, is to be directly attributed to the spectre's intervention. Mary A. Woods, writing on Shakespeare's ghosts generally, says,[1] "They are no mere stage accessories. They have a function and a dignity that compel the awe-struck recognition of the most careless. They are Messengers from the Unseen, Ministers of Justice, Avengers of crimes that but for them might have remained unpunished. They stand for the nemesis which is a prime factor in all the Plays, though here, as in real life, it may seem to work slowly, falteringly, even at times capriciously."

The Ghost in *Hamlet* is an instructive case of the effective employment of the spectral in dramatic craftmanship, and an excellent example of the skill with which Shakespeare endowed his supernatural beings with all the prevalent superstitions. But it is more than that. It is a revelation of the inner Shakespeare and his changing and darkening mental attitude towards the Unseen at the beginning of his middle life and his great tragic period.

[1] *Studies in Shakespeare*, p. 51.

V

"MACBETH"

Macbeth is the Shakespearean play into which the Supernatural enters most largely. The form adopted is that of witches; and the wholly evil designs of these half-earthly, half-metaphysical beings control events and exert an ever-present and irresistible influence over the characters. Even when the witches are not visible, the audience remains acutely conscious of their presence. They seem to hover unseen in the background, producing that sense of gloom and terror which permeates the tragedy.

Macbeth was written four years after *Hamlet* and belongs to the latter part of the tragic period which *Julius Cæsar* and *Hamlet* introduced. The plays nearest *Macbeth* in point of writing are the grim tragedies of *Othello* and *King Lear*. We can, therefore, form some estimate of the state of melancholy through which the poet was slowly passing when these great but solemn masterpieces were composed.

In the course of our study we have found that the dramatist's general outlook upon life has been fairly reflected in his treatment of the Supernatural. In *Midsummer Night's Dream*, begun while he was still in the twenties, we saw the Fairies handled in the gay, buoyant, irrepressible spirit of youth. *Hamlet*, written in the late thirties, showed a grave and serious attitude towards the Supernatural. *Macbeth*, the product of Shakespeare in the forties, reveals the darkest and most pessimistic phase of his life. He does not appear to doubt or question the power of the forces of evil as he did in the *Hamlet* period. Now he seems to believe that human beings are surrounded by foul and terrible influences and temptations, aimed at their betrayal and undoing. At this time Shakespeare was almost overwhelmed by his contemplation of all the sin, pain, and cruelty which seemed to beset mortal existence. His fear of the Supernatural is no longer physical; it is moral. It is the ability of evil to destroy the soul which so oppresses him that scarcely a ray of light pierces the cloud.

In *Macbeth*, therefore, we find the supernatural beings exercising greater powers than ever, and succeeding in their fell purposes. Whereas Titania's fairies had little or no influence over mortals, and the *Hamlet* Ghost had such limited power that his mission was really a failure, the Weird Sisters of *Macbeth* accomplish their vile purpose in the ruin of a great and noble character. Nevertheless, even in his darkest hour, the spirits of evil, according to Shakespeare, only exercised a limited power. Man still retained the gift of free-will; he could not be deprived of life, but only lured to self-destruction.

Shakespeare reveals his mental state during this time of heaviness and ill-foreboding in those famous lines which he puts into Macbeth's mouth when the usurper is approaching his doom (v. 5. 19–28):

> To-morrow, and to-morrow, and to-morrow,
> Creeps in this petty pace from day to day,
> To the last syllable of recorded time;
> And all our yesterdays have lighted fools
> The way to dusty death. Out, out, brief candle!
> Life's but a walking shadow, a poor player,
> That struts and frets his hour upon the stage,
> And then is heard no more: it is a tale
> Told by an idiot, full of sound and fury,
> Signifying nothing.

In what different mood is the foregoing to the famous
speech of Jaques in *As You Like It*—"All the world's
a stage"—an acknowledgment of law and order and
divine direction!

Another instance of the hopeless outlook comes
from one of the murderers of Banquo (III. 1. 108–111):

> I am one, my liege,
> Whom the vile blows and buffets of the world
> Have so incensed that I am reckless what
> I do to spite the world.

No form of the Supernatural would match Shakespeare's blackest humour so well as witches. The
dramatist had not in mind the old and toothless
hags who told fortunes and dealt in charms and
spells. Probably he had little faith in such creatures,
persecuted though they were for their occult practices.
Shakespeare entertained a higher conception for the
witches in *Macbeth*. It is significant that he does not
call them witches anywhere in the play. They are
always the "Weird Sisters," or the "Weird Women,"
or sometimes merely the "Sisters." Whereas the
ordinary witch was dreaded because she could injure
with a glance, make a child sick, cause losses among
livestock, or otherwise inflict physical harm, Shakespeare intended that his Weird Sisters should terrify
by their threat to the human soul.

Although Shakespeare did not confuse the supernatural beings in *Macbeth* with those wretched
creatures who were forced by torture to confess to
witchcraft and burned at the stake for their evil
deeds, he was compelled, in order to be intelligible
to his audience, to attach to his Weird Sisters the
popular ideas of witch-lore. Many of these—for

example, that witches were withered, bearded women
in wild attire—are included in the first words of
Banquo, when he and Macbeth perceive the Sisters
for the first time (I. 3. 39–47):

> What are these
> So wither'd, and so wild in their attire,
> That look not like the inhabitants o' the earth,
> And yet are on't? Live you? or are you aught
> That man may question? You seem to understand me,
> By each at once her choppy finger laying
> Upon her skinny lips: you should be women,
> And yet your beards forbid me to interpret
> That you are so.

Witches appeared in dark, dismal, and creepy circumstances. In *Macbeth* they are always accompanied
by thunder, which from earliest times has sent a
superstitious shudder through the minds of mortals.
They choose a blasted heath overcast by fog for their
first meeting with Macbeth. When he seeks them out
for a second interview, he finds them in a black
cavern, with a boiling cauldron in its centre, and
the rumblings of thunder still in the distance. He
greets them with the words, "How now, you secret,
black, and midnight hags!" (IV. I. 48).

Witches can vanish as easily and suddenly as they
appear. After delivering their first prophecies to
Macbeth, they fade away (I. 3. 79–82):

> *Ban.* The earth hath bubbles as the water has,
>   And these are of them: whither are they vanish'd?
> *Macb.* Into the air; and what seem'd corporal melted
>   As breath into the wind.

Describing the experience in a letter to his wife,
Macbeth writes, "When I burned in desire to ques-

tion them further, they made themselves air, into which they vanished" (I. 5. 3–5).

From speeches of the Weird Sisters we learn that they possess most of the powers credited to the popular witch. They can, for instance, assume all sorts of shapes; they have both the cat and the dog as familiars; they can raise storms and command the winds. Their control of the elements, as well as their other feats of magic, are acknowledged by Macbeth (IV. I. 50–61):

> I conjure you, by that which you profess,
> Howe'er you come to know it, answer me:
> Though you untie the winds and let them fight
> Against the churches; though the yesty waves
> Confound and swallow navigation up;
> Though bladed corn be lodged and trees blown down;
> Though castles topple on their warders' heads;
> Though palaces and pyramids do slope
> Their heads to their foundations; though the treasure
> Of nature's germins tumble all together,
> Even till destruction sicken; answer me
> To what I ask you.

A further reference to witches' power over wind and wave occurs in Scene 3 of Act I, where the Second Witch promises the First Witch "I'll give thee a wind" (11). The First Witch, in her railing against the sailor, whose wife had insulted her, threatens (24–25):

> Though his bark cannot be lost,
> Yet it shall be tempest-tost.

The lines, while further defining the wide powers of evil possessed by witches, suggest at the same time that these powers were limited and did not cover the taking of human life.

There are many minor points of witch-lore in the text of *Macbeth*, as we have it, which are more in keeping with vulgar superstition than with Shakespeare's mature conception of the Supernatural. The explanation is interesting and may be stated shortly.

Scholars are now nearly all agreed that some other hand than Shakespeare's meddled with the tragedy. This other hand is particularly noticeable in certain of the Witch scenes. Some of the appearances of the Weird Sisters serve no dramatic purpose whatsoever, while in Hecate a meaningless and superfluous character is introduced who is inconsistent with the other supernatural beings. The verse of these redundant scenes is assuredly not by Shakespeare; and the conclusion has been reached that they are interpolations. Such scenes are Act I, Scene 1 and the beginning of Scene 3; Act III, Scene 5; and the appearance of Hecate in Act IV, Scene 1.

Macbeth, as written by Shakespeare, was a short play and intended, no doubt, for presentation at Court on some special occasion—perhaps the visit of the Queen's brother, the King of Denmark, in 1606. It is assumed that it was such a success that production in the public theatre followed as a matter of course. But for this purpose the piece was too short, and the script was given to one of the company's dramatists to expand and enlarge. Textual examination points to Middleton as the man who was given the job. On considering the script, Middleton saw that his best opportunity for effective padding lay in the scenes of the Weird Sisters. Not only would this go down well with the audience, who always applauded anything in the nature of ghosts and witches, but Middleton himself was something of an expert on witch-lore and wrote a play of his own on the subject. The passages he added contain a lot of matter about witches that seems trivial compared with the grand ideas of Shakespeare; and any reader of the tragedy who has been puzzled by the silly talk about the sailor at the beginning of I. 3, or the unimpressive character of Hecate, who introduces herself as mistress of the very impressive Weird Sisters, will not hesitate to agree with the theory of interpolation.

Shakespeare had included sufficient of the current superstition about witches to render his Weird Sisters understandable enough before Middleton made his additions. These additions were dictated merely by the popularity of the Supernatural on the Elizabethan stage. Shakespeare was economical in his use of accepted witch-lore, because he was aiming at something higher than ordinary types of the dealers in magic and spells. He had chosen his points with care —looks, attire, appearance in darkness and thunder, the power to vanish, control of the elements. The minor points mentioned in the interpolated scenes have no significance. One aspect of witchcraft Shakespeare did lay great emphasis upon, because it was of first importance in the construction of his plot; and that aspect was the supposed gift of prophecy. At the first meeting with the Weird Sisters, Banquo says to them (I. 3. 58–61):

> If you can look into the seeds of time,
> And say which grain will grow and which will not,
> Speak then to me, who neither beg nor fear
> Your favours nor your hate.

The whole play thereafter turns upon the prophecies

of the Sisters. The first group, that Macbeth will be thane of Glamis, thane of Cawdor, and king hereafter, persuades the ambitious man to murder Duncan and seize the Crown. The promise to Banquo that he shall be father of a line of kings leads to his death at the hands of Macbeth and the return of his ghost to assist in the murderer's undoing. This concludes the first half of the tragedy; and the second half is prefaced by a new set of prophecies: beware Macduff; none born of woman shall harm Macbeth; and Macbeth shall not be vanquished till Great Birnam Wood shall come to Dunsinane Hill. Macduff eventually rids Scotland of the wicked king; Macduff also reveals that his birth was premature; and Malcolm's army marches on Dunsinane behind a screen of branches cut from Birnam Wood. It was essential, then, to make much of the powers of prophecy with which the people credited the witch. Moreover, these prophets were shown to be actuated by hate and spite so that their predictions, though fair-sounding, should prove to be clever and unscrupulous deceptions.

Another department of witchcraft which Shakespeare found useful in the composition of *Macbeth* was the power to raise spirits. He bases his great Incantation Scene upon it—probably the finest supernatural spectacle ever written for the stage. The smoky cavern, the bubbling cauldron, the growling thunder, the chanting witches, combine to form a setting revealing Shakespeare's gift of dramatic creation at its highest. For this was all the playwright's own invention, not copied nor suggested by other writers. Into this scene Shakespeare certainly poured a goodly dose of witch-lore. But he did not work at random. For example, when he talks about the whining hedge-pig, he remembers that according to folk-lore witches drew omens from the hedgehog; and Macbeth is coming, as we know, to learn what the fates have in store for him. Here again we have another demonstration of the use of music to impress an audience with the mysterious and incomprehensible nature of the Supernatural. The chanting of the Sisters in a sinister minor key, the coarse cry of the hautboys as the cauldron descends, the rhythm of the wild dance in which the unearthly creatures vanish—all intensify the feeling of awe and disquietude which the witch scenes inspire. (The songs given to Hecate (III. 4 and IV. 1) are probably, like the character itself, interpolations.)

In introducing Witches into his play, Shakespeare knew that he was on safe ground. He could feel particularly confident if the play was written for a Court function, as most critics believe it was. King James, as we have noted in an earlier chapter, was the bitter enemy of witches. He had answered Reginald Scot's attack on the witchcraft superstition by his own volume *Demonologie*, published in 1597. Only a year or two before *Macbeth* was written a statute had been passed for the suppression of witches. The subject was, therefore, popular and topical; and the famous dramatist admitted such concessions to popular superstitions as were useful in making his Weird Sisters intelligible and attractive without introducing anything that was in conflict with the dramatic rôle he intended them to fill.

It was one of the marvels of Shakespeare's genius that the touch of his master-hand, even the lightest of touches, could transform the commonplace into

something commanding respect and attention. His
handling of the Supernatural in *Macbeth* is no exception. His decision to use witches taken, he avoids
anything coarse, gross, or sensual. There is much in
his Weird Sisters that raises them far above the
conventional witch of the theatre. We have seen that
he was careful not to call them witches. He gives
them no names. Though they are "Weird Women"
in the text, the description is taken from Holinshed
and used for want of a better. He meant them to
be without sex, without passion, without age. Except
in so far as they are disseminators of evil, they can
be said to be without motive. Yet these strange
beings, sufficiently like the popular conception of
witches to be recognizable, are so great an advance
upon the customary presentation as to be truly
impressive and even dignified.

Shakespeare's original genius is well exemplified
in the way in which he makes his Weird Sisters
speak. Coleridge writes:[1] "The exquisite judgment
of Shakespeare is shown in nothing more than in
the different language of the Witches with each other,
and with those whom they address: the former
displays a certain fierce familiarity, grotesqueness
mingled with terror; the latter is always solemn,
dark, and mysterious." Schlegel also notes this
characteristic:[2] "Among themselves the witches con-
verse like women of the lowest class, for this they
are intended to be; with Macbeth, however, their
tone is elevated."

We have had occasion to mention the dramatist
Middleton, who wrote a play of considerable merit

[1] *Coleridge's Shakespearean Criticism* (Raysor), II. 270.
[2] *Werke*, VI. 255.

entitled *The Witch*, and is generally believed to be responsible for the interpolated scenes in *Macbeth*. Middleton was a clever writer and handled his witches with marked ability. But with all his cleverness, he fell far short of the genius of Shakespeare. On this point Charles Lamb wrote:[1] "Their names and some of the properties, which Middleton has given to his hags, excite smiles. The Weird Sisters are serious things. Their presence cannot co-exist with mirth. But in a lesser degree, the Witches of Middleton are fine creatures. Their power, too, is in some measure over the mind."

The recognition of the subtle difference and superiority of the Shakespearean witch is found in all critics and commentators. Coleridge said of the Sisters,[2] "They were awful beings, and blended in themselves the Fates and Furies of the ancients with the sorceresses of Gothic and popular superstition. They were mysterious natures: fatherless, motherless, sexless." And again,[3] "Shakespeare's Witches are threefold—Fates, Furies, and earthly Hags o' the cauldron." W. W. Lloyd, in his essay on *Macbeth*, writes, "Creative imagination has blended together the revolting horrors of the witchcraft known or imagined by the penal statutes, and the boding solemnity of the nobler superstitions of the Highlands and the Western Isles without any incongruity."

Shakespeare's dramatic use of the Weird Sisters is as ingenious as his original conception of them. His handling of them shows his treatment of the Supernatural in its most masterly form. Once having

---

[1] *Specimens of English Dramatic Poets.*
[2] *Coleridge's Shakespearean Criticism* (Raysor), II. 269.
[3] *Ibid.*, II. 356.

made his audience acquainted with his awesome
beings, he does not cheapen them by permitting
them to be seen too often. As in other instances, his
use of the Supernatural is restrained. He never over-
does it, never allows it to become frivolous. He
contents himself with two appearances of the Sisters,
introducing each half of the tragedy. (We have seen
that the superfluous witch scenes are interpolated.)
By so doing he brings the powerful influences before
us and then leaves the rest to our imaginations. This
device is the inspiration of genius. It imbues us with
a feeling of the omnipresence of the Supernatural
and deepens the sense of fear and revulsion.

Suppose Shakespeare, over-anxious to please and
lacking in self-confidence, had repeated the thrilling
Incantation Scene, how the drama would have been
spoilt! Lesser dramatists were often induced to do
this sort of thing and were surprised at their failure.
Shakespeare realized that any repetition would
damage the impression which the single presentation
had created, while frequent reappearances would
end in rendering the whole supernatural element
ludicrous. The Poet knew that the real struggle
between good and evil is not between angels and
demons; and did not, therefore, bring angels and
demons on to the stage to fight their battle out. The
real struggle is always decided in the human heart.

At the time *Macbeth* was written Shakespeare's
powers had attained their zenith. His mature conception of tragedy was the ruin of a grand and noble
nature through the existence of some serious, inherent
weakness, brought into contact with the special
hostile circumstances calculated to defeat it. *Macbeth*
follows the lines of all the great dramas of this period.

The thane is a man of considerable elements of greatness. But he has one weakness—ambition. The Weird
Sisters provide in their glamorous and cleverly disguised prophecies the temptation which Macbeth's
ambitious yearnings cannot resist. He yields, and the
end is tragedy.

We must ask ourselves how Shakespeare meant
us to interpret his Weird Sisters. We see, of course,
witches, with most of the attributes associated with
these unfortunates. We are conscious, however, that
though outwardly witches, they are something apart
from any other stage witches we have seen. How
did the dramatist intend us to view them? It seems
to me that Shakespeare meant his Weird Sisters to
be the symbolic representation of the inward temptation of Macbeth's restless ambition; for, to quote
once more from Coleridge,[1] "they lead evil minds
from evil to evil, and have the power of tempting
those who have been the tempters of themselves."

In *Hamlet* we saw that the supernatural agent
worked by connecting with the latent thought of the
human being who was to carry out its purposes. So
it is in *Macbeth*. The Sisters appear to Macbeth in
his weakest moment, that is to say, when he is flushed
with victory. The hour of success is always the most
dangerous for those who are madly ambitious. In
their prophecies they echo Macbeth's secret hopes
and desires. He cannot disguise the fact. Banquo
notices it and asks (I. 3. 51–52):

> Good sir, why do you start, and seem to fear
> Things that do sound so fair?

Nevertheless, Macbeth is not bound to surrender.

[1] *Coleridge's Shakespearean Criticism* (Raysor), II. 270.

He has power to resist. Mortals, as we have said before, have always freedom of choice. As Gervinus writes, "The Weird Sisters have no authority with fatalistic power to do violence to the human will." But to resist temptation means a fight, and often a bitter one, as Shakespeare had learned in the school of life. Macbeth, though shaken, does not intend to yield without a struggle. It is made more difficult for him by the immediate confirmation of one of the prophecies. Lords arrive from Duncan with the news that the successful general has been created thane of Cawdor by his grateful sovereign. He muses (I. 3. 130–137):

> This supernatural soliciting
> Cannot be ill; cannot be good: if ill,
> Why hath it given me earnest of success,
> Commencing in a truth? I am thane of Cawdor:
> If good, why do I yield to that suggestion
> Whose horrid image doth unfix my hair,
> And make my seated heart knock at my ribs,
> Against the use of nature?

He fights down the horrible suggestion of assassination (*ibid.*, 143–144):

> If chance will have me king, why, chance may crown me,
> Without my stir.

Temptation, however, does not mean to leave Macbeth alone. Through his wife he has strong and legitimate claims to the crown. Duncan himself is a usurper; and when the king appoints his son Malcolm as his heir, Evil winds another tentacle round the thane (I. 4. 48–53):

> The Prince of Cumberland! that is a step
> On which I must fall down, or else o'erleap,
> For in my way it lies. Stars, hide your fires!
> Let not light see my black and deep desires:
> The eye wink at the hand; yet let that be
> Which the eye fears, when it is done, to see.

Macbeth finds temptation assail him through another channel—the incitements of his wife. Although Duncan and Lady Macbeth are instruments for bringing further pressure to bear on the thane, we realize all the time that the wielders of those instruments are the unseen Sisters. Lady Macbeth shares with her husband the fault of ambition; but when temptation comes to her with the report of the prophecies, she, unlike her husband, makes no attempt at resistance, but is all impatience to snatch the promised fruit.

Though he is hardly pressed, Macbeth is not conquered without a struggle. He tries to delay matters—"We will speak further" (1. 5. 72). When Lady Macbeth has urged him to the breaking-point, he makes a last desperate effort to resist the devil—"We will proceed no further in this business" (1. 7. 31). Every excuse for going back upon his word is put forward: Duncan has honoured him; he is a guest in his house; he has been a kind and gentle king; he himself has won golden opinions from all sorts of people which he wants to keep. It is all of no avail. Lady Macbeth wins him to the foul deed, and succeeds because Macbeth *wants* to be king, and believes he must move Duncan out of his way. Duncan is murdered and the Weird Sisters chuckle over the success of their cruel trick. Unlike the *Hamlet* Ghost, they have succeeded, although the Supernatural in the one case intervened to revenge a great wrong, while in the other there was merely a motive-less desire to ruin and destroy. Yet the Sisters said nothing of the means Macbeth was to adopt to gain his end. They did not even hint that the reigning king must be assassinated to open the way to the throne. This wickedness grew out of Macbeth's fault in not hurling the temptation from him.

Once having stepped on the downward path, resistance for Macbeth became more difficult. Though the Sisters appeared not again, their words still rang in Macbeth's ears. Banquo shall beget kings though he be none. Macbeth, now stained with evil, sees danger in a living Banquo. He plans and carries out his murder. But the son, Fleance, escapes. So crime follows crime, and still the voices of the Sisters lure the sinner on.

Banquo serves a useful dramatic purpose in the attitude he adopts towards the prophecies, for he is in direct contrast to the susceptible Macbeth. He asks the Sisters to speak to him, though he neither begs nor fears their favours nor their hate (1. 3. 60). He does not, however, treat their predictions seriously. He does not really credit their existence (1. 3. 79–80) :

> The earth hath bubbles as the water has,
> And these are of them.

Banquo recognizes something of the true nature of the prophecies, when he says (1. 3. 123–126) :

> . . . oftentimes, to win us to our harm,
> The instruments of darkness tell us truths,
> Win us with honest trifles, to betray us
> In deepest consequence.

Shakespeare gives the different reaction of the three

leading characters to temptation. Macbeth is deeply moved, but struggles against it; Lady Macbeth surrenders without any resistance at all; Banquo rejects it and keeps his "bosom franchised and allegiance clear." But even Banquo has ambitions and toys with the thought of founding a line of kings. For this small weakness he has to pay the penalty.

On the second appearance of the Supernatural, which opens the latter half of the tragedy, it is Macbeth who seeks the Sisters out, not the Sisters Macbeth. Duncan has been assassinated, Banquo has been murdered, horrible and foul crimes have been committed, but even now Macbeth has opportunity to repent. He can still turn over a new leaf and make reparation. Instead of doing so, he deliberately places himself again within reach of temptation. He does not wait for it to come to him. He goes to the Sisters like Saul to the Witch of Endor.

In the Incantation Scene the prophecies have a different character. At the beginning of the play the Weird Women suggested no line of action to Macbeth. The violence which followed was the product of his own wicked mind. Now, however, the apparitions conjured up by their magic do urge Macbeth to "be bloody, bold, and resolute." Moreover, their predictions are cleverly worded with the deliberate intent to deceive. They begin by connecting with Macbeth's secret fear, as the Ghost connected with Hamlet's latent thought, and warn him to beware Macduff. Then, his attention won, they tell him that no man of woman born can harm him, thereby encouraging him to think that he can be bold, bloody, and resolute with impunity. The prophecy that he shall never be vanquished till Birnam Wood comes to Dunsinane lifts his self-confidence to such a height that his fall is all the greater, more sudden and unexpected.

Deep in sin as he is, Macbeth has even yet the power to reform. But he plunges from one crime to another until he brings about his own destruction. The prophecies, which so heartened him, prove to be the most ingenious and unscrupulous frauds; and when this realization comes to him he cries (v. 8. 19–22):

> And be these juggling fiends no more believed,
> That palter with us in a double sense;
> That keep the word of promise to our ear,
> And break it to our hope.

Macbeth does not blame the Sisters. He knows that he had the power to resist temptation, and that his present misfortunes are the result of not resisting it. He realizes all that he has lost; and, criminal as he is, we can hardly deny him our pity, when he says (v. 3. 22–28):

> I have lived long enough: my way of life
> Is fall'n into the sear, the yellow leaf;
> And that which should accompany old age,
> As honour, love, obedience, troops of friends,
> I must not look to have; but, in their stead,
> Curses, not loud but deep, mouth-honour, breath,
> Which the poor heart would fain deny, and dare not.

For this most impressive and successful use of the Supernatural Shakespeare worked upon a sentence he found in Holinshed's Chronicles, which included the story of Macbeth in the section dealing with the history of Scotland.

The historian told how Macbeth and Banquo,

returning from the wars, were met by "three women in straunge and ferly apparell, resembling creatures of an elder world." It was, he said, believed that these women were "eyther the wierd sisters, that is ye Goddesses of Destinie, or else some Nimphes or Feiries endowed with knowledge of prophecie by their Nicromanticall Science." Shakespeare takes the incident and also the name of Weird Sisters, and places his own interpretation upon the supernatural manifestation.

For the second stage appearance of the Weird Sisters, Shakespeare adopted a different course. Holinshed describes the second lot of prophecies as coming in respect of the warning to beware Macduff from "certeine wizzards," and in respect of the others from "a certeine witch, whome hee had in great trust." Shakespeare here rejects Holinshed, invents the Incantation Scene, and places the new prophecies also with the Weird Sisters, thus developing his high conception of the tragedy and the important symbolic part the Supernatural was to play.

The Weird Sisters are not the only unearthly characters of *Macbeth*. In the banquet scene, where the usurper and his queen are entertaining the Scottish nobles in the palace at Forres, there enters the ghost of the murdered Banquo. Macbeth's horror at seeing it is so great that he betrays his guilty secret to his subjects.

Banquo's shade is a subjective ghost. No one sees it but Macbeth. It is an illusion of his own perturbed thought. He has had a similar experience earlier, for just before the murder of the king, he believed he saw a dagger floating in the air before his eyes. He recognized it then as "a false creation, proceeding from the heat-oppressed brain" (II. I. 38–39): and Lady Macbeth, speaking contemptuously, says of the ghost (III. 4. 60–63):

> O proper stuff!
> This is the very painting of your fear:
> This is the air-drawn dagger, which, you said,
> Led you to Duncan.

Macbeth alone knows of the foul murder of Banquo; and on each occasion that he refers to him, his imagination conjures up the ghastly vision of his gory locks.

Some critics have been dissatisfied with the double appearance of Banquo's ghost and would prefer to substitute that of Duncan on one occasion, arguing that an apparition would lose some of its power to terrify by showing itself twice in so short a time. But Macbeth's mind is full of the very recent murder of Banquo, and his horror and fright are understandable enough. Moreover, contemporary evidence has much to say of Banquo's ghost, while that of Duncan is not mentioned.

Whether Banquo's ghost should actually appear on the stage is an open question. As a subjective ghost, invisible to all but Macbeth, the more accurate and artistic interpretation would be to leave the audience to be made aware of its presence by the fear in the actor's eyes. We might think that Shakespeare himself would prefer such a rendering. However, it seems that when the tragedy was performed in the author's lifetime, the ghost actually entered and sat in Macbeth's seat, unseen by the rest of the company. Dr. Simon Forman, who saw *Macbeth* at the Globe in 1610, left a full account in his work, *The Booke of Plaies and Notes thereof*, and is not at all ambiguous about the appearance of Banquo's ghost. Moreover, the stage directions are plain enough: "The Ghost of Banquo enters and sits in Macbeth's place." Shakespeare would have probably preferred a subjective representation, but realized the demand it made on the actor and the limited intelligence of the greater part of his audience.

Many other strange happenings occur in *Macbeth.* The night of Duncan's murder was disturbed and fearful (II. 3. 59–68):

> *Len.* The night has been unruly: where we lay,
>   Our chimneys were blown down, and, as they say,
>   Lamentings heard i' the air, strange screams of death,
>   And prophesying with accents terrible
>   Of dire combustion and confused events
>   New hatch'd to the woful time: the obscure bird
>   Clamour'd the live-long night: some say, the earth
>   Was feverous and did shake.
> *Macb.*   'Twas a rough night.
> *Len.* My young remembrance cannot parallel
>   A fellow to it.

The next morning Ross, outside Macbeth's castle, meets an old man, who says (II. 4. 1–4):

> Threescore and ten I can remember well:
> Within the volume of which time I have seen
> Hours dreadful and things strange, but this sore night
> Hath trifled former knowings.

Ross and the Old Man proceed to relate some of the strange and eerie things that are reported to have happened, and agree "'Tis unnatural."

Shakespeare surrounded the Supernatural with marvels of all kinds, and succeeded in inspiring his audience with a feeling of awe beyond the power of sub-genius to excite. There is no play in any language which handles the Unseen with such consummate skill as *Macbeth*, nor one that produces so profound an effect upon the audient mind. It was a work of Shakespeare's darkest years, when his own attitude towards the Supernatural was one of gloomy detestation and anxious foreboding.

VI

"THE TEMPEST"

THE last of the four great plays dealing with the Supernatural was the Poet's swan-song. *The Tempest* reveals Shakespeare's final attitude, not only towards the Unseen, but towards life in general. It was an attitude very different from the bitter, pessimistic, cynical frame of mind in which he wrote *Macbeth*. Some five or six years have passed since then. The dramatist is approaching his half-century, and has practically retired from the busy world of London to the peace of his native Stratford.

It is the experience of most men that age, bringing with it a wider knowledge and understanding of life and its potentialities, changes, or at least modifies, their views on the deep questions confronting them. We have followed Shakespeare through such fluctuations in regard to his beliefs in the Supernatural. In *Midsummer Night's Dream* we saw a somewhat frivolous handling of this profound subject, but one consistent with the joyous irresponsibility of youth. Six or seven years later gaiety has given place to the gravity and seriousness that infold *Hamlet*, a play of his late thirties. Five years later still, this solemn mood has darkened to the one of deepest depression which overshadows *Macbeth*. Another half-dozen years have passed, and we find in *The Tempest* a Shakespeare emerged from the doubt and fear and gloom which had burdened him, and a poet returning to the freedom and happiness of his youthful fairy fantasy.

Studying Shakespeare's history from the super-natural plays alone, we surmise that he embarked upon life with all the easy optimism of youth; that he soon came face to face with obstacles, temptations, and difficulties which sobered his light-heartedness; that, as he battled with all the disillusionment and disappointment which seem to be the inevitable concomitants of human life he found himself the prey of cynicism and despair; and finally, that he passed through the valley, and came once more to the peace and calm of a new faith and a new confidence in a benign Providence. This victory made all the struggles and tears and heartbreaks worth while, for it contained the realization that soul-growth results from times of stress and trial.

The last drama itself is suggestively allegorical of the experience of his closing period. It opens with a raging tempest, threatening death and disasters, as tempests do. But these threats never materialize; and the thunder, the lightning, and the mountainous seas give place to the still beauty of the enchanted island. So Shakespeare turns from the bitter contemplation of the stark and hideous realities of life to toy again with an ideal. But he does not allow his imagination to lead him whithersoever it pleases. It is now under the control of belief, in the reins of a steadfast faith and a mature joy. He uses the same materials of which he compounded his early success of *Midsummer Night's Dream*. The fairies, magic, spells, and enchantment, are all present; but they are wielded now by a restrained and practised hand, which has made itself master of the dramatic art.

The idea that seems to have been uppermost in Shakespeare's mind at this period of his life is that of forgiveness. The New Shakespeare describes it as "Reconciliation, with pardon and atonement for the sins or mistakes of one generation in the young love of the children and in their promise."[1] It is the theme, not only of *The Tempest*, but of *Cymbeline* and *The Winter's Tale*, also plays of his closing years. Prospero, addressing his enemy brother, Antonio, at whose hands he has suffered such terrible wrong, says, "I do forgive thee, unnatural though thou art" (v. 1. 78–79). The forgiveness extends even to Caliban, and to those who plotted the master's death in order to make the island their own. All are pardoned. No trace of anger or resentment is allowed to linger. With forgiveness goes freedom. Ariel is promised that he shall be "as free as mountain winds" (1. 2. 498). "I'll deliver all" is the magnanimous promise of Prospero at the end of this beautiful play.

When Shakespeare first used the Supernatural in *Midsummer Night's Dream*, he endowed the Fairies with little power over human beings. They could annoy with childish mischief, but they exerted no moral influence. In *Hamlet* the Ghost counted for very much more. It could connect with and strengthen thoughts and feelings latent in the individual, but it could not command the action it desired. In *Macbeth* the Weird Sisters had still greater potentiality for evil. They were particularly dangerous because they deceived with luring temptation and revealed the Supernatural making its strongest bid for authority over man. But even the Weird Sisters could not rob the human mind of the sovereign gift of free-will, nor could it destroy a human life, but only entice

[1] *The Tempest*, Intro., p. l.

man to self-destruction. In *The Tempest* the last phase
is reached in the evolution of Shakespeare's attitude.
In this final play the supernatural agencies are entirely
beneath the control of man; they cannot run counter
to his wishes; indeed, they cannot act at all without
his permission and direction.

This ultimate stage was made possible by the return
of Shakespeare's trust in good. In his prime he won
a renewed confidence in men and women and the
glory of their eventual destiny. His thoughts turned
to a ruling Providence that was wholly beneficent
and well-intentioned. When telling Miranda the story
of how they were callously cast adrift at sea, Prospero
answers the girl's question, "How came we ashore?"
with the explanation, "By Providence divine" (I. 2.
159). "By foul play were we heaved thence; but
blessedly holp hither" (I. 2. 62–63). It is "bountiful
Fortune," again (I. 2. 178), that "hath mine enemies
brought to this shore." In the last Act, when the
inquisitive Alonso cross-questions Ferdinand about
Miranda, the Prince replies to his father, "By immortal
Providence she's mine" (v. 1. 189). Irrefutable
evidence of Shakespeare's reverent acceptance of
orthodox Christian teaching will be found in the
second part of this book. Here it will suffice to quote
from his Will. It reads, "I commend my soul into
the hands of God my Creator, hoping, and assuredly
believing, through the only merits of Jesus Christ my
Saviour, to be made partaker of life everlasting."

All authority is taken from the spirits in *The
Tempest*. The Supernatural is now wholly under
human government. The power to harm has gone.
Caliban says to Trinculo and Stephano (III. 2.
143–144):

> Be not afeard; the isle is full of noises,
> Sounds and sweet airs, that give delight, and hurt not.

Prospero reveals how man has at last attained dominion over the forces of evil. He has been able to free Ariel, imprisoned for twelve years in a cloven pine by the sorceries of the "damned witch" Sycorax, mother of Caliban.

> It was mine art,
> When I arrived and heard thee, that made gape
> The pine, and let thee out.
>
> (I. 2. 291–293.)

The monster Caliban is also subject to Prospero:

> his art is of such power,
> It would control my dam's god, Setebos,
> And make a vassal of him.
>
> (I. 2. 372–374.)

In many passages Prospero acknowledges his own sovereignty. For example:

> Spirits, which by mine art
> I have from their confines call'd to enact
> My present fancies.
>
> (IV. I. 120–122.)

Ariel can employ none of his superhuman talents unless Prospero first gives permission. The sprite must obey and carry out his mortal master's command, as the price of obtaining his ethereal freedom. In summoning the spirits to do his bidding, Prospero sometimes transmits his orders through Ariel and at other times issues them direct. The obedient spirits are kept busily employed. In III. 3, according to the Stage Directions, several strange shapes bring in a banquet and invite Alonso to feed. But Ariel arrives and causes the banquet to vanish. At the end of Act IV again, "Enter divers Spirits in shape of dogs and hounds, hunting" the rascals, Stephano and Trinculo. In this spirit realm Prospero's word is law.

Shakespeare reaches the final conclusion that man need not fear the Supernatural. It is within his capacity to order it. But, according to Prospero—and we cannot doubt that he is expressing Shakespeare's own view—the forces of magic and mystery are best left alone. When we watch Prospero voluntarily renouncing his useful and hard-won powers, we understand that this is the course which wisdom dictates. It is the only safe course; and the Poet, with the authority of his bitter life experiences behind him, advocates it emphatically and sincerely.

"Who is Prospero?" is a question that has agitated the minds of countless thousands who have been charmed by *The Tempest*. Some have wondered whether he is intended to be the personification of Destiny. Others have conjectured that he is Shakespeare himself, who has now laid down his pen, and will no more control his characters, arranging their "exits and their entrances," and hastening them to victory or defeat, to tears or laughter. The poet Campbell was the first to suggest this explanation of Prospero; and while it is certainly attractive, we cannot advance beyond surmise in presenting it, for the meaning of *The Tempest* has never been wholly unravelled.

The scholarly Prince, who has come through misfortune to the kingship of an enchanted island, is unlike any other Shakespearean character. No mortal shares his enviable authority over the realm of the Supernatural. There is nothing equivocal about his position. His domination is complete. The witch

Sycorax, the sprite Ariel, the half-human monster Caliban, the spirits, the elves, have all to spring to his word of command and obtain his leave for whatsoever they wish to do.

Prospero was not born with any peculiar or exceptional supernatural gifts. His command over the Spirits is the result of deliberate study. Learning and the reading of books of magic have taught him the use of his magician's mantle and his wondrous wand. He says of himself that he was all dedicated to closeness and the bettering of his mind, neglecting worldly ends (1. 2. 89–90); and he concludes Act III, Scene 1, with the words:

> I'll to my book;
> For yet, ere supper-time, must I perform
> Much business appertaining.

Prospero's learning seems to have included a knowledge of astrology, one of the main channels by which an understanding of the Supernatural could be reached, according to Elizabethan belief. He says to Miranda (1. 2. 180–184):

> And by my prescience
> I find my zenith doth depend upon
> A most auspicious star, whose influence
> If now I court not, but omit, my fortunes
> Will ever after droop.

The first thing we learn about his extraordinary powers is his control over the elements. Miranda opens the second scene of the play with the words:

> If by your art, my dearest father, you have
> Put the wild waters in this roar, allay them.

Prospero comforts her, calming her anxiety for the

safety of the unhappy people in the sinking ship. He tells her "There's no harm done," and, laying aside his magic powers by the simple process of removing his mantle, reveals their whole personal history previous to the opening of the play. (This scene shows a clever piece of dramatic construction by Shakespeare, by which he was able to observe the unity of time, and yet in that space make the audience fully conversant with a story that extended over several years.)

Prospero resumes his mantle, and we are introduced to Ariel, the Sprite who has carried out his command to raise the tempest and has brought his "potent master's" enemies to land at different points of the island. The ship and the sailors are also saved, but Alonso's escort has been conveniently scattered and persuaded homewards.

Prospero's power over Ariel is typical of the control over the supernatural agencies which is possible to the enlightened mortal. Ariel is in Prospero's debt and bound to be obedient. If he becomes a little restless and over-anxious for the freedom that is promised him, his lord has to be stern and remind him of his cause for gratitude. Ariel is easily brought back to a willing and gracious obedience (1. 2. 296–298):

> Pardon, master:
> I will be correspondent to command,
> And do my spiriting gently.

Prospero has also the ability to charm humans—a knowledge of hypnotism, we might call it. When Ferdinand draws upon him, he transfixes him, sword in hand (1. 2. 466). He can also read the treachery in the hearts of Sebastian and Antonio. "The devil speaks in him," declares the frightened Sebastian (v. 1. 129) when he learns that their guilty secret is known to the exiled Duke. Again, he has no difficulty in unmasking and defeating the plot against himself, hatched by Stephano and Trinculo with the help of Caliban. He remarks with a satisfaction he cannot conceal (iii. 3. 88–91):

> My high charms work,
> And these mine enemies are all knit up
> In their distractions: they are now in my power;
> And in these fits I leave them.

Another useful trick that Prospero has learned in his necromantic studies is the ability to make himself invisible. He employs it frequently to his own advantage and the extreme discomfiture of others, whether for overhearing the planning of some diabolical piece of treachery or watching the love-making of Ferdinand and Miranda.

It is greatly to Prospero's credit that, while possessed of these exceptional gifts, he does not use them with any evil or malignant design. He is not a wizard who has dealings with Satan, nor is he a possessor of the Evil Eye. His self-control is admirable. With all his grounds for hatred, he is not maliciously resentful towards those who have wronged him. He does not use his superior knowledge to effect a sweet revenge. His purposes are higher. When retribution has been made, he is only too happy to forgive and forget; and, his end attained, he voluntarily resigns his occult powers and becomes no more than a learned prince (v. 1. 33–57):

Ye elves of hills, brooks, standing lakes, and groves;
And ye that on the sands with printless foot
Do chase the ebbing Neptune, and do fly him
When he comes back; you demi-puppets that
By moonshine do the green-sour ringlets make,
Whereof the ewe not bites; and you whose pastime
Is to make midnight mushrooms, that rejoice
To hear the solemn curfew; by whose aid—
Weak masters though ye be—I have bedimm'd
The noontide sun, call'd forth the mutinous winds,
And 'twixt the green sea and the azured vault
Set roaring war: to the dread rattling thunder
Have I given fire, and rifted Jove's stout oak
With his own bolt; the strong-based promontory
Have I made shake, and by the spurs pluck'd up
The pine and cedar: graves, at my command,
Have waked their sleepers; oped, and let 'em forth
By my so potent art. But this rough magic
I here abjure; and, when I have required
Some heavenly music—which even now I do—
To work mine end upon their senses, that
This airy charm is for, I'll break my staff,
Bury it certain fathoms in the earth,
And, deeper than did ever plummet sound,
I'll drown my book.

The above summarizes the wonderful powers that
Prospero had acquired through diligent study of
books of magic. He worked through the elves and
spirits, who were "demi-puppets" and "weak masters," and the most prominent of his airy servants
was the sprite Ariel. From his history up to the
opening of the play, of which many details are given,
we learn that Ariel was no match for the witchcraft
of Sycorax, and only escaped from a cruel imprisonment of twelve years with the aid of Prospero. By
way of repaying this kindness, he has to serve his
benefactor for a season before obtaining his full

freedom. Servitude of any kind is unnatural and irksome to Ariel. Gratitude convinces him of the necessity of a temporary, willing obedience to Prospero, but it cannot prevent him from constantly looking forward to that day of absolute and lasting freedom, when his debt will have been paid. During his service he has certain powers delegated to him by his master, but he can exercise none of them without his consent.

From his first words we learn that Ariel is really a sylph. His very name reveals it. Says Schlegel,[1] "In the zephyr-like Ariel, the image of air is not to be mistaken; even his name alludes to it: as, on the other hand, Caliban signifies the heavy element of earth." Coleridge describes the sylph in the same strain;[2] "In air he lives, from air he derives his being, in air he acts; and all his colours and properties seem to have been obtained from the rainbow and the skies. There is nothing about Ariel that cannot be conceived to exist either at sunrise or at sunset: hence all that belongs to Ariel belongs to the delight the mind is capable of receiving from the most lovely external appearances." His first speech to Prospero reveals his character (1. 2. 189–193):

> All hail, great master! grave sir, hail! I come
> To answer thy best pleasure; be't to fly,
> To swim, to dive into the fire, to ride
> On the curl'd clouds, to thy strong bidding task
> Ariel and all his quality.

He gives a description of how he has carried out

---

[1] *Werke*, VI. 236–237.
[2] *Coleridge's Shakespearean Criticism* (Raysor), II. 176.

Prospero's orders in raising the tempest (I. 2. 196–201):

> I boarded the king's ship; now on the beak,
> Now in the waist, the deck, in every cabin,
> I flamed amazement: sometime I'ld divide,
> And burn in many places: on the topmast,
> The yards and bowsprit, would I flame distinctly,
> Then meet and join.

(Ariel is supposed in these lines to relate how he appeared in the form of the famous St. Elmo fires.) The sprite brings the important passengers to land at the various points of the beach and in the various groups as Prospero needs them; he harbours the ship safely in a deep nook, "the mariners all under hatches stow'd"; and the escort he sends "bound sadly home for Naples." Prospero is pleased with his sprite: "Ariel, thy charge exactly is performed."

In Ariel Shakespeare reverts to his conception of the fairies as little people, infinitesimally small, which he had originated when writing *Midsummer Night's Dream*. "In a cowslip's bell I lie," sings the sprite (v. 1. 89). The demi-puppets, "whose pastime is to make midnight mushrooms" (v. 1. 40), also belong to the diminutive Shakespearean tribe, so different to the fairies of folk-lore. The elves, however, conform to popular superstition in their bad temper and hostility to mortals.

The fairy artifices of evanescence and metamorphosis are permitted to Ariel. Prospero says (I. 2. 301–304):

> Go make thyself like a nymph o' the sea: be subject
> To no sight but thine and mine; invisible
> To every eyeball else. Go, take this shape,
> And hither come in 't.

So well does Ariel fulfil the command that his master exclaims, "Fine apparition!" He then proceeds to work his will upon the mortals, for whom he has scant respect.

It is consistent with Shakespeare's use of the Supernatural that the delicate, ethereal Ariel is never brought into direct contact with the lovely but human Miranda. He realized that the beauty and individuality of each would suffer. His instinct led him rather to contrast the sprite with the gross and earthy Caliban.

Prospero has found it convenient to give Ariel authority over the other spirits, and the sylph is often the bearer of the master's commands (iv. 1. 37–39):

> Go bring the rabble,
> O'er whom I give thee power, here to this place:
> Incite them to quick motion.

Ariel, in his relation to Prospero, is reminiscent of Puck, the messenger of Oberon; and in both cases Shakespeare attached many of the old folk-lore beliefs to his fairy character. In the last act Ariel sings (v. 1. 88–95):

> Where the bee sucks, there suck I:
> In a cowslip's bell I lie;
> There I couch when owls do cry.
> On the bat's back do I fly
> After summer merrily.
> Merrily, merrily, shall I live now
> Under the blossom that hangs on the bough.

Just as Puck "misleads night-wanderers, laughing at their harm," so Ariel entices Stephano, Trinculo, and Caliban through "tooth'd briers, sharp furzes, pricking goss, and thorns" and "the filthy-mantled pool"

(IV. I. 180), until Stephano grumbles that he "has done little better than played the Jack with us" (IV. I. 198).

When Prospero breaks his staff and drowns his book, then Ariel has repaid in service the good deed of his master in liberating him, and with the forgiveness of past wrongs all round, hears the joyful news, "My Ariel, chick, . . . be free, and fare thou well!" (V. I. 318).

Critics have examined *The Tempest* to discover a symbolical interpretation for Ariel. Miss Helen H. Stewart suggests[1] that the sprite is "the quintessence of the higher laws of Nature, those forces which, invisible yet irresistible, work in all material things." She adds, "In his constant longing for liberty and Prospero's repeated promise that he shall be free, we are reminded of the well-known tendency of all the elements and forces of Nature to escape, unless held prisoner by the ingenuity of man." We can only safely say that Ariel is, quite obviously, drawn in contrast to Caliban. Whereas the monster is earthy, misshapen, and sensual, the sylph is ethereal, graceful, and refined. Hazlitt writes,[2] "Nothing was ever more finely conceived than this contrast between the material and the spiritual, the gross and delicate."

The actor (or actress) who plays Ariel must have considerable musical gifts. Into no play of Shakespeare's does music enter so largely as into *The Tempest*, and the sprite is the chief performer. Mr. Richmond Noble writes,[3] "It is *The Tempest* which

---

[1] *The Supernatural in Shakespeare*, pp. 152 and 153.
[2] *Characters of Shakespeare's Plays*, p. 98.
[3] *Shakespeare's Use of Song*, p. 14.

marks the culminating point in the use made of song by Shakespeare. The more Shakespeare gained in experience, the more relevant did he make his songs to their context and the more important was their office in promoting his dramatic ends." Critics and commentators have been generous with their praise of his clever, artistic, and dramatic use of ballad and incidental music in his last delightful fantasy. It would seem that the Poet's love and knowledge of music were exploited to the best advantage when handling a supernatural theme. Not Ariel alone, but all the characters of *The Tempest* are musical. Music plays no small part in unravelling the plot. To quote Mr. Noble again,[1] "There are frequent opportunities not only for vocal music, but also for orchestral as well." As with the enchanted wood of *Midsummer Night's Dream*, so Prospero's magic island is made more mysterious, impressive, and fascinating through the medium of music. Caliban says (III. 2. 144–149):

> The isle is full of noises,
> Sounds and sweet airs, that give delight and hurt not.
> Sometimes a thousand twangling instruments
> Will hum about mine ears; and sometime voices,
> That, if I then had waked after long sleep,
> Will make me sleep again.

Prospero finds music a valuable aid in his magic practice. He employs it for enchanting and disenchanting, just as Oberon employs it when he removes the spell from the confused lovers. Releasing Alonso, Gonzalo, and their companions from his charm, Prospero says (v. 1. 51–54, 58–59):

---

[1] *Shakespeare's Use of Song*, p. 99.

When I have required
ty music—which even now I do—
e end upon their senses, that
arm is for, I'll break my staff

.   .   .   .

air, and the best comforter
nsettled fancy, cure thy brains.

of *The Tempest* are Ariel, Stephano,
a the characters in the Masque of Act IV.
Ariel is the chief; and his singing and playing are
native to his character. His appearances are nearly
always accompanied by melodic strains—technique
that reveals how closely Shakespeare connected music
with supernatural manifestation. When the sprite
entices Ferdinand ashore by his song, "Come unto
these yellow sands," and then persuades him by his
second song, "Full fathom five thy father lies," that
Alonso is drowned, Ferdinand remarks, "This is no
mortal business, nor no sound That the earth owes"
(i. 2. 406-407). Ariel's musical contributions recur
frequently throughout the play, ending with that
exquisite refrain, "Where the bee sucks, there suck
I," which I have quoted in full above.

The drunken butler, Stephano, sings rough sailor
songs with nothing supernatural about them. He is,
however, much taken aback when starting the catch,
"Flout 'em and scout 'em," in III. 2, to hear the
invisible Ariel play the tune on a tabor and pipe.
When he is assured by Caliban that the island music
harms not, he is delighted and observes, "This will
prove a brave kingdom to me, where I shall have
my music for nothing" (153). It is a striking fact
that many of Shakespeare's rogues are musical.
Autolycus is another case in point.

Caliban is moved to song by the influence of drink, a song of rebellion against his daily, menial tasks. "No more dams I'll make for fish; Nor fetch in firing" (II. 2. 184). "Soft music" accompanies the Masque in Act IV—the usual practice for all such interludes, which dealt most generally with the Supernatural. Two characters of the Masque, Juno and Ceres, are given what looks like a duet, but it is doubtful if any of this Masque is the work of Shakespeare. To summarize, it would be hardly an exaggeration to describe *The Tempest* as a musical play.

The authorship of the Masque has for some years been a matter of debate. If Shakespeare did indeed write it himself, it is thought to have been inserted by him in deference to the wishes of a royal audience, who delighted in pageantry. *The Tempest* was performed at Court during the festivities held in honour of the marriage of Princess Elizabeth to the Prince Palatine Elector in the winter of 1612–1613. The play was probably written a year or two previously; and the dramatist may have been persuaded against his inclination and in defiance of his sense of the artistic to interpolate the Masque for the celebration. If the lines are Shakespeare's, he evidently wrote them without inspiration and possibly with distaste. They may, on the other hand, be the work of another man.

The sharp contrast in Shakespeare's attitude towards the Supernatural, as revealed by the two plays of *The Tempest* and *Macbeth*, is fully pointed by comparing the influence of the Weird Sisters over Macbeth with Prospero's power over Caliban's mother, the witch Sycorax. We learn (I. 2. 263–266):

> This damn'd witch Sycorax,
> For mischiefs manifold, and sorceries terrible
> To enter human hearing, from Argier,
> . . . was banish'd:

That Sycorax was something of the conventional witch we understand from Caliban's curse (i. 2. 339–340):

> All the charms
> Of Sycorax, toads, beetles, bats, light on you!

Moreover, Prospero says of her, when speaking of Caliban (v. i. 269–271):

> His mother was a witch; and one so strong
> That could control the moon, make flows and ebbs,
> And deal in her command, without her power.

Nevertheless, Prospero was able to counter her sorceries, release Ariel from her toils, tame Caliban, and take from her possession the enchanted island, which she had appropriated.

Several actual islands have been identified as Prospero's Island, but the balance of opinion is in favour of Bermuda. Not only does Ariel mention the "still-vex'd Bermoothes" (i. 2. 229), but Shakespeare undoubtedly drew material for *The Tempest* from the wreck of an English ship, the *Sea Adventure*, at the Bermudas in 1609. Accounts of the disaster and the life of the mariners, marooned for ten months on the island, were written by William Strachey and Sil Jourdain and published in 1610. According to Stow, Bermuda was "said and supposed to be inchanted and inhabited with witches and deuills, which grew by reason of accustomed monstrous thunder, storme, and tempest." Bermuda seems to have been in Shakespeare's mind when he wrote of the island, "Here is everything advantageous to life" (II. I. 49), "the isle is full of noises, sounds, and sweet airs" (III. 2. 143), and in Caliban's offer to Stephano (II. 2. 164–165):

> I'll show thee the best springs; I'll pluck thee berries;
> I'll fish for thee, and get thee wood enough.

It is an interesting fact that Shakespeare in his second fairy play, as in his first, relied, as far as is known, upon his own creation for plot and characters.

When he wrote *The Tempest*, Shakespeare had attained the ambition of his life. He was a prosperous citizen of Stratford, wealthy, respected, famous, friendly with his rich neighbours, the proprietor of a delightful house in New Place, as well as the owner of other property. He was now content, at peace with the world; and this peace and contentment are reflected in the spirit of tolerance, reconciliation, and forgiveness which shines through the last of his plays. The struggles, the sufferings, and disappointment are all behind and forgotten. His superstition has been supplanted by a mature and reasonable faith, and his improved belief in the Supernatural makes him kind, patient, and forbearing to his fellow-beings. The beautiful, fascinating Miranda reveals the Shakespeare of the last years. No Lady Macbeth, Cleopatra, Goneril, or Regan now engages his analytical mind. He is satisfied to worship at the throne of loveliness and innocence.

To summarize Shakespeare's attitude towards the Supernatural in a sentence is impossible, because that attitude underwent a series of profound changes as the years passed and new experiences claimed him. As revealed in the first of the supernatural plays, *Midsummer Night's Dream*, we find the poet as a young man confessing an uncritical and ready acquiescence in the superstitions of his time. In *Hamlet* we see the philosopher questioning, doubting, reasoning, and viewing the Supernatural with a new-born seriousness. In *Macbeth* we discover the successful, middle-aged dramatist, pessimistic and despairing of man's ability to withstand the unseen agencies ranged against his well-being and happiness. In *The Tempest*, the Poet's epilogue, we are confronted with a renewed faith in the omnipotence and ever-presence of Good and a confidence in the possibility of man's dominion over evil.

VII

"JULIUS CÆSAR"

WHILE a study of Shakespeare and the Supernatural necessarily concerns itself chiefly with the four great dramas in which fairies, ghosts, and witches play a principal part, there are at least a dozen others from which the poet was unable to exclude the influences of the unseen world. Probably the most famous of these is *Julius Cæsar*.

A tragedy dealing with the conflict between monarchical and democratic parties in the political world of Rome may seem a somewhat unpromising stage on which to introduce the Supernatural. It must be remembered, however, that the Romans were extremely superstitious, a trait that is emphasized over and over again in *Julius Cæsar*. The marvellous and unnatural are not represented solely by the appearance of Cæsar's Ghost in IV. 3. They are given special prominence by the terrifying astrological portents that accompany the storm on the eve of the assassination, the prophetic dream of Calphurnia, and the warnings uttered by Artemidorus and the Soothsayer.

Perhaps Shakespeare would not have introduced the principal supernatural event—the appearance of the Ghost—if he had not found it in his authority, Plutarch. The Greek biographer describes in uninspired language the circumstances and manner of the spectral visit, and goes on to say, "Brutus boldly asked what he was, a god or a man, and what cause brought him hither? The spirit answered: 'I am thy evil spirit, Brutus, and thou shalt see me by the city of Philippi.' Brutus being no otherwise afraid, replied again unto it: 'Well: then I shall see thee again.' The spirit presently vanished away."

This somewhat matter-of-fact account of an unusual phenomenon was transformed—as was all of Plutarch—into something impressive and dramatic by the master touch of Shakespeare. The Poet realized that the circumstances were favourable for some unusual and eerie experience. It was late at night and dark. Great events were pending. The memory of a crime, as yet unpunished and unavenged, hovered about the tent of Brutus. The republican leader has had a tiring day. He has just emerged from a violent quarrel with his brother-in-law, Cassius. He has received news of the death of his beloved and noble wife, Portia. His cause is not going well. Octavius and Antony are marching against him with a powerful army. He is tired and drowsy and troubled by a premonition of his own death at Philippi. His page, Lucius, has dozed off in the middle of playing to him "a sleepy tune." He tries to settle himself to read, when the Ghost, for whose appearance the music has helped to prepare the audience, enters (IV. 3. 275–281):

> *Bru.* How ill this taper burns! Ha! Who comes here?
> I think it is the weakness of mine eyes
> That shapes this monstrous apparition.
> It comes upon me. Art thou any thing?
> Art thou some god, some angel, or some devil,
> That makest my blood cold, and my hair to stare?
> Speak to me what thou art.

Thereafter Shakespeare transcribes Plutarch to the exit of the spectre.

Cæsar's Ghost is a conventional ghost judged by Elizabethan superstition. It arrives in the depth of the night, heralded by solemn music, and must be addressed before it can speak. Like other ghosts, it is condemned to walk the earth until its death is avenged. Shakespeare's mind was very much upon these disturbing visitors at this period, for *Julius Cæsar* and *Hamlet* were written much about the same time.

There is, however, a difference between Cæsar's Ghost and the *Hamlet* Ghost. Cæsar's Ghost is subjective. It appears only to Brutus. Hamlet's Ghost, on the other hand, is objective—it only becomes subjective on its later visit—and is seen by all present. Cæsar's Ghost is more like the ghost of Banquo. Both Macbeth and Brutus recognize the subjective nature of the apparition before their eyes. Macbeth knows it is an "unreal mockery," the very painting of his fear; and Brutus declares "it is the weakness of mine eyes" that "shapes this monstrous apparition."

In the two plays, *Macbeth* and *Julius Cæsar*, Shakespeare deals with the assassination of the head of state, and is not so interested in the one slain as in the results of the crime upon the murderer. In picturing these results he has found the Supernatural (suggested in each case by his authority) of the highest dramatic value. Julius Cæsar alive is not a character that commands great respect and admiration. He is vain, boastful, irresolute, and a prey to flatterers. But Julius Cæsar dead is an all-important influence in the drama. We are conscious throughout of the ever-presence of his restless, inexorable spirit hovering, like the Weird Sisters of *Macbeth*, over the whole action, and leading the assassins relentlessly to final doom and retribution. Brutus feels the power of the dead Cæsar constantly. Even he, the hero of the tragedy, cannot escape from it. He cries (v. 3. 94–96):

> O Julius Cæsar, thou art mighty yet!
> Thy spirit walks abroad, and turns our swords
> In our own proper entrails.

Marc Antony expresses the same thought (III. 1. 270–275):

> . . . Cæsar's spirit ranging for revenge,
> With Ate by his side, come hot from hell,
> Shall in these confines with a monarch's voice
> Cry "Havoc," and let slip the dogs of war;
> That this foul deed shall smell above the earth
> With carrion men, groaning for burial.

There is no doubt, I think, that Shakespeare meant us to understand that when the inward voice warns Brutus that his end is near, then his consciousness of the ever-presence of Cæsar's spirit is so intensified that it brings him into closer contact with the Unseen and results in a visible manifestation.

When Cæsar's Ghost tells Brutus that he will see him at Philippi (IV. 3. 283), he means that he will meet him on the same plane of existence—in other words, in the spirit world of the hereafter. Shakespeare, with his customary economy in the use of the Supernatural, does not show us this further spectral appearance on the stage; but we learn that it has happened from Brutus' speech to Volumnius (V. 5. 17–20):

> The ghost of Cæsar hath appear'd to me
> Two several times by night; at Sardis once,
> And this last night here in Philippi fields:
> I know my hour is come.

Brutus seems to interpret the second manifestation as a command from the spirit of his victim to take his own life. Wherefore he runs upon his sword, and dies, exclaiming, "Cæsar, now be still" (v. 5. 50).

Superstitious fear is wonderfully depicted by Shakespeare in the horror of Casca at the terrifying violence of the thunderstorm in I. 3, and the ghastly prodigies accompanying it—all intended as a sign of the anger of the gods at the dastardly conspiracy against Cæsar. To an Elizabethan audience, steeped as it was in astrology, these celestial disturbances would bear a profound significance. Only the level-headedness of Cicero prevents Casca from becoming panic-stricken, until the shrewd Cassius arrives to place an interpretation upon the phenomena that appears to justify the dark conspiracy against Cæsar. Here we have an instance of the *friendly* intervention of the Supernatural in an endeavour to prevent man from committing blunders that will prove disastrous to himself. Man, however, cannot be deprived of his freewill and independence, even when such deprivation would be to his own advantage. He can choose to ignore the helpful warning from the metaphysical world, silencing it with his own obstinacy and wilfulness. This course the conspirators against Cæsar pursue, and eventually pay for their mistake with their lives.

Much store was laid by Shakespeare's contemporaries on dreams and their interpretation. Here was a favourite channel of communication between the mortal and immortal, and free use was made of it by the playwrights. Calphurnia's dream (II. 2) would strike the average playgoer as a clear warning from the spirit world which no sensible man should ignore

We learn of Calphurnia's troubled sleep in the first lines of the scene. Cæsar says:

> Nor heaven nor earth have been at peace to-night:
> Thrice hath Calphurnia in her sleep cried out,
> "Help, ho! They murder Cæsar!"

But the first arguments that Cæsar's wife uses to dissuade her husband from leaving their house on the fatal day are the violent thunderstorm and the "horrid sights" which accompanied it.

> When beggars die, there are no comets seen;
> The heavens themselves blaze forth the death of princes.
>
> (30–31.)

To these Cæsar turns a deaf ear. He is terribly afraid of being thought afraid. But Calphurnia's pleading is insistent. She tells him, "Your wisdom is consumed in confidence" (49), and on bended knee begs him to call it *her* fear, and not his own, that keeps him at home. Cæsar is persuaded; but at that moment, unfortunately, the wily conspirator, Decius, arrives to learn of his decision. Realizing at once that it must involve the utter failure of the conspiracy, he presses Cæsar to give him the reason for absenting himself from the senate-house. It is then we hear of Calphurnia's dream in detail (75–82):

> Calphurnia here, my wife, stays me at home:
> She dreamt to-night she saw my statuë,
> Which like a fountain with a hundred spouts
> Did run pure blood, and many lusty Romans
> Came smiling and did bathe their hands in it:
> And these does she apply for warnings and portents
> And evils imminent, and on her knee
> Hath begg'd that I will stay at home to-day.

I

With remarkable presence of mind and ingenuity Decius places an entirely new and favourable construction on the dream, and one that flatters Cæsar. He tells the dictator that the Senate intend to offer him a royal crown, and is scornful that this final triumph of his career should be frustrated by the foolish fears of a weak woman. Cæsar is persuaded to change his mind once again. Smilingly he says to Calphurnia (105–106):

> How foolish do your fears seem now, Calphurnia!
> I am ashamed I did yield to them.

He waves aside her presentiment and allows his vanity to lead him to his death. Cæsar's action in rejecting so clear an offer of metaphysical aid would sound like madness in Elizabethan ears, and would fill the audience with excited anticipation of the inevitable penalty.

Another hand from the Unseen is outstretched to save Cæsar. Through Artemidorus and a Soothsayer further warnings are given of the danger threatening him. Prophecy was one of the recognized branches of witchcraft; and the picture of Cæsar recklessly turning from these well-intentioned and clairvoyant counsellors would be, in the modern phrase, "good theatre."

Although the Supernatural is not dominant in *Julius Cæsar*, it has an important rôle to fill in the unfoldment of the tragedy. It intervenes in an endeavour to prevent men from committing irrevocable blunders. But it fails, for it has no power to coerce the free-will of man. Its warnings are disregarded, and disaster ensues.

VIII

"RICHARD III"

SHAKESPEARE uses the ghost form of the Supernatural in effective manner in the final Act of *Richard III*, the last play dealing with that great national catastrophe, the Wars of the Roses. The usurping Richard, a man of commanding intellect and overweening self-confidence, embittered by his physical deformity, and carried forward by a reckless ambition and iron will, has stooped to crime after crime to win the throne for himself and keep it. He is, as the present Poet Laureate describes him, "a 'bloody dog' let loose in a sheep-fold."[1] Without compunction he has removed from his path all possible rivals, all those whom he suspected or feared, hurrying them to a miserable, dishonourable death without trial or mercy. But the country rises against him; and the forces cf dissatisfaction find a rallying-point round Henry Tudor, Earl of Richmond, a leader with claims of his own to the English crown.

The rival armies confront each other on Bosworth Field, and battle is to be joined on the morrow. The two leaders give their final orders, dismiss their followers, and try to snatch a few hours' sleep to gain strength for the ordeal confronting them. Richard finds consolation in a bowl of wine, which makes him drowsy. Richmond prays to God for help before he lets fall the windows of his eyes (v. 3. 116).

Shakespeare, by the insertion of words and phrases into the dialogue, speeds the passage of time in this

[1] *William Shakespeare*, p. 96.

scene. We first learn that the "weary sun hath made a golden set" (19). Soon afterwards, "It's nine o'clock" (46). Then, "the silent hours steal on" (85). "It is now dead midnight" (180): and finally, "The early village cock Hath twice done salutation to the morn" (209–210). It is in the very darkest hours of midnight that the Ghosts appear. They first address the dreaming Richard, prophesying defeat and Nemesis; then turn to the sleeping Richmond, foretelling reward and victory.

The first immortal visitant is the Ghost of Prince Edward, son to Henry the Sixth, whom Richard stabbed to death at the battle of Tewkesbury. He threatens to sit heavy on the Crookback's soul, but bids Richmond be cheerful "for the wrongèd souls of butcher'd princes fight in thy behalf" (121–122). The next ghost is that of Henry the Sixth himself, who accuses Richard of punching his "anointed body," "full of deadly holes." To Richmond he recalls his (the Ghost's) prophecy that he would be king. There follow the Ghosts of the Duke of Clarence, Richard's murdered brother, of Earl Rivers, Lord Grey, and Sir Thomas Vaughan of the exterminated party of the Queen, of Lord Hastings, of the young Princes murdered in the Tower, of Lady Anne, his wife, and of his latest sufferer, the Duke of Buckingham. All repeat Prince Edward's prediction of disaster for Richard and triumph for Richmond. Miss Helen Hinton Stewart describes the effect of this scene faithfully when she writes,[1] "There is something appalling in the thought of the active conscienceless man, tied to his couch by the chain of slumber, helpless to shake off the terrible memories

---

[1] *The Supernatural in Shakespeare*, p. 50.

compelled to act over again each crime, to see the very form of each sufferer, ghastly, reproachful, threatening. Awake, he would have defied them with some new crime or violent action, but asleep he was at their mercy—he could only gaze and melt in an agony of fear."

When the Ghosts vanish, King Richard "starts out of his dream" and cries (177–181):

> Give me another horse! bind up my wounds!
> Have mercy, Jesu! Soft!—I did but dream.
> O coward conscience, how dost thou afflict me!
> The lights burn blue. It is now dead midnight.
> Cold fearful drops stand on my trembling flesh.

The effect on Richmond of the encouraging predictions of his ghostly visitors is to strengthen his confidence in the justice of his cause and the belief that he is executing the Divine Will. Compare his speech on waking up (226–233, 240–242) with that of Richard:

> The sweetest sleep, and fairest-boding dreams
> That ever enter'd in a drowsy head,
> Have I since your departure had, my lords.
> Methought their souls, whose bodies Richard murder'd,
> Came to my tent, and cried On! victory!
> I promise you, my soul is very jocund
> In the remembrance of so fair a dream.
>
> .   .   .   .   .
>
> God and our good cause fight upon our side;
> The prayers of holy saints and wrongèd souls,
> Like high-rear'd bulwarks, stand before our faces.

Although Shakespeare had the authority of Holinshed for the ghostly procession in the tents at Bosworth, he invested the scene with much of his skill for dramatic presentation. It would have been all too easy to write something impossible and ridiculous, but the master has earned the most generous praise for his successful and convincing handling of so incredible an incident.

The Ghosts of *Richard III* are not endowed with any real power over mortals. Their influence is limited to producing discouragement in Richard and confidence in Richmond. They prophesy, but they do not, they cannot, take any steps to assist the fulfilment of their prophecies. The fulfilment is the expected and logical crisis arising from the whole history and characters of Richmond and Richard. There is nothing supernatural about it; but the supernatural forecast of a natural event was a powerful dramatic aid, since the power of spirits to see into the future was allowed by the Elizabethans. Moreover, sleep was the condition and dreams the medium in and by which these forecasts reached human intelligence. To-day we should be inclined to trace such experiences to the workings of the subconscious mind; but in Shakespeare's day the existence and reality of good and evil spirits was freely admitted by the highest philosophy. Certain thinkers claimed that mankind could come to know something of the aims, natures, and methods of spirits; and only a few would question the possibility of the return of a dead man's shade to prophesy on so outstanding an event as a battle for a crown.

Prophecies fall also from the lips of unhappy Margaret, "the cursing queen," as she has been nicknamed. In I. 3. 241–246, she says to Queen Elizabeth:

> Poor painted queen, vain flourish of my fortune!
> Why strew'st thou sugar on that bottled spider,
> Whose deadly web ensnareth thee about?
> Fool, fool! Thou whet'st a knife to kill thyself.
> The time will come that thou shalt wish for me
> To help thee curse that poisonous bunch-back'd toad.

How literally this prediction was fulfilled is revealed in the sorrowing words of Queen Elizabeth in IV. 4, 79–81.

> O, thou didst prophesy the time would come
> That I should wish for thee to help me curse
> That bottled spider, that foul, bunch-back'd toad.

Again, the far-seeing Margaret warns Buckingham (I. 3. 297–301):

> What, dost thou scorn me for my gentle counsel?
> And soothe the devil that I warn thee from?
> O, but remember this another day,
> When he shall split thy very heart with sorrow,
> And say poor Margaret was a prophetess.

Buckingham does remember and remarks bitterly (V. I. 25–27):

> Now Margaret's curse is fallen upon my head;
> "When he," quoth she, "shall split thy heart with sorrow,
> Remember Margaret was a prophetess."

Many are the dreams in Shakespeare's plays, and many are the dramatic purposes to which he puts them. Popular belief regarded dreams as the most intelligible form of supernatural warning. They were aids to the righteous, threats to the wicked, consolation to the sorrowing, and premonitions to those about to die. The recital of Clarence's dream in Act I, Scene 4, of this play is a typical instance.

The unhappy prince is confined in the Tower and recites his strange dream to the Lieutenant, Brakenbury, just before the murderers, hired by his wicked brother, Richard, enter to rob him of his royal life. It is a long, vivid, ugly story of the treachery of Richard, the horrors of drowning, the entry into the kingdom of death, the meeting with former enemies, and tormenting punishment by a legion of foul fiends. The effect is to frighten Clarence into repentance for past misdeeds before swift and violent death overtakes him.

Throughout this early play it is revealed how Shakespeare's mind is already touching upon the mysteries of existence beyond the grave and the connection between mortal man and the metaphysical world. But some years were to elapse before he concentrated seriously on these fathomless subjects.

IX

THE SUPERNATURAL IN OTHER PLAYS

WHILE the Supernatural is of vital dramatic importance in *Midsummer Night's Dream, Hamlet, Macbeth,* and *The Tempest,* and is a less prominent, but still salient feature of *Julius Cæsar* and *Richard III,* quite half of Shakespeare's plays contain some mention of ghosts, spirits, witches, fairies, dreams, divinations, or prophecy. Miss Helen Hinton Stewart writes in her book on *The Supernatural in Shakespeare,*[1] "Apparitions appear only in a limited number of the dramas, but through almost the whole of Shakespeare's plays a subtle breath of metaphysics may be apprehended in the form of dreams and presentiments." The Poet seems to have found difficulty in wholly excluding the mystical and superhuman from his plots, probably because of the universal belief in those agencies, and their consequent popularity with theatre audiences. In the four great plays dealing with the Supernatural we have endeavoured to discover Shakespeare's own views as opposed to the views he attributed to his characters. Where the metaphysical is so much in evidence this presented no great problem. In the following plays, however, where the use of the Supernatural is brief and incidental, it is not always possible to declare whether the viewpoint presented is the Poet's own or not. Sometimes two opposite opinions are contrasted.

Shakespeare's own attitude towards the difficult questions of the spirit world are fully covered in the

[1] P. 3.

dramas considered under their separate chapters. The following plays are added to make our study complete and to throw further light on the superstitions of the age, to many of which the Poet subscribed.

The plays are dealt with in their chronological order.

"1 HENRY VI"

History relates that Joan of Arc was burned by the English as a witch, with the approval of the French priests of the Roman Catholic Church, who condemned her as a heretic. In *1 Henry VI* she is represented as one of those withered and toothless hags who were thought by the credulous multitude to wield diabolical powers. Says Talbot in III. 2, 38–40:

> Pucelle, that witch, that damned sorceress,
> Hath wrought this hellish mischief unawares,
> That hardly we escaped the pride of France.

Joan (called La Pucelle throughout this play) confesses that she is a witch (v. 3. 2–7):

> Now help, ye charming spells and periapts;
> And ye choice spirits that admonish me,
> And give me signs of future accidents.
> You speedy helpers, . . .
> Appear and aid me in this enterprise.

The fiends then appear and act in dumb show. Joan continues (8–12):

> This speedy and quick appearance argues proof
> Of your accustom'd diligence to me.
> Now, ye familiar spirits, that are cull'd
> Out of the powerful regions under earth,
> Help me this once.

But the Spirits refuse obedience, for La Pucelle's star is setting.

We have noted that this is the only instance where fiends are introduced on to the stage in a play of Shakespeare. The Poet's favoured practice was to portray the battle between right and wrong fought out in the human heart. The truth is that very little of *1 Henry VI* is from the hand of the "Swan of Avon." Nearly all scholars now agree that the play was written by an inferior dramatist, name unknown, and that Shakespeare made valuable additions, such as the famous scene of the plucking of the roses in the Temple Garden, where his master-touch can be detected. For the coarse and vulgar portrait of Saint Joan, which is given in the latter part of the drama, Shakespeare is certainly not responsible.

"2 Henry VI"

In this play the dramatist introduces a case of spirit-raising. Humphrey, Duke of Gloucester, and next-of-kin to the Sovereign, has a dream, which his ambitious and unscrupulous wife, Eleanor, interprets as a promise of the crown. Gloucester puts these thoughts aside, but Eleanor is ready to enlist supernatural help to further her designs. When the wily priest, Hume, enters and addresses her as "your majesty," she answers (I. 2. 74–77):

> What say'st thou, man? has thou as yet conferr'd
> With Margery Jourdain, the cunning witch,
> With Roger Bolingbroke, the conjurer?
> And will they undertake to do me good?

Hume replies that they have promised to raise a spirit from the underground which will answer any questions the duchess may wish to put to it. The superstitious Eleanor accepts the offer, and the crafty Hume gloats at the prospect of profit for himself.

In Act I, Scene 4, Margery Jourdain, Bolingbroke, Hume, and a fellow-priest named Southwell, meet in Gloucester's garden to carry out their promise to the duchess. When she welcomes them, Bolingbroke, conversant with the practices of witchcraft, says (18-22):

> Patience, good lady; wizards know their times:
> Deep night, dark night, the silent of the night,
> The time of night when Troy was set on fire;
> The time when screech-owls cry, and ban-dogs howl,
> And spirits walk, and ghosts break up their graves,
> That time best fits the work we have in hand.

Here, according to the Stage Directions, "they do the ceremonies belonging, and make the circle; Bolingbroke or Southwell reads, 'Conjuro te, etc.' It thunders and lightens terribly; then the Spirit riseth."

Jourdain calls it by the name of Asmath and orders it to answer all questions, for "till thou speak, thou shalt not pass from hence." The spirit, evidently present against its will, and anxious to be off, complies. It foretells the fate of King Henry, the Duke of Suffolk, the Duke of Somerset, and then groans, "Have done, for more I hardly can endure." Bolingbroke dismisses the spirit, who disappears in thunder. Its prophecies are all fulfilled later in the play.

The séance is broken up by the entry of the Duke of York and the Duke of Buckingham with their guard (1. 4. 44-45):

York Lay hands upon these traitors and their trash.
Beldam, I think we watch'd you at an inch.
[i.e. caught you in the act.]

The magicians and the duchess are led off guarded, while Buckingham leaves to report to the King (II. 1. 167–175):

> A sort of naughty persons, lewdly bent,
> Under the countenance and confederacy
> Of Lady Eleanor, the protector's wife,
> The ringleader and head of all this rout,
> Have practised dangerously against your state,
> Dealing with witches and with conjurers:
> Whom we have apprehended in the fact;
> Raising up wicked spirits from under ground,
> Demanding of King Henry's life and death.

The accused are brought to trial, found guilty and sentenced. The duchess is banished, and as for the rest (II. 3. 5–8) the King says:

> You four, from hence to prison back again;
> From thence unto the place of execution:
> The witch in Smithfield shall be burn'd to ashes,
> And you three shall be strangled on the gallows.

In this play the true and false Supernatural are brought together and contrasted; and while the false is confounded, the true is confirmed. Shakespeare treats reliable manifestations of the Unseen with due respect, but forgers and charlatans are humorously handled, as Saunder Simpcox in II. 1, who asserts that he has been cured of blindness and protests he is lame, until persuaded by the Beadle's whips to leap over a stool.

"1 HENRY IV"

Another comparison between the believer and the sceptic makes the first part of *Henry IV* worthy of notice in connection with Shakespeare's attitude towards the Supernatural. In Scene 1 of Act III, Glendower, the powerful Welsh leader, who shares the superstitions of his race, has a heated argument with Harry Hotspur, the blunt, matter-of-fact soldier. Glendower remarks (13–17):

> . . . at my nativity
> The front of heaven was full of fiery shapes,
> Of burning cressets; and at my birth
> The frame and huge foundation of the earth
> Shaked like a coward.

The prosaic Hotspur, who has little faith in astrological portents, replies (18–20), "Why, so it would have done at the same season, if your mother's cat had but kittened, though yourself had never been born." Glendower angrily repeats that at his coming, "The heavens were all on fire, the earth did tremble." Hotspur substitutes a possible scientific explanation of the disturbance. Both men become furious; and Mortimer has to intervene and put an end to "this unprofitable chat," which threatens to ruin the conference called to decide on the military campaign against the King.

In the above scene it is impossible not to suspect that Shakespeare inclined to the enlightened, scientific view and was quietly laughing at the old, absurd superstitions.

Another incident with a supernatural flavour occurs in this play on the battlefield of Shrewsbury. The rebel Hotspur is mortally wounded by the Prince of Wales; and as he expires, exclaims (v. 4. 83–86):

> O, I could prophesy,
> But that the earthy and cold hand of death
> Lies on my tongue: no, Percy, thou art dust,
> And food for——   [dies

Dying men were credited with the ability to foresee the future. John of Gaunt is another instance of death-bed clairvoyance.

"THE MERRY WIVES OF WINDSOR"

About five years after writing *Midsummer Night's Dream* Shakespeare's mind wandered back to the fairies. But they are not those Lilliputian, immortal flower-and-insect beings which his genius had originated in his first supernatural play. In the new comedy the fairies are very human boys dressed up to look the part; their queen is Anne Page, now a woman of marriageable age; their leaders are Sir Hugh Evans, the Welsh parson, and Mistress Quickly; and their Robin Goodfellow, here called Hobgoblin, is no other than the sharper, Pistol.

Except in a few minor, flowery characteristics the fairies of the *Merry Wives of Windsor* revert from the *Midsummer Night's Dream* conception to the fairies of folk-lore. Shakespeare draws generously on vulgar superstition for the writing of the Windsor Park scenes. The size of the children is in keeping with the popular idea of fairy stature. The surroundings of Herne's Oak, where Mrs. Ford has persuaded the wicked, old Falstaff to keep yet a third assignation with her, is typical of the fairy dwellings. The time of meeting, midnight, is the accepted fairy time. None were so qualified to punish a case of unchastity as fairies, since most of their earthly life was supposed to be occupied in dealing with such delinquents. Indeed, it is probable that this very belief suggested the final scene of the play to Shakespeare.

The actual existence of fairies was widely accepted

among the Elizabethans, and their visibility to certain people was not seriously questioned. The aim of the Fords and the Pages was to convince Falstaff that he was one of those so gifted. To this end, as M. W. Latham writes,[1] "much trouble and great pains were taken to make Anne Page and her troupe instantly recognizable as fairies. . . . They finally appeared 'mask'd and vizarded' and 'loose enrob'd' in 'white and green' with 'ribbands pendant, flaring 'bout' their heads upon which were 'rounds of waxen tapers.' " White and green costumes were, it seems, the conventional dress of Elizabethan fairies.

Falstaff falls into the well-laid trap. He arrives at the oak at twelve and meets the ladies. Almost at once, however, the fairies appear, led by Mistress Quickly, to the inevitable accompaniment of fairy music. She sings (v. 5. 41–44):

> Fairies, black, grey, green, and white,
> You moonshine revellers and shades of night,
> You orphan heirs of fixed destiny,
> Attend your office and your quality.

Mistress Quickly then calls to Pistol, "Hobgoblin, make the fairy oyes"; and Pistol addresses the elves (46–50):

> Elves, list your names; silence, you airy toys.
> Cricket, to Windsor chimneys shalt thou leap:
> Where fires thou find'st unraked and hearths unswept,
> There pinch the maids as blue as bilberry:
> Our radiant queen hates sluts and sluttery.

The elves, to judge from this play and *Midsummer Night's Dream*, were apparently subject to the fairy queen, although distinct from the fairies proper and

[1] *The Elizabethan Fairies*, p. 89.

rather more wicked than they. Here they are ordered
to carry out their sovereign's sentence on those guilty
of the sin of uncleanliness, against which the fairies
were particularly virulent.

All these folk-lore beliefs were intentionally included
in order to convince Falstaff of the reality of the
fairies who had interrupted his love-making. The
trick succeeds. Terrified, he remembers that fairies
punish those who talk to or spy upon them:

> They are fairies; he that speaks to them shall die:
> I'll wink and couch: no man their works must eye.
>
> (51–52.)

He lies trembling upon his face. For the moment
the fairies are busy with their own concerns; but
on discovering the frightened mortal, they burn him
with tapers to test his chastity. He howls with pain,
and in consequence they are convinced that he is a
sinner. Mistress Quickly cries:

> Corrupt, corrupt, and tainted in desire!
> About him, fairies; sing a scornful rhyme;
> And, as you trip, still pinch him to your time.
>
> (94–96.)

With their habit of breaking into a dance on the
least provocation, and often singing to their measure,
the fairies surround Falstaff, chanting as they trip,
"Fie on sinful fantasy! Fie on lust and luxury!" They
visit him with their characteristic punishment of
pinching, which was often extremely painful:

> Pinch him, and burn him, and turn him about,
> Till candles and starlight and moonshine be out.

In the end Falstaff realizes how he has been tricked

K

and fooled, and in chastened mood hears this good
advice from Sir Hugh Evans, "Sir John Falstaff,
serve Got, and leave your desires, and fairies will not
pinse you" (137–138).

"Troilus and Cressida"

The point that calls for notice in this apparently
unfinished play of the Trojan War is the prophetic
powers of Cassandra, Priam's daughter. In II. 2, she
predicts the fall of Troy, if the Grecian Helen is not
restored to her people (108–112):

> Cry, Trojans, cry! practise your eyes with tears!
> Troy must not be, nor goodly Ilion stand;
> Our firebrand brother, Paris, burns us all.
> Cry, Trojans, cry! a Helen and a woe:
> Cry, cry! Troy burns, or else let Helen go.

The young Troilus represents the sceptical attitude
in this play. Hector asks (113–115):

> Now, youthful Troilus, do not these high strains
> Of divination in our sister work
> Some touches of remorse?

Troilus has been opposed to all surrender to the Greeks
and favours a pursuance to the end of what Hector
describes as "a bad case." Cassandra's prophecy moves
him not at all (122–125):

> . . . Cassandra's mad: her brain-sick raptures
> Cannot distaste the goodness of a quarrel
> Which hath our several honours all engaged
> To make it gracious.

Cassandra is again inspired in V. 3, and foretells the
death of Hector. Troilus in exasperation bids her

"Away! away!" Brother and sister enact another clash .between belief and unbelief; and in this instance the powers of divination are allowed and corroborated.

"KING LEAR"

The Elizabethans, like the Jews of Palestine in the time of Our Lord, were wont to say that insane people were possessed with a devil. It is, therefore, natural that we should hear much of devils in that grand but wild tragedy of *Lear*. The poor old king, driven to madness by grief and resentment at the cruelty and ingratitude of his faithless daughters, is cleverly contrasted with Edgar, who feigns madness for self-protection against injustice.

The devils traced their origin back to the gods of heathen mythology. They were full of all malice and wickedness, the inspirers of terror and agents of disaster. In *King Lear* the fiends appear to hold sway over the characters. For material regarding the various devils Shakespeare consulted Harsnett's category in the *Declaration of Egregious Popish Impostures*, published in 1603, two years before the writing of the tragedy. From this book he took the strange names that we come across in the text—Smulkin (III. 4. 146), Modo and Mahu (III. 4. 149), and Frateretto (III. 6. 7). The pseudo-lunatic Edgar is always howling that the fiends are after him and attacking him. A typical instance occurs in III. 6, 31–34:

The foul fiend haunts poor Tom in the voice of a nightingale. Hopdance cries in Tom's belly for two white herring. Croak not, black angel; I have no food for thee.

In IV. 1, we hear something of the nature of these fiends. Says Edgar, still pretending to be out of his mind (61–65):

Five fiends have been in poor Tom at once; of lust, as Obidicut; Hobbididance, prince of dumbness; Mahu, of stealing; Modo, of murder; Flibbertigibbet, of mopping and mowing [i.e. making grimaces].

King Lear is not only interesting from the supernatural point of view on account of its mention of devils. The tragedy is very full of astrology; and Shakespeare contrasts the old believer in Gloucester, who fears that the recent eclipses "portend no good" (1. 2. 112) with the more enlightened and advanced ideas of Edgar, who declares, "This is the excellent foppery of the world, that, when we are sick in fortune—often the surfeit of our own behaviour—we make guilty of our disasters, the sun, moon, and the stars" (128–131). He sums it up as "an admirable evasion" on man's part of the responsibility for his misfortunes.

The astrology of *King Lear* is fully discussed in my book, *Shakespeare and Science*.

"ANTONY AND CLEOPATRA"

There is not a great deal of the supernatural order in the second of the splendid Roman dramas; but what there is, is interesting. Firstly, we have a conversation between Antony and his ever-attendant Soothsayer, who has accompanied him from Egypt to Rome and remains with him in Cæsar's house. The Romans were firm believers in omens and divination; and it was natural enough for Antony to ask his seer, "Say to me, Whose fortune shall rise

higher, Cæsar's or mine?" and for the Soothsayer
to reply without fear or favour (II. 3, 17–23, 25–30) :

> Cæsar's.
> Therefore, O Antony, stay not by his side:
> Thy demon, that thy spirit which keeps thee, is
> Noble, courageous, high, unmatchable,
> Where Cæsar's is not; but near him thy angel
> Becomes a fear, as being o'erpower'd: therefore
> Make space enough between you.
>
> .   .   .   -   .
>
> If thou dost play with him at any game,
> Thou art sure to lose; and, of that natural luck,
> He beats thee 'gainst the odds: thy lustre thickens,
> When he shines by: I say again, thy spirit
> Is all afraid to govern thee near him;
> But, he away, 'tis noble.

The Soothsayer's advice to return to Cleopatra is
welcome to Antony since it corresponds with his own
inclination. The point of supernatural interest, however, is the mention of Antony's "demon" or atten-
dant spirit. Although Shakespeare drew his materials
for this scene from Plutarch, he knew that it would
suit very well an Elizabethan audience. The Church
taught that every human being was watched over
by his good genius or guardian angel, with whom
the spirits of evil were constantly at war. Such was
the common explanation of the inward mental conflict between good and evil, a conflict referred to
constantly by Shakespeare, notably in Sonnet CXLIV,
where the figure of a "better angel" and "worser
spirit" is used.

In *Antony and Cleopatra*, too, we have another
instance of the association of music with the Supernatural. Working on a hint from Plutarch, Shakespeare
introduces a short scene showing the sentries on guard

before the palace of Cleopatra—a situation reminiscent of the eerie opening of *Hamlet*. It is the eve of the battle which must decide whether Antony or Octavius shall rule the Roman world. The mental strain of the soldiers and the sense of impending disaster find expression in the strains of mysterious music. The men, unable to explain it, are perturbed and anxiously debate its meaning. One suggests, " 'Tis the god Hercules, whom Antony loved, Now leaves him" (IV. 3. 15). The strange melody floats away, and the puzzled soldiers follow it. The Stage Directions read, "Music of hautboys as under the stage." According to Mr. Edward W. Naylor,[1] "hautboys" is an important musical term which always implies a special significance in the music. To Shakespeare few musical uses were more important than that of convincing his audience of the reality of his supernatural manifestations.

"PERICLES"

In this drama, not unjustly described by Ben Jonson as a "mouldy tale," the goddess Diana intervenes to unravel the intricacies of the plot. Pericles believes that his wife, Thaisa, is dead. When apparently lifeless, she is thrown overboard in deference to the superstitious demands of the sailors on Pericles' ship. The body floats to Ephesus, where a physician revives it. Thaisa, thinking she has lost her husband, enters Diana's temple as a votaress.

Diana appears to Pericles in a vision as he lies aboard his ship, then off Mytilene. The goddess orders the Prince to her temple at Ephesus. He obeys, and

[1] *Shakespeare and Music*, p. 175.

there is reunited to the wife he believed he had lost for ever many years before.

Although Shakespeare is certainly responsible for portions of *Pericles,* the greater part of the drama is by another man, probably George Wilkins. Even the Shakespearean portions do not reveal the Poet at his best; and it would appear that he took little interest in the play, and that probably commercial.

"Cymbeline"

Cymbeline was one of those plays written at the end of Shakespeare's life when the idea of forgiveness and reconciliation was uppermost in his mind. Apart from the Soothsayer's prophecy of the success of the Roman arms in IV. 2, 346–352, and the passing references to fairies, the supernatural element is confined to Posthumus' vision in V. 4.

Posthumus, who has been wrongly led to suspect his wife, Imogen, lies in a British prison following the defeat of the Roman forces, to which he joined himself. While waiting for death to release him from his gaolers, he falls asleep and dreams.

In his vision, introduced by solemn music, he sees the ghost of his father, Sicilius Leonatus, attired like a warrior, and of his mother enter hand-in-hand, "with music before them." Then, "after other music," follow his two young brothers, as they died in the wars. They surround the sleeping Posthumus; and after recounting his history and present woes in verse, appeal for help to Jupiter. The great god of Rome descends with his eagle, and promises that all shall be well with Posthumus, that his time of trouble will make his joy all the greater when a blameless Imogen is restored to him. The Ghosts have received the glad tidings on their knees; and when Jupiter re-ascends to heaven, they also vanish, leaving behind them a book with a cryptic message upon it. This message is interpreted later by the Soothsayer (v. 5. 436), and is found to contain prophecies that have all been fulfilled; hence the promise of a happy "issue out of all their affliction" is assured to all.

There is some doubt as to Shakespeare's authorship of the Posthumus vision. Like the Masque in Act IV of *The Tempest*, it was probably inserted to please a Court audience, who, apparently, could not have too much of the pageant type of entertainment. It is interesting to remark that these masques dealt most often with the Supernatural, and were, as in the case of *Cymbeline*, sometimes interpolated into plays which, apart from them, had little or nothing to do with the metaphysical world. Whoever the author, the value of music in awakening a sense of awe towards the Supernatural is once more demonstrated.

The allusions to fairies include Belarius' remark, when he and Guiderius and Arviragus discover the disguised Imogen in their Welsh cave: "But that it eats our victuals, I should think here were a fairy." The line is interesting as confirming the popular idea as to the size of fairies. Further on in the play Posthumus refers to the well-known bounty of the fairies, when he awakens from his vision and finds the book and its strange wording: "What fairies haunt this ground?" (v. 4. 133). The folk-fairies often rewarded their favourites with sixpences placed in shoes and other useful and valuable gifts.

"THE WINTER'S TALE"

Dreams are common enough in Shakespeare's plays, but the dream of Antigonus in *The Winter's Tale* has features of its own which make it particularly interesting.

From his own account (III. 3. 16–53) we learn that the spirit of Hermione has visited Antigonus in his sleep and told him to take her child, to be called Perdita, to a desolate spot in Bohemia and there abandon her. This incident was, no doubt, suggested by the very common method of dealing with the fairies' changelings. It is not so much the seemingly heartless request that distinguishes the dream, as the fact, which transpires later, that Hermione is not dead. Although Antigonus says:

> I have heard, but not believed, the spirits o' the dead
> May walk again: if such thing be, thy mother
> Appear'd to me last night, for ne'er was dream
> So like to waking.

Hermione does not, like conventional ghosts, mention the circumstances of her death, for the very good reason that she is not yet dead. This is the only instance in the whole of Shakespeare where the supernatural presence of a living person is recorded.

It would be interesting to know if Shakespeare had any belief in what we can call telepathy, or ever speculated on the workings of the subconscious mind. Mr. Paul Gibson raises the point in his essay on *Shakespeare's Use of the Supernatural*,"[1] and it does not seem a wholly improbable theory.

Music assists what appears to be a supernatural occurrence when the statue of Hermione, supposedly

[1] P. 36.

slain fifteen years ago by her jealous husband, Leontes, comes to life. The musical accompaniment persuades us to accept the miracle, whereas we might otherwise summarily reject it before reaching the explanation that Hermione never really died.

Another incident occurs in this play of the bounty of the fairies, who were believed to bestow fortunes on certain lucky individuals. The shepherd goes out grumbling to collect his sheep and comes upon a child's mantle full of fairy gold (III. 3).

"HENRY VIII"

To decide what portions of *Henry VIII* were written by Shakespeare and what portions by Fletcher is a task which has engaged scholars without resulting in unanimity. The balance of opinion, however, is in favour of assigning the only supernatural scene in the drama to the lesser dramatist.

The scene (IV. 2) is that showing the sorrowful and deposed Katharine of Aragon in retirement at Kimbolton. The wronged Queen is sick and weary of life and requests the good Griffith:

> Cause the musicians play me that sad note
> I named my knell, whilst I sit meditating
> On that celestial harmony I go to.
>
> (IV. 2. 78–80.)

To "sad and solemn music" she falls asleep and sees a vision in which angels visit her. The Stage Directions describe it thus:

The vision. Enter, solemnly tripping one after another, six personages, clad in white robes, wearing on their heads garlands of bays, and golden vizards on their faces; branches of bays or palm in their hands. They first congee unto her, then dance; and, at certain changes, the first two hold a spare garland over her head; at which the other four make reverent curtsies; then the two that held the garland deliver the same to the other next two, who observe the same order in their changes, and holding the garland over her head: which done, they deliver the same garland to the last two, who likewise observe the same order: at which, as it were by inspiration, she makes in her sleep signs of rejoicing, and holdeth up her hands to heaven: and so in their dancing vanish, carrying the garland with them. The music continues.

These unusually elaborate directions give a good description of the type of interlude that both Court and public demanded from the playwrights. Once again recourse is had to the Supernatural, and once again use is made of music to make the presentation impressive. The soft, mournful strains suggest that the dying queen is already standing on the threshold of the hereafter, and is conscious of the spiritual harmony to which she knows she is soon to go. But the "spirits of peace," as Katharine calls the angels, depart without her, for her work on earth is not quite finished. She is distressed that the bright faces which promised her eternal happiness have vanished, and in her disappointment cries: "Bid the music leave; They are harsh and heavy to me." But Katharine's life is ebbing, and she welcomes death as a deliverer from her sorrows, only begging her faithful attendants to:

> embalm me,
> Then lay me forth; although unqueen'd, yet like
> A queen, and daughter to a king, inter me.
>
> (IV. 2. 170–172.)

PART II

SHAKESPEARE AND RELIGION

X

RELIGION UNDER ELIZABETH

A STUDY of Shakespeare's religion may most profitably be commenced with a recapitulation of the various influences by which he was surrounded, especially during his most impressionable years.

Under Elizabeth England became definitely and for all time Protestant. Her reign is, therefore, the most important epoch in our religious history. Although the English Reformation was launched by her father, Henry VIII, the movement in its earliest stages was inspired more by political than religious motives. It was not primarily enthusiasm for, nor even smouldering sympathy with, the Lutheran doctrines making such rapid headway on the Continent that influenced England to revolt against the rule of Rome. It was the irritation of the King at the papal thwarting of his plans, particularly in the matter of his divorce from Katharine of Aragon.

Henry VIII made no revolutionary changes in doctrine. The supremacy of the Pope was overthrown, pilgrimages were forbidden, the old superstitions connected with relics and images were confuted, the Romish purgatory was rejected, and the Bible was translated into the English tongue, and a copy set up in every church where all could read it. But, apart from these points, the old teachings of the Catholic Church were retained together with many of its rites and ceremonies.

A more decided move towards Protestantism occurred during the reign of Henry's son. The members of the Regency Council for Edward VI favoured further progress along Reformation lines. The inoffensive first Prayer Book was introduced, to be followed a few years later by the more radical second Prayer Book, which made such fundamental changes as the substitution of Holy Communion for the Mass, and laid the foundation stone of the Church of England.

The untimely death of Edward brought his sister Mary to the throne in 1553. The new sovereign had remained faithful all her life to the religion of her mother, Katharine of Aragon. Under Mary's influence the Reformation was checked and turned back, and for five years England experienced all the miseries of reaction. The country returned to its papal allegiance; the old laws against heresy, abolished by Edward VI, were revived; and there commenced that ghastly series of religious murders, when Cranmer, Latimer, Ridley, and a host of other Protestant martyrs were burnt at the stake for their opinions. Further, Mary's marriage to Philip of Spain made England a pawn in the struggles of the Continental Powers, and lost her Calais, her solitary remaining possession in France.

The bitter experiences of Mary's reign compared ill with the peaceful establishment of the independent Church of England under her father and brother. The explosions of fanatical hatred against the Protestants and the cruelty of the persecutions created that fear, distrust, and hatred of Rome which have guided English church history ever since. Those who had hitherto been lukewarm towards the Reformation were found on Mary's death looking hopefully towards Elizabeth, whose sympathies were reputed to be on the side of progress.

Nevertheless, Elizabeth had to proceed with care and discretion. The flames of Smithfield and the disasters abroad had made the people ready to welcome any changes that the acceding Sovereign might devise for peace and security. But the new Queen did not wish to repeat the mistakes of her unhappy sister by restoring the Protestants and taking a horrible revenge upon the Catholics. That would have been to prolong indefinitely the dismal story of wrong and persecution. Elizabeth aimed at conciliating and winning the Catholics, not alienating them. Her changes were, therefore, introduced gradually and pertained more to outward observance than to dogma.

The year after her accession the supremacy of the Sovereign over the Church in England and the repudiation of the authority of the Pope were reaffirmed. This was final. England was free of Rome for ever. Nor was she alone in this assertion of her independence. Scotland, her inveterate enemy, stood by her side and broke with the Scots' hereditary ally, France. Scotland was being swept by the fervour of John Knox; and her religious alliance with England was the first step on the path to political union.

Edward VI's Prayer Book was reintroduced, and the Act of Uniformity passed, which compelled all private and public worship to conform to the new ritual. A few years later the Thirty-Nine Articles, with their strong Protestant flavour, stated in final form the creed of the National Church. Apart from one or two important points, such as the repudiation of the sacrifice of the Mass, and the rejection of the overlordship of the Pope, there were no such violent reversals in dogma as to make it impossible for Catholics to obey the new laws as loyal subjects of the Queen. It was on this ground rather than on the ground of Christianity that their obedience was demanded and expected. Many of the old Roman practices were retained in pursuance of the policy of compromise; and the extremist Protestant wing, followers of Calvin and soon to be known as Puritans, found themselves more opposed to the Queen than the Catholics on certain points. Even her own clergy were in conflict with Elizabeth over the discard of some of the old uses, which she herself was anxious to retain. The most notable instance was the celibacy of the priests.

As "supreme governor" of the Church, Elizabeth called upon all her subjects to conform, outwardly at any rate, to the new rules of religious observance; and fines were exacted from those who absented themselves from public worship. As was to be expected, the Bishops who had served under Mary refused obedience, and were deposed and imprisoned. The clergy generally, however, accepted the Prayer Book and submitted to the Act of Supremacy. Some two hundred only[1] were compelled by their conscience to reject the compromise. As for the laity, they came easily into line; and for the first few years of her reign Elizabeth's policy of moderation and gradualness seemed to have solved a most perplexing problem.

Steering the middle course between extreme Catholicism on the one hand and extreme Calvinism on the other was resulting in the peace and order throughout her realm for which Elizabeth had hoped, when Rome interfered and ruined the bright promise. The Pope forbade all good Catholics to attend the new worship. The unfortunate people, torn between

---

[1] Camden gives the total as 189.

the old allegiance and the new, were forced into an opposition for which they had no desire and no liking. Fines were imposed on those who refused to conform, and the new name of "recusants," or nonconformists, was found for them. (At first "recusant" was almost synonymous with "Catholic," but later on there were Puritan recusants, against whom the Church proceeded with equal energy. Shakespeare's father was arraigned as a recusant, a fact that has led some to suppose that he was a Catholic. His Protestantism, however, is undoubted, and will be proved in a later chapter.)

Although the majority of Catholics were outwardly conformists, it was too much to expect that many were not secretly hoping for a restoration of the old religion. When such a restoration had seemed to pass beyond the bounds of possibility, an event occurred which gave encouragement, though false encouragement, to these suppressed longings. In 1568 Mary, Queen of Scots, fled to England; and her presence in Carlisle led to a great Catholic rising in the North under the Earls of Northumberland and Westmorland. Although attended with initial success, the great mass of Catholics throughout the country failed to join the rebellion, which was consequently crushed. It was the first invasion of that peace and order which was the great aim of the Elizabethan religious compromise. It made the policy of toleration impossible and brought evil days to the Catholics of England.

The chagrin of Pope Pius V at the failure of the English Catholics to turn the northern rebellion into a general rising, prompted him to take sterner measures against the recalcitrant queen. In 1570 he

issued the Papal Bull excommunicating Elizabeth.
By this step he finally destroyed her hope of winning
the Catholics to conformity and drove them into
permanent opposition to the National Church. Until
Rome interfered, there had appeared every chance
that the whole country would settle down and
acquiesce in the tolerance and moderation which had
guided the sovereign's religious policy. There was
very keen resentment, therefore, that the Pope had
meddled in English affairs, rekindled the hostility
of the Catholics, and placed them in a position
where obedience to the temporal power conflicted
with obedience to their Church. The feelings of the
country as a whole upon the excommunication of
the Queen and foreign interference in local and
internal affairs are well expressed by Shakespeare
in that famous anti-Roman speech from *King John*,
where the English monarch is made to declare that
"No Italian priest shall tithe or toil in our dominions."
(We shall have occasion to return again to this passage,
for few utterances are so significant in determining
the pronounced Protestant leanings of Shakespeare
himself.)

The Bull of 1570 initiated the wretched prosecu-
tion, with its curtailment of the liberties of the English
Catholics, which lasted until serious danger of a
reassertion of papal supremacy was passed. This series
of misfortunes could have been avoided if Rome had
minded her own business and abstained from interference in the affairs of the Church of England. The
Queen replied to the Papal Bull by obliging all
magistrates and public officers to subscribe to the
Articles of Faith. It is because John Shakespeare
continued to hold municipal office at Stratford long

after this decree was issued that we know he was a conforming member of the State Church.

Two years after the excommunication, an event occurred abroad which strengthened the English hostility to Rome. The queen-mother of France, Catherine de' Medici, was determined to crush once and for all the rising power of the French Huguenot, or Protestant, party. When these unfortunate people had swarmed into Paris for the marriage of Henry of Navarre and Marguerite de Valois, Catherine persuaded her son, Charles IX, to consent to their wholesale massacre on St. Bartholomew's Day, 1572. This sweeping extermination was not confined to Paris, but extended to the Provinces and lasted for many weeks. The dastardly deed evoked horror and anger in England, who noted that Catherine de' Medici received the congratulations of Pope Gregory XIII and all the great Catholic powers upon it.

England, free, self-dependent, and prosperous, entered what is known as the golden age of Elizabeth, when mighty achievements on the sea and in the New World, as well as in the world of art and literature, awakened the hearts and minds of Englishmen to the high destiny before the race. During these years of wealth, social energy, artistic triumph, and expansion, the traditionary Catholicism, to which nearly three-quarters of the people belonged at Elizabeth's succession, gradually decayed. The old Catholic priests, who had accepted the new religion outwardly while hating it in their hearts, died off; and their places were taken by young, zealous men; men, whose enthusiasm for Protestantism and energetic propagation of Reformation ideas carried the

new generation farther and farther from Rome.
Archbishop Parker cleverly and unobtrusively guided
this tendency to the strengthening of the National
Church, of which he was at this juncture the ideal
head. Moderate, tolerant, modest, scholarly, pious,
and virtuous, but withal a disciplinarian, he interpreted accurately the Elizabethan policy of steering
a middle course between the Catholic and Puritan
extremes.

The fact that matters were shaping well for the
future of the Church of England fired the Catholics
to make even more strenuous efforts to check its
progress and recover the ground that had been lost.
The Papal Bull of excommunication had only embarrassed the English Catholics, while strengthening
the determination of the rest of the people to have
nothing further to do with Rome. The crime of St.
Bartholomew's Day had increased the anti-papal
spirit. The new and desperate efforts of the Catholics
to stem the Protestant flood commenced about 1577,
when preachers, English for the most part, filtered
into England from Catholic seminaries abroad, and
began to sow seeds of religious revolt and political
treason among the recusant Catholics. They gained
a sufficient hearing to necessitate the strongest expe-
dients against them to preserve the safety of the realm.

The danger of disturbance from the activities of
the seminary preachers was increased from 1580
onwards by the coming of the Jesuits. Their leaders
were Edmund Campion and Robert Parsons, men
who certainly had the courage of their convictions,
but were unwise enough to engage in subversive
intrigue, playing upon the feelings of the Catholic
minority, and enticing them away from the new

service. Stern measures were taken against them; and in the next year Campion was arrested and executed at Tyburn, while Parsons was forced to flee the country. Despite the eclipse of the leaders, the Jesuit proselytizing continued; and by 1584 the Catholic reaction had assumed dimensions which called forth vigorous steps to counter it. Jesuit missionaries were declared guilty of high treason, and anyone found harbouring them was severely punished.

A relation of Shakespeare's on his mother's side, Edward Arden of Park Hall, was caught in the Jesuit trap and suffered the extreme penalty at Smithfield in 1583. He had been found guilty of inciting the young squire of Edston, John Somerville, to journey to London to shoot the heretical queen. He was but one of those, many of them revolting priests, who suffered for their religion between the coming of the Jesuits and the accession of James I. Nearly two hundred Catholics were put to death during this period, largely through the efforts of Sir Francis Walsingham, who organized an effective intelligence service, hunting the emissaries of Rome out of their hiding-places, exposing and frustrating their plots, and bringing them to execution as traitors to the Queen. Although English Protestantism stood firm against these attacks, the compromise and hope of union under the Church of England were destroyed; and the Jesuits succeeded in cutting off the Catholics for ever from their fellow-countrymen in the important sphere of religion.

The feeling of resentment against the Catholics which inspired the persecutions—persecutions which seem mild and restricted enough compared with the Bolshevist massacres in modern Russia—can be the more readily understood and excused when the foreign relations of Elizabethan England are considered. Rome allied herself invariably with the enemies of this country—a fact which justified the Queen and her ministers in regarding Catholics as political traitors. Most formidable among our foes was Spain; and while the Armada was dispatched primarily to drive the English from the New World and preserve the Spanish monopoly, yet religion was an important motive, for victory was to bring defeated England once more beneath the heel of the Pope. The great triumph of our sailors in 1588 did not only guarantee our political freedom, but preserved our religious liberty, which we shall never surrender to anyone.

It is an interesting fact that the people at large, who had already made up their minds that the new religion satisfied their needs, were indifferent to the Jesuit persuasiveness and the sufferings of the unfortunate Catholics who listened to them. The priests made no converts beyond the ranks of those fervent religionists who had never accepted the new creed and only attended the Church observances to avoid fines and imprisonment. In the whole of his writings Shakespeare makes no allusion to the measures taken against the Catholics; and only in one passage are there lines which are sometimes interpreted as a possible reference to the martyrs of the day. They occur in Sonnet CXXIV and run:

> . . . the fools of time,
> Which die for goodness, who have lived for crime.

These words may refer as well to political as to religious martyrs; and some critics see in them an allusion to the unfortunate Earl of Essex. The truth is, that by the time Shakespeare commenced his career, England had definitely chosen to pursue her destiny along the path of Protestantism. The futile excommunicating and fulminations of the Pope, the energies of the seminary priests and the Jesuits, the attacks of the great Catholic Power of Spain, had all failed to shake the New Faith; and Englishmen were now so confident of themselves that they feared no longer the machinations of Rome.

Moderates are not only assailed by the reactionaries, but also by the advanced wing of their own party. So it was with Elizabeth. Not only had she to conciliate the Catholics, but also to pacify the impatience and extravagant demands of the Calvinists or Puritans. Indeed, she was often more annoyed by the Protestant extremists than by the Roman party in steering her middle course; and herself had almost as little sympathy with Calvinism as Catholicism.

During the reign of "bloody Mary," England had not been a safe place for the advanced members of the Reformation party. Numbers of them fled for refuge abroad, Geneva being their most favoured sanctuary. At Geneva was stationed the great Swiss reformer, John Calvin, who led the most forward wing of the Reformed Church, and differed from the Lutherans in holding the doctrines of absolute predestination, of the spiritual presence only in the Eucharist, and of the independence of the Church in matters of government. Calvin and his followers practised the severest austerity, while the Calvinist ecclesiastical rule was distinguished by its rigour and iron discipline.

The English refugees at Geneva imbibed the Cal-

vinistic influence and heard even the Protestant
Prayer Book of Edward VI criticized by the great
reformer for its moderation. Saturated with extreme
opinions, they returned to England on Elizabeth's
accession, eager to avenge themselves upon the
Catholics and obliterate Popery throughout the land.
Naturally they were disappointed to find the Queen
bent on compromise. While they demanded and
expected a clean sweep of all Roman doctrine and
ritual, they discovered that many of the old teachings
and practices were retained in the interests of uniformity. They missed from the new creed some of
the advanced tenets of Calvin, and strongly objected
to such ritual as the wearing of the surplice, kneeling
at the Communion Table, and other observances,
which appeared to them unnecessary and harmful
survivals of a discredited religion.

In England the Calvinist party grew rapidly in
strength, but failed to win the sympathy of the
pleasure-loving Queen, to whom the asceticism of
their lives made little appeal. In Scotland the doctrines of Calvin were propagated by the ardent and
fearless reformer, John Knox. In his violent attack
upon the Churches he carried all before him, and
desolated his enemies with his withering invective.
Elizabeth had little liking for Knox, and was especially
displeased by his diatribe against woman, whom he
considered fundamentally unfitted for any position
of power or authority. The coldness of the Queen
and her insistence on conformity to the English Prayer
Book, which contained so much that they disliked,
drove the extremists to holding their own meetings
and worshipping in their own way. It was then,
about 1567, that they first became known as

Puritans, and as nonconformists were liable for the same fines and penalties that awaited obstinate Catholics.

Calvin died in the same year in which Shakespeare was born; and in some countries the movement which he founded swept all opposition aside and attained supreme power. Owing to the religious policy of Elizabeth, the Calvinist triumph in England was delayed until the next century. The Puritans were, however, a growing party; and the recusants in their ranks were a thorn in the side of the Church of England.

To the average Englishman of Elizabethan times the Puritan asceticism appealed no more than it did to the Queen. Converts were, of course, constantly being made, but they had to be worked for and did not flock to the Calvinist standard. The outlook of the extremists was strict and narrow. They believed that life should consist only of work and religion. They frowned upon all pleasures. They allowed no leisure for sport and art, which, they asserted, exposed men and women to temptation. Moreover, art was particularly associated in their minds with the medieval Church, whereas they wished to efface all relics and reminders of the old Faith. This point of view naturally led the Puritans to wage war upon the theatres—a war that eventually succeeded in closing them. Happily, this disaster did not overtake the stage until years after Shakespeare's career as a dramatist was closed. When they wished to deprive him of his very means of livelihood and destroy the ladder by which he had climbed to success and fame, we can understand why the Poet had little love for the Puritans. It is, indeed, a testimony to his humanity to find his treatment of them tempered with so much kindly tolerance.

The foregoing briefly surveys the religious position in England during the early part of the life of Shakespeare. For the purpose of our study it was important to remind ourselves of the various creeds and parties which manœuvred for position and intrigued against each other, either to force uniformity in the interests of the State Church, or to avoid conformance and seek opportunity to worship in their own way according to their particular beliefs. Only by so refreshing our memories can we appreciate how the warring influences in the England of the Poet's youth were likely to mould his own religious opinions.

To summarize in a very general manner, it would be fair to say that Elizabeth's reign was a period of peace and compromise. It marked a pause in the gigantic revolution from medieval Catholicism to advanced Protestantism; and during its comparative quiet and order, art, literature, the drama, discovery, exploration, colonization, naval triumphs, trade and commerce were given an opportunity of which they took the fullest advantage. In the wealth, prosperity, and success which came to England under the great Queen, that national consciousness was born, which eventually extended the rule of our race over one-quarter of the globe.

In the Elizabethan interregnum there were, we have seen, three creeds to which Shakespeare could have subscribed. He could, like some of his mother's relations, have identified himself with the Roman Catholics, who were always hoping and plotting and scheming for the overthrow of the Church of England and the return of the country to allegiance to the

Pope. Such an association, however, would have involved Shakespeare in treason and disloyalty to his Queen, whose favours he enjoyed and on whose patronage he and his fellow-actors depended. He could, again, have adopted the austere code of the Puritans, who were aiming at control of the State machine and the obliteration of everything that savoured of Popery in the Established Church. By so doing he would have worked against his own business interests, centred as they were in the theatre, at which the Puritans hurled angry fulminations with intent to raze it to the ground. Thirdly, he could have chosen to be a conforming Protestant of the Church of England, obediently following his sovereign down the middle course between Rome and Geneva. In this way he would have displayed his patriotism and loyalty; and this, I think there is no doubt, is the path he took and the truth about his religion.

JOHN SHAKESPEARE'S RELIGION[1]

In a majority of cases a person's religion is determined by the influences that surround his childhood. It is true that spiritually minded men and women are often known to reach a crisis in their religious experience, where they leave the faith of their fathers to follow the light of a new revelation. To most of us, however, it is not given to feel so intensely upon these divine questions; and we are content to give an uncritical adherence to the creed of the Church in which we have been reared—if, indeed, we continue to be interested in religion at all.

From what we know of the life of Shakespeare, of the people with whom he mixed, and the atmosphere in which he worked, we should be very surprised to learn that he was obtrusively pious. From the scraps of information, of which most of his biographies are of necessity compiled, we conjure up a picture of a man who enjoyed the good things of life, was extremely broad-minded, a jovial companion, and very far from being an ascetic. If we try to find the man through his writings, we get the impression of a kindly, tolerant nature, one imbued with a feeling of good will towards all men, and blessedly free from those deep-seated prejudices which have spread hatred and persecution through the ranks of religionists.

There is no reason to believe, then, that Shakespeare was ever tempted to change his form of religion or

[1] For many new facts in this chapter I am indebted to Edgar I. Fripp's *Shakespeare Studies*.

to desert the Church in which he was brought up. His real religion consisted of mental questionings on the great problems of life and death, and was not guided, controlled, or influenced by dogma and ritual. While efforts to determine his religious views have engaged the minds of many great Shakespearean scholars, and ingenious attempts have been made to prove that he became a Roman Catholic, the truth of what he really felt towards the differing claims of Catholicism, orthodox Protestantism, and Calvinism has never been revealed in a way to command general acceptance. He has denied us a direct confession of faith; and we can most safely arrive at an estimate of his views by determining what he definitely was *not* among the religious labels of the period.

It is possible to decide, with confidence in the accuracy of our decision, the form of religion which the young Shakespeare was taught during his early years in Stratford. It was surely the religion of his father; and, as I shall now show, John Shakespeare in those years was, without question, a staunch, loyal, conforming Protestant.

John Shakespeare was born at Snitterfield, some four miles from Stratford, about 1529. His father's name was Richard, a farmer by calling, who had another son named Henry. Snitterfield was one of the places in the Midlands where the English Reformation obtained an early footing. Nearby, too, was Hampton Lucy, whose rector, Edward Large, preached a Protestant sermon, which led to his arrest and trial for heresy by the Catholic authorities, as early as 1537. A tense battle was fought between the Catholic Squire Clopton, who desired Large to be punished, and the Protestant Squire Lucy, who worked indefatigably for his pardon. By enlisting the aid of those famous leaders of the Reformation party, Cromwell and Latimer, William Lucy was at last successful in his efforts on behalf of his Protestant parson.

From this we see that, even before he came to Stratford to be apprenticed to a glover, John Shakespeare must have learnt something of Reformation ideas, and been fully aware of the points of controversy between the old Church and the new. He set up in business for himself in the reign of Edward VI, and was already in Henley Street in 1552, in which year he was fined for making a dunghill to the annoyance of his neighbours.

John Shakespeare was well established in business —his activities were many and various—when Queen Mary succeeded her brother, restored the old religion, and inaugurated those horrible persecutions which have seared the pages of our history. The very first victims of the new tyranny were Warwickshire men. Very early among the martyrdoms was that of Hooper, the Bishop of the diocese, who was burnt before his own Cathedral at Gloucester. The well-loved Latimer, known to many at Stratford, was burnt at Oxford. Others suffered a like fate at Coventry, Leicester, Banbury, Wotton-under-Edge, and neighbouring towns. Relations and friends of the sufferers dwelt in Stratford itself, and the people were much stirred by these hideous crimes committed in the name of religion. There were riots, feuds, and fierce fights in the streets, which were only quelled by fines and imprisonment, and the strict order that none was to carry arms within the precincts of the borough. The Catholic authorities had the utmost difficulty in keeping the situation under control, even the Corporation itself being out of hand and ripe for revolt.

In this difficult period John Shakespeare entered upon his long and honourable career of municipal service. Among his earliest appointments was that of Constable, a duty requiring courage and firmness, since he was responsible for the maintenance of order and for seeing that the decree against the carrying of arms was obeyed. At this period John Shakespeare seems to have expressed no religious opinions distasteful to his Catholic masters, whatever his private opinions may have been. In marrying Mary Arden in 1557 he chose the daughter of a Catholic for his bride. Mary's father, Robert Arden, had, however, died the previous year; and we have no information at all as to what Mary's own religious views were. Her sister seems to have married a Protestant; but we find her relations, Edward and Mary Arden of Park Hall, concerned in a plot to shoot the Protestant Queen in 1583. John Shakespeare evidently had no sympathy with traitors such as these, even though they were connections of his wife's, for when his son William wished him to impale the arms of Arden with his own in 1599, he refused the Park Hall arms and substituted those of Simon Arden, the only Protestant member of the family.[1]

When Mary died and Elizabeth succeeded, Stratford, like all the rest of England, looked anxiously for the new Queen to reveal her policy. John Shakespeare was still Constable; and during this critical period the performance of his official duties must have called for much tact and steadiness. When

[1] See *Shakespeare Studies* (Fripp), p. 98.

Elizabeth gave the lead towards Protestantism, the Stratford Corporation were not slow to follow it. They dismissed their Catholic Steward, one Edgeworth. They got rid of their Catholic vicar, Father Dyos. They elected that stout Protestant, Adrian Quyney, as their bailiff (or mayor). Surely it is ample proof of John Shakespeare's Protestantism that when all these changes were taking effect, he continued to hold municipal office.

From 1561–1562 he was one of the two chamberlains to whom the finances of the town were entrusted. He continued as acting-Chamberlain until 1565. He was engaged in important activities during this period which leave no doubt as to his religious leanings. After the death of the great Catholic Squire, Sir William Clopton, in 1560, and the flight of his son abroad, the Corporation turned their attention to the Guild Chapel, which had been rebuilt by the Cloptons, but was within the town's jurisdiction. Under the supervision of John Shakespeare, acting-Chamberlain, the Protestantizing of the chapel was carried out, and in no mild fashion, for the frescoes and statues were disfigured, the rood-loft was taken down, and the Communion Table substituted for the altar.

John Shakespeare must have been an exceptionally busy man at this period of his life. His father died in the winter of 1560–1561; and he seems to have continued the family farm at Snitterfield. In addition to his business as a glover, apparently he also dealt in wool and agricultural produce, and, according to some accounts, in butcher's meat as well. In addition, his municipal duties were extensive and responsible; and he is found putting all the Corporation property in a proper state of repair, particularly the house of the new Protestant vicar, the Rev. John Bretchgirdle.

Bretchgirdle was a graduate of Oxford and was up at Christ Church, the college famed for its fervent support of the Reformation. Between him and John Shakespeare there was not only the bond of a stout Protestantism, but a more intimate relationship, for the vicar baptized two of the Chamberlain's children —his second daughter, Margaret, and his world-famous son, William. Both baptisms followed the English form of service as contained in the reintroduced Prayer Book, and marked a contrast to the Catholic ceremony performed by Father Dyos over the first-born, Joan, in 1558. In 1564, soon after the birth of William Shakespeare, Stratford experienced a terrible visitation of the plague; and John rendered invaluable service to the overworked vicar, who himself died the following year, probably as a result of the strain imposed upon him.

In 1565 the Corporation showed their appreciation of the services of John Shakespeare by making him an Alderman. He had now a thriving business, was the holder of considerable property in the town, and the husband of an Arden heiress. In 1568 he reached the highest honour to which the municipality could raise him when he was elected mayor—or bailiff, as it was then called. Since no such office could have been held at that date by a Catholic, or any non-conformist, it is incontrovertible evidence that John Shakespeare was then a loyal member of the Church of England. Most certainly he was no Catholic in 1568, whatever outward consent he may have given under Queen Mary to papist doctrine and ritual.

(His marriage and the baptism of his eldest child according to Roman rites show that in those early days he was not disposed to place unnecessary obstacles in his path by quarrels over religious forms and ceremonies.) And Mayor Shakespeare was no Puritan either, for we find him welcoming companies of players to Stratford during his year of office.

The Corporation needed a loyal, reliable Protestant as their chief officer, for 1568–1569 was a time of danger and excitement, when Catholic hopes were raised by the rebellion of the northern earls, and when the Queen of Scots herself was held prisoner at Coventry. The Northumberland and Westmorland rising was put down by men of the Midlands led by the Earls of Warwick and Leicester; and Stratford's sympathies are revealed clearly by the dismissal of their vicar, curate, and schoolmaster, who were all suspected of being papist.

In another time of peril and anxiety John Shakespeare held high office and bore witness to the staunch Protestantism of Stratford. On this occasion (1571–1572) he was deputy bailiff to that unshakable Protestant, Adrian Quyney, while Henry Rogers, a Puritan, filled the post of steward. Parliament was loudly demanding the execution of Mary, Queen of Scots, and the whole country was shocked and horrified by the ghastly massacre of St. Bartholomew's Day. It is during this period that the town chronicles record the disposal of the Romanist vestments at the Chapel by Quyney and Shakespeare.

For some four or five years after this date (1572) John Shakespeare attended the meetings of the Town Council, occupied, as a past bailiff, a seat on the magistrates' bench, and generally continued his interest in municipal affairs. As early as 1576 he applied for the coat of arms, which would rank him as a gentlemen and entitle him to place "esquire" after his name. Apparently the application was successful, but John Shakespeare appears for some reason to have let it drop. At the same time he retired from the Corporation, ceased to act as a "Queen's Officer," and entered that retirement which has caused so much speculation and perplexity among biographers of the Poet.

The most usual way of explaining the sudden eclipse of John Shakespeare is to attribute it to financial difficulties consequent upon some quick reversal of fortune. Mr. Edgar I. Fripp points out, however, in his *Shakespeare Studies*[1], that he owned at this time time the whole of the block of buildings now known as the Birthplace, worth in modern equivalent between £3,000 and £4,000, and was, besides, the husband of the favourite daughter and heiress of the well-to-do Robert Arden. The long-accepted theory of impecuniosity is therefore suspect; and a belief that the change was caused by some form of religious dissent has taken its place in many people's minds.

The assumption that John Shakespeare was financially embarrassed rested on certain information extracted from the records of Stratford. In January 1578 the townsmen were taxed to provide extra pikemen and gunmen rendered necessary by the growing restlessness among the Catholics. Master Shakespeare was assessed at 3s. 4d., and refused to pay. He was proceeded against, but there is no record that he paid up. Later in the same year he was

[1] P. 88.

assessed at 4d. a week as his contribution to the poor rate. Despite the smallness of the assessment, he again objected. Probably the Council let him off, as they let him off his fine for absenting himself on Election Day in the previous September. About this time, too, we find him conveying his wife's property at Asbies and Snitterfield to relations; and this step, it is now suspected, was not dictated by pressure of creditors, but to outwit those who would distrain upon his goods on account of his recusancy.

The above proceedings were of a minor character compared with the misfortune that befell John Shakespeare in 1580. He was bound over to appear before the Court of Queen's Bench at Westminster and to give sureties that he would keep the peace. He failed to obey the summons and was fined the considerable sum of £40.[1] It is not to be supposed that the Court would trouble to impose a penalty of the equivalent of £500 in our money on a ruined tradesman. It was evidently expected that the fine would be paid, as in fact it was, when the hope that he could escape the consequences of his seditious speech or illegal act (or whatever his indiscretion was) was found to be vain.

Between 1582 and 1586 the records show that the Poet's father was involved in tiresome legal proceedings and was frequently sued for monies said to be owing by him. In one case it is reported that he has nothing on which to distrain. This is a curious verdict because it is known that he owned at least the three houses constituting the Birthplace. As Mr John Semple Smart writes in *Shakespeare—Truth and Tradition*,[2] some of these entries probably do not refer

[1] *Coram Rege Roll*, Anglia, 20, 21.   [2] Pp. 65–66

to Alderman Shakespeare at all, but to another and younger John Shakespeare, a shoemaker by trade, who is known to have lived in Stratford contemporaneously. It is often difficult, if not impossible, to distinguish in the records between the two men; but from what we know of Master Shakespeare's holding in real estate, it seems that the *nihil habet* of the Sergeant's report in this case must indicate the shoemaker.

There is no doubt, however, that actions for recovery of monies were brought against the ex-bailiff, nor any doubt that he stolidly refused to settle them. Whether the refusal was prompted by inability to pay or just obstinacy is the interesting problem. The fact that he stood surety for his brother Henry for £10 in June 1586, and in the next month went bail for £10 at Coventry in order that a tinker of Henley Street might be let out of prison—and forfeited his money, too—does not suggest a want of cash to meet his liabilities. Further, the continual friendliness of his old colleagues of the Corporation, shown in excusing him his payments and making every allowance for his obdurate attitude, would probably have given place to quite a different feeling if he had failed in business and become bankrupt. But, as it happened, their consideration was so marked, and their hope of his renewed interest in municipal affairs so strong, that they kept his name on the roll of Aldermen for ten years after he had ceased to attend the Council meetings.

A close examination of the evidence fails to bring conviction that the long-held theory, that a financial cloud darkened the later years of John Shakespeare's life, is true. The mystery is much more satisfactorily explained by a lapse into recusancy. Modern critics are becoming more and more inclined to accept this explanation; but whereas Mr. J. S. Smart in *Shakespeare —Truth and Tradition*, following Halliwell-Phillipps and others, believes the Poet's father became a Catholic recusant, Mr. Edgar I. Fripp in *Shakespeare Studies* is equally sure that he was a Puritan recusant.

In deciding the type of recusancy of which John Shakespeare was guilty, it will be advisable to recall briefly the point reached by Elizabeth's policy of compromise at the time the ex-bailiff withdrew from municipal office. By 1575 the nonconformity of the extreme Protestants had grown to be as troublesome, if not more troublesome, than the obstinacy of the extreme Catholics. The Presbyterian party, which enjoyed the powerful support of the Earl of Leicester, had been a severe obstacle in the path of the old Archbishop Parker. Leicester's influence in the Stratford country was enormous; and men of the Midlands were offended by the renewed efforts of the Queen in 1576 to force uniformity by declaring illegal all departures from the Prayer Book and by imposing fines and penalties on all those who wilfully and obstinately absented themselves from Church. Those who objected to this dictatorial presumption in matters of religion were dismayed to see the appointment to the vacant bishopric of Worcester of Whitgift, an iron disciplinarian, who dubbed all nonconformists of whatever creed traitors to the Crown.

The new bishop made energetic attempts to catch the recusants in his diocese and force them to pay the penalty for their non-attendance at Divine Service. Opposition to the rules of the State Church was then construed by the law as a treasonable act against Her Majesty. Whitgift and his men found their efforts unrewarded by any conspicuous success. There was a wholesome distaste of religious compulsion among the Midlanders, who were encouraged in their attitude by the support of the Earl of Leicester and his brother of Warwick. The Puritan recusants were difficult to bring to book because most of those in office secretly sympathized with them and refused to give evidence against them. The officers were unwilling to denounce even their Catholic neighbours to the Bishop and his nominees. Thus Catholic and Puritan recusant, diverse as their religious views were, had the bond of a common objection to outside interference in local affairs.

While the powerful Dudleys ruled at Kenilworth and Warwick the recusants of Stratford felt secure, for Whitgift was afraid openly to challenge the great nobles on this issue. In 1588, however, Leicester died, and was followed to the grave by Warwick two years later. The delighted Bishop acted at once and swept down upon the luckless nonconformists, who had relied on the earls' protection. Escape was now impossible, and Catholic and Puritan recusants were called to answer for their disobedience. In 1592 a mixed party of men belonging to both creeds were presented for non-attendance at Church, John Shakespeare among them. But churchwardens and magistrates were so well disposed towards their unfortunate neighbours that they made every excuse on their behalf and let off as many as they could. John Shakespeare with eight other men, some of them known for their extreme Protestantism, were sheltered under the explanation, "We suspect these nine persons absent themselves for fear of process."[1] Six months later there was another presentment of recusants, and for Shakespeare and his eight companions the same excuse was advanced. This verdict has helped to strengthen the theory that the Poet's father was financially embarrassed at the time. But some of his companions in misfortune, notably John Wheeler and Nicholas Barnhurst, are known to have been very well-to-do. Even supposing it were true that they were afraid to come to church "for fear of process for debt" at the first presentment at Easter, it is very unlikely that such men of substance would still be in the same state at the second presentment at Michaelmas. It appears that Squire Lucy and his fellow-commissioners were using any plausible excuse to protect their friends from Whitgift, and fell back upon one that had done good service on many occasions in avoiding indictment. These burghers, who were afraid to show themselves in public on Sunday, moved about freely on all other days of the week in pursuance of their ordinary vocations; and the hollowness of the plea is, therefore, manifest.

Four years later the recusants of Stratford were in trouble with the new bishop, Thomas Bilson, who complained that the Protestant rebels were as troublesome as the obstinate Catholics. In the 1596 returns John Shakespeare's name is not included; and Fripp points out[2] that he was now nearly seventy years old and "probably was left in peace as incorrigible." But we hear of John Shakespeare in this year of 1596 in a different connection, for he renewed his application to the heralds for a coat of arms, the grounds being the services rendered to

[1] Warwick Castle MSS. [2] *Shakespeare Studies*, p. 97.

Henry VII by his grandfather, his own position as an ex-bailiff of Stratford, and his connection through his wife with the influential and ancient Arden family. His application was successful, which it is difficult to believe would have been the case had he been a bankrupt tradesman or a notorious Catholic rebel.

It is well known that William Shakespeare sought permission to impale the arms of Arden in 1599. It is also true that no use of the Arden arms was made by the Shakespeares, although the request was granted and a sketch embodying the ermine, a fess checky, of the Park Hall family was made. Now Edward Arden of Park Hall had been executed on December 20th, 1583, for urging John Somerville, Margaret Arden's husband, to kill the Queen. His wife, also called Mary Arden, was found guilty of complicity in this Catholic plot, but was pardoned. Old John Shakespeare evidently had no sympathy with open treason such as this, and had a new sketch made substituting the arms of the one Arden who was a Protestant, namely, Simon of Yoxall in Staffordshire.[1] This was not adopted either; but it is valuable testimony of the anti-Catholic feelings of John Shakespeare, Esquire, at the close of his life.

In 1597 William Shakespeare purchased New Place. Up to then his wife and children had apparently been living under the parental roof of the Birthplace, while he himself was at work in London. That John Shakespeare ended his days in happy circumstances, unmolested and free of all perplexing religious controversy, we know from a record left by a visitor to

[1] French, *Shakespeareana Genealogica*, 416–430; *Camden Miscellany*, IX, 3, 1–8, 39, 44 ff.

his shop, which tells of "a merry cheek'd old man, that said *Will is a good, honest fellow, but he durst crack a jest with him at any time.*"[1] He died in 1601.

Briefly reviewing the life of the Poet's father on its religious side, we find him born in an early home of the Reformation and serving his apprenticeship and commencing his own business in Stratford in the Protestant reign of Edward VI. During the Catholic reaction under Mary, his marriage and the christening of his daughter at the Church by Father Dyos according to the old rites suggest an outward conformance at any rate to the religious requirements of the day. During this period he commenced his municipal service, but all his principal offices were held after the accession of Elizabeth, when he identified himself wholly with the intensely Protestant programme planned by the Corporation. He was largely instrumental in carrying this programme out, and for seventeen or eighteen years was a loyal conforming member of the State Church. During this period William Shakespeare was born, and these were the religious views he learned from his father during his most impressionable years. The great Protestant influence, active in the Midlands later, attracted the elder Shakespeare along the pathway of Puritanism; and he found himself in conflict with the authorities and under the shadow of recusancy. His son, however, remained faithful to his early teaching and was a conforming Protestant all his days.

[1] The Plume MS.

XII

SHAKESPEARE'S ANTI-PAPAL VIEWS

So great is Shakespeare that all nations, sects, and classes are eager to claim affinity with him and prove that he identified himself with their particular views and outlook. Some of the attempts have been more ingenious than convincing, some extravagant, some even ludicrous, as witness the determined effort revived during the War to give the Poet a German origin. Most of these claims do not command nor deserve serious attention. They betray on the surface an over-anxiety to establish the incredible. Others, however, require close scrutiny and examination, particularly those which profess to determine the Poet's religion. Since it was possible for Shakespeare to have been a conforming Protestant, a Roman Catholic, a Puritan, or a Presbyterian, and since he carefully refrained from making any unequivocal confession of his religious preferences, the point has given occasion for much discussion and speculation. As I have said before, it is much easier to determine the creeds he is most unlikely to have subscribed to, than to find in his writings any deep attachment to one particular form of worship. The truth is that Shakespeare's real religion, the religion of his heart, was of the type that transcended creed and dogma. At the same time, he certainly conformed outwardly to the requirements of the Church of which his Sovereign was the head.

No Church has been more anxious to establish Shakespeare as one of their fold than the Roman

Catholic. Ever since 1700, when Davies[1] handed down the rumour that the Poet died a Papist, there have been continuous efforts to claim him for the old Faith. As Professor Creizenach suggests,[2] the rumour that Davies seized upon was probably a Puritan invention to discredit one who followed a profession which they hated, and arguments based upon that rumour carry little weight. But fresh grounds for establishing Shakespeare's Catholicism have been advanced and demand refutation, more especially as the point appears to have assumed a new prominence of late. The feeling on the matter is surprisingly intense—so intense that in the early part of the last century some Catholic advocate allowed his enthusiasm to run away with him to the extent of forging a document that purported to be a copy of Shakespeare's will.[3] This manuscript used to be exhibited with the other relics at Stratford-on-Avon, but after it had been compared with the real will deposited in Doctors' Commons and found to be spurious, it was removed. The difference between the real will and the forgery, both in tone and expression, and length of the preamble, shows quite clearly that the object was to support the old rumour that Shakespeare died a Papist. There was another questionable document in existence, claimed to be from the pen of John Shakespeare, and brought to light about 1770, which was also an obvious attempt to prove the Catholicism of the family. This, again, was rejected by the critics as a fabrication.[4]

[1] Cf. *Shakespere Allusion Book*, II. 335.
[2] *The English Drama in the Age of Shakespeare*, p. 102.
[3] *Shakespeare's Knowledge and Use of the Bible*, p. 222.
[4] *The Life and Poetry of William Shakespeare*, Gilfillan, p. xv.

There is so little external evidence to support the theory that Shakespeare was a Catholic that we can understand, while not approving, the efforts to make a Papist of John Shakespeare. Halliwell-Phillipps and his followers encouraged the theory of a Catholic recusancy. This I hope I have answered by marshalling all the arguments and probabilities against it in our chapter on the Poet's father. It only remains to re-emphasize that in those impressionable years before William Shakespeare reached the age of discretion when he could be accepted into the Church, John Shakespeare held high office in Stratford, office which in those days could be filled by no one who had not taken the oath of supremacy. When John became a recusant—and a Puritan, not a Catholic recusant— William had entered upon young manhood and was competent to decide these affairs of conscience for himself.

Much is made by the Catholic champions of the attachment to Rome of Shakespeare's relations on his mother's side. It is true that his grandfather, Robert Arden, died a Catholic in 1556. It must not be forgotten, though, that at that time Queen Mary still ruled, and to confess Protestant sympathies, even if one felt them, was to run the risk of torture and burning. Even John Shakespeare, stalwart Protestant as he afterwards showed himself, conformed in his marriage and the baptism of his first-born to the rites of what was then the State religion. The branch of the family at Park Hall were, we have seen, sufficiently staunch Catholics to suffer for their beliefs. But there is no evidence that others of the Ardens did not, with the great mass of the English people, accept the new religion as loyal subjects of the Queen.

Mary Arden's religious sympathies we do not know. Her father was a Catholic: her husband was Protestant. Her eldest child, Joan, was baptized by Father Dyos according to the Roman ceremony. Her next children were christened by the Rev. John Bretchgirdle according to the form in the new Prayer Book. Her son William was married and her grandchildren were baptized with due conformity. Some, at least, of her brothers-in-law were Protestant. There is no record that Mary Shakespeare ever showed signs of dissent; and it is difficult to believe that she did not conform when the great change came, remembering that during the next few years John Shakespeare was most thorough-going in his Protestantizing activities. Such whole-hearted enthusiasm would hardly be found in the husband of a Catholic wife.

Externally, then, there is very little evidence to support the Catholic claim. It is so little that its advocates have attempted to strengthen their case by additional evidence mined from the Poet's works. Three points are stressed which, it is held, tell in favour of Catholicism. First, the Catholics argue, Shakespeare displays no animosity or antipathy to the Church of Rome despite the tense religious feelings of the time. Secondly, he reveals a close acquaintance with Catholic ritual. Thirdly, his treatment of the Catholic friars is characterized by an extreme kindliness and sympathy. Let us examine these claims.

It is undoubtedly true that Shakespeare was not intolerant nor antagonistic to the Catholic or, indeed, any form of religion. He was kindly and forbearing towards all creeds, an attitude that arose from the deep humanity within him. If he had been inclined to be bitter, narrow-minded, and sectarian, he would have exhibited these unlovely traits against the Puritans, who threatened to close the theatres and cut him off from his means of livelihood, and who looked upon the actors, dramatists, and their kind as servants of the Devil. But even towards such dangerous enemies to his interests as these, Shakespeare is wonderfully patient and long-suffering. He laughs at them and teases them, but he is never spiteful nor malicious. He was too great for feelings of that kind. If, then, he could treat the Puritans, who were a real danger to his success and business activities, with such goodwill and tolerance, still less would he display any hostility towards those of his fellow-countrymen who were Roman Catholics, some of whom were nearly related to him, and none of whom had ever done him any harm. Shakespeare's attitude is not proof of Catholic sympathies but of the true Christian charity which was his by nature.

The Poet had no dislike for Roman Catholics on religious grounds. The fact that he was ready to impale the arms of the Park Hall Ardens with the Shakespeare crest shows he had no such bias. His countrymen and countrywomen were English firstly and Roman Catholics, Protestants, or Puritans secondly. He did, however, find his patriotism and loyalty roused to opposition by papal interference in the internal affairs of England, by the excommunication of his Queen, and the alliance of Rome with the enemies of his Motherland.

Shakespeare, it can be admitted, was familiar with the ritual of Romanism. He would naturally be interested in it, as he was interested in every phase of life and thought. It is easy to imagine that it appealed to him; but it is much more likely to have appealed to him as a spectacle, and one that would be extremely effective in the theatre, than as a method of awakening spiritual devoutness or impressing religious truth. There is nothing to show that he had any close acquaintance with Roman dogma; and, as I shall show in a later chapter, he apparently had no knowledge at all of the Roman Catholic Bible.

As the dramatist of the Chronicle Plays, Shakespeare had necessarily to know something of Popish ritual. All of the pieces, except *Henry VIII*, of which he was only part-author, are pre-Reformation, and do not touch Protestant times. The Cardinals, Bishops, and Archbishops are all, of course, members of the Roman Church; and the characters with which many of them are endowed do no credit to their religion. But the Poet does not handle them solely as churchmen. He takes a broader view of them as men, swayed by passion, hate, and ambition, men engaged not so much in the saving of souls as in the tortuous paths of politics and feud. Discussing the artist's use of the broader canvas, the Rev. George Gilfillan says, "The spirit of his plays is far too wide and far too human for one who had been nurtured in the contracted and withering atmosphere of the Popish Church."[1]

The third argument, that Shakespeare's papal spirit is revealed in his gentle treatment of such intrinsic types of Catholicism as Friar Laurence of *Romeo and Juliet* and Friar Francis of *Much Ado about Nothing*, is answered by the simple truth that he does not invest these characters with any religious significance whatsoever. He approaches them on their

[1] *The Life and Poetry of William Shakespeare*, p. xvi.

human side and commends them for their good qualities and their readiness to help their fellow-men. It is quite possible that the poet in him saw the beautiful side of the sheltered life in the monastery and convent, with its opportunities for quiet meditation and appreciation of all that was most lovely in nature—that he compared it in a mood of wistful longing with the turmoil of his own existence. Certainly he expunged from the old play of *King John*, which he re-wrote, those passages reflecting on the morals of monks and nuns. But we cannot read into that a prejudice in favour of Catholicism. It was the poet that was uppermost here, not the religionist.

Shakespeare treated the clergy and priests with respect whenever he could. Catholics say that he treated members of their persuasion, the monks and the friars, with more deference than the Protestant, parish clergy of the Sir Hugh Evans type. The answer is that he withheld all respect from some of the high officers of the Catholic Church in the Chronicle Plays when their subtlety, greed, and untruthfulness justified it. On the other hand, he often smiled at the country parsons, not because they were Protestant, but because they were ignorant. In the previous reign the parish priests had been Catholic and just as ignorant. The majority of them quietly conformed to the new order, but Elizabeth had to delay one of the changes on which she had set her heart, namely, the sermon, because most of the priests were not sufficiently educated to be allowed to preach. Again, it was not a religious preference that dictated his attitude, but his wonderful understanding of the very human men and women who lived, loved, and suffered around him.

It was convenient to answer the arguments for
Shakespeare's Catholicism before turning to the play
of *King John*, in which the anti-papal spirit is so strong
that it is difficult to understand how any fair-minded
critic can doubt the Protestantism of the dramatist.
The Catholic argument is based upon points that
seem very small indeed compared with the famous
"No-Popery" speech in the first, historically-speaking,
of the Chronicle Plays.

King John is primarily a political play and deals
with the struggle of John, who has assumed the
English Crown, with the French King Philip, who
supports the claim of Prince Arthur, the son of John's
elder brother. Shakespeare delivers himself of much
patriotic sentiment, principally through the mouth of
Faulconbridge, whom he has drawn as a fine type
of English character. To some John may appear a
usurper, but it must be remembered in his favour
that he was king with the consent of the English
Parliament and that the hereditary principle was not
then accepted as inviolable. He enters into the war
with Philip with the great majority of the nation
behind him, and speaks for England. After a phase of
indecisive fighting, the two kings meet to negotiate
a patched-up peace, by which John's kingship is
recognized and the Dauphin is to marry his niece,
Blanch of Spain.

Although the action is primarily concerned with the
political feud between France and England, the papal
influence hovers in the background throughout the
play; and, as was the way of Popes in those medieval
times, intervention in these temporal matters seriously
complicates the situation. The two monarchs have
met at the pavilion of the French king to carry out the

most important provision of their agreement, namely, the royal marriage, when the papal legate, Pandulph, enters. Ignoring treaty matters he proceeds at once to voice the Pope's complaint against John, demanding an explanation of his opposition to the will of Rome and his refusal to appoint her chosen candidate, Stephen Langton, to the archbishopric of Canterbury. Pandulph, after a brief greeting to the "two anointed deputies of heaven," turns to England's sovereign and says (III. 1. 137–146):

> To thee, King John, my holy errand is.
> I, Pandulph, of fair Milan cardinal,
> And from Pope Innocent the legate here,
> Do in his name religiously demand
> Why thou against the church, our holy mother,
> So wilfully doth spurn; and force perforce
> Keep Stephen Langton, chosen archbishop
> Of Canterbury, from that holy see?
> This, in our 'foresaid holy father's name,
> Pope Innocent, I do demand of thee.

John makes a spirited reply, and speaks, not as an individual, but as the voice of England—and not the England of the early thirteenth century, but of the Protestant Elizabethan England, of which Shakespeare was a loyal and patriotic son. John hurls this defiance in the teeth of the Pope's representative (147–160):

> What earthy name to interrogatories
> Can task the free breath of a sacred king?
> Thou canst not, cardinal, devise a name
> So slight, unworthy, and ridiculous,
> To charge me to an answer, as the pope.
> Tell him this tale; and from the mouth of England
> Add thus much more, that no Italian priest
> Shall tithe or toll in our dominions;

> But as we, under heaven, are supreme head,
> So under Him that great supremacy,
> Where we do reign, we will alone uphold,
> Without the assistance of a mortal hand:
> So tell the pope, all reverence set apart
> To him and his usurp'd authority.

That any Catholic could pen such a speech as the above is an utter impossibility. No one, hoping for salvation through the Roman Church, would have dared to fling such insults at the Pope. The emphatic Protestantism of the King's answer could never have emanated from anyone holding Catholic sympathies, even if they were held in secret. Note how the main planks in the Reformation programme are stressed— the repudiation of papal dominance, the assertion of freedom and independence, the declaration of the monarch as head of the native Church in conformity with the Elizabethan Act of Supremacy. It cannot even be argued in this instance that it is the character and not the dramatist speaking, for King John would never have employed such terms, while Shakespeare's own Sovereign did employ them. Here we have the one occasion in the whole of his writings where the Poet comes nearest to an unambiguous declaration of his own views; and they are views impossible in a Roman Catholic.

In writing the play of *King John* Shakespeare worked upon an old drama entitled *The Troublesome Raigne of John, King of England*, written about 1589— that is to say about half a dozen years before his own version. Although *The Troublesome Raigne* had some merit, the Poet transformed it with the touch of his genius, ennobling the characters, beautifying the language, and improving the construction. It is true

that he found in his original John's outburst of resentment at papal interference. Instead of suppressing it,
as he suppressed the passages reflecting on the moral
atmosphere of monastic establishments, he re-wrote it.
And in his re-writing he did not draw the sting, he
did not even moderate the language, but left it as
biting and offensive as before. This was not the act of
a man with Popish sympathies. Moreover, it shows
that the slanders on monks and nuns were not omitted
by him for religious reasons, but either from humani-
tarian feelings, poetic sympathies, or dramatic
exigencies.

At the close of John's protest, the dramatist shows
us at once how such strong anti-papal language would
affect the professing Catholic. The shocked King
Philip exclaims: "Brother of England, you blaspheme
in this." But John follows with another diatribe, in
which he catalogues the abuses and corruption in the
Roman Church that brought about the Reformation
(162–171):

> Though you and all the kings of Christendom
> Are led so grossly by this meddling priest,
> Dreading the curse that money may buy out;
> And by the merit of vile gold, dross, dust,
> Purchase corrupted pardon of a man,
> Who in that sale sells pardon for himself,
> Though you and all the rest so grossly led
> This juggling witchcraft with revenue cherish;
> Yet I alone, alone do me oppose
> Against the pope and count his friends my foes.

It was very true that the Pope's friends were the foes
of Elizabethan England, a fact that a patriotic
Englishman had ever in mind. *The Troublesome
Raigne* was written the year after the country had

gloriously surmounted the peril of the Armada, dispatched by Catholic Spain. Six years afterwards England had not begun to forget that the Pope had counted on a Spanish victory to restore his authority over Elizabeth's realm. To oppose the Pope, then, seemed practical politics to Englishmen, dictated by common sense and the love of independence.

To John's heretical invective Pandulph replies by using the time-worn weapon of papal retaliation— excommunication. It had been used against Elizabeth by Pope Pius in 1570, and the memory rankled in the breast of each one of her loyal subjects. Pandulph says (172–179):

> Then, by the lawful power that I have,
> Thou shalt stand cursed and excommunicate:
> And blessed shall be he that doth revolt
> From his allegiance to an heretic;
> And meritorious shall that hand be call'd,
> Canonized and worshipp'd as a saint,
> That takes away by any secret course
> Thy hateful life.

King Philip is urged by Pandulph to break his truce with England on pain of like excommunication. The French monarch is very loath to throw away the fruits of their peace compact. But he is afraid of the power and threats of the Roman Church; and the crafty Cardinal succeeds in embroiling them once again in the interests of the Pope's political aims in England. Shakespeare's England had found her purposes so often thwarted and hindered by Roman opposition that the Protestant audiences at the theatre would find themselves in full agreement with the anti-Catholic tenor of *King John*.

Patriotism and Popery were not compatible in the

new England which was growing up during the latter half of the sixteenth century; therefore the spirit of the people, their loyalty, their concern for the highest interests of their country, and their love of freedom and independence, are effectually portrayed by the dramatist and shown to be directly opposed to the claims of papal supremacy and adherence to the old Faith. A perusal of *King John* can leave no doubt in any open mind on which side Shakespeare's own sympathies were ranged. The play could not, definitely, have been written by a Roman Catholic.

King John is sufficient answer of itself to Catholic claims that Shakespeare was of that persuasion. It is as well, however, to add further proofs, not least of which is his fulsome admiration and flattery of England's Protestant Queen. One can safely identify King John's sentiments as those of Elizabeth; and one senses that it is of his own sovereign that the playwright is thinking and not of the monarch of Magna Carta fame. Such unstinted praise and homage as Shakespeare bestows upon Good Queen Bess would be somewhat forced in a Catholic towards one excommunicated by his spiritual leader. There is no mistaking, however, the sincerity and warmth of Shakespeare's affection. True, the theatre owed much to the Queen, whose patronage it enjoyed. But there is something deeper than expediency in the Poet's eulogies.

Writing for a Protestant patron and an overwhelmingly Protestant audience, perhaps we should hardly expect the playwrights to reveal Catholic propensities. Those, however, who felt strongly on the matter of their faith were unable to prevent signs of their real feelings appearing in their work. There are distinct traces in Chapman. Massinger leaves us in no doubt of his Catholicism. Lodge confessed himself an adherent of the old religion after his retirement from the theatre. It may be that his conversion was subsequent to his retirement. Shakespeare, on the other hand, search as we will, reveals nothing that is not in harmony with a robust Protestantism.

A much-quoted anti-Roman passage occurs in *Titus Andronicus*, where Aaron says (v. 1. 74–78):

> Yet, for I know thou art religious,
> And hast a thing within thee called a conscience,
> With twenty popish tricks and ceremonies,
> Which I have seen thee careful to observe,
> Therefore I urge thy oath.

In fairness it must be admitted that the Shakespearean authorship of these particular lines is open to grave doubt. The same remark applies to the following extract from *Henry VIII*, which is now generally attributed to Shakespeare's collaborator, Fletcher (III. 2. 310–312):

> First that, without the king's assent or knowledge,
> You wrought to be a legate; by which power
> You maim'd the jurisdiction of all bishops.

While it is probably true that Shakespeare did not actually pen these passages himself, yet he handled both these plays, contributed much of the dialogue, and presumably concurred in those portions which were not his own work, but appeared nevertheless under his name, as witness their inclusion in the First Folio.

But we do not have to rely on doubtful passages to

support the anti-Catholic sentiment of *King John*. There are echoes in many plays, the genuine character of which is not contested. In *Macbeth*, for example, written in 1606, are touches that recall the famous Gunpowder Plot, the Catholic attempt to blow up Parliament, which so excited public opinion in the previous November. Among those implicated, arrested, and placed on their trial was Father Garnet, leader of the English Jesuits. Before his judges Garnet confessed his adherence to the Jesuitical doctrine of equivocation. The doctrine evoked widespread execration, and the dramatist satirizes it in the words of the Porter (II. 3. 8–13):

Who's there, in th' other devil's name? Faith, here's an equivocator, that could swear in both the scales against either scale; who committed treason enough for God's sake, yet could not equivocate to heaven: O, come in, equivocator.

That this is a reference to Garnet, who was executed in May 1606, there is little doubt. They are impossible words for a Catholic. Some critics have, we must admit, rejected the Porter's speech as an interpolation; but the majority have followed De Quincey in recognizing its importance in the construction of the play; and, as Sir Israel Gollancz writes in *The Temple Shakespeare*,[1] "both the character and the speech are thoroughly Shakespearean in conception."

Professor Creizenach[2] mentions other passages which strength the Protestant case. These include the speech of Edgar in *King Lear* (IV. 1. 58–66), where the foul fiends, Obidicut, Hobbididence, Mahu, Modo, and Flibbertigibbet are mentioned. These names were taken by Shakespeare from the category of devils in

[1] P. vii.   [2] *The English Drama in the Age of Shakespeare*, p. 130.

Samuel Harsnett's "Declaration of Egregious Popish Impostures"—an impossible work for a Catholic to peruse and quote from.

We must also note the dramatist's disinclination to mitigate in the smallest degree the character of the villainous Cardinal Beaufort in *Henry VI*, Parts I and II. To this we may add Tarquin's remark in *Lucrece* (line 354), "The blackest sin is clear'd with absolution," spoken as he contemplates the gravest wrong of which a tyrant is capable. In another early poem, *A Lover's Complaint*, the Poet writes a description of a love-sick nun (line 232 *et seq.*)—a subject that would scarcely occur to an ardent Catholic.

In the face of such overwhelming evidence, and particularly with the play of *King John* before us, we can come to no other conclusion than that Shakespeare was neither in youth nor middle age, openly or secretly, a Roman Catholic. The proofs of his Protestantism are irrefutable; and a marshalling of the arguments must always defeat the understandable anxiety to claim him for the Church of Rome.

XIII

SHAKESPEARE NO PURITAN

AT the tender age at which the child mind gathers the first gleanings of spiritual truth, the influences surrounding the youthful Shakespeare were undoubtedly those of orthodox Protestantism. John Shakespeare, holding high office in the Stratford Corporation, was then active in the restoration of the Reformed Religion and the suppression of Popery. When bailiff of Stratford in 1568–1569, he received the players to his town and made them welcome—proof that he had no tendency at this period towards the extremist views which he adopted more than a decade later.

Mary Shakespeare's religion has never been definitely established. We can only assume, from the decided Protestantism of her husband and her own immunity from fines and persecution, that she conformed to the new Church, although brought up as a Catholic.

Both parents agreed to the baptism of their son William according to the rites of the Church of England. There is no record that young Shakespeare was ever in difficulties with the authorities for non-attendance at divine service. He obeyed the law of the land and outwardly, at any rate, was a conforming Protestant.

During the first twelve years of Shakespeare's life the Puritan movement was young. Neither in numbers nor in the strength of its fanaticism did it give promise of the menace to the Established Church that it was soon to become. Only as the danger of a Catholic restoration receded did the Puritans launch their fierce attacks upon their fellow-Protestants and endeavour to sweep away from the Reformed Religion those relics of Catholicism which they feared and hated. The use of coercive measures to compel their conformity only succeeded in adding to their numbers; and, as we have seen, one of those driven to revolt by persecution was the Poet's own father.

If the young Shakespeare had felt in the least degree attracted towards the ascetic creed of Calvin, he would certainly have followed his father along the thorny path of recusancy. Not only would a lad in his teens naturally be eager to concur in his father's opinions, but also in those of his teacher; for, as Thomas Carter reminds us in *Shakespeare and Holy Scripture*,[1] "We know that from the age of eight to that of thirteen William Shakespeare was under the tuition at Stratford of Thomas Hunt, a Puritan well qualified to train his scholars in Biblical knowledge, who was afterwards deprived of his living of Luddington for contumacy."

The Biblical knowledge referred to seems (as I hope to show fully in a later chapter) to have been imparted from the Genevan or Puritan Bible. This was the most popular version for home use in the early part of Elizabeth's reign. That Shakespeare was familiar with it the comparison of numerous lines in his works with the Scriptural originals proves beyond doubt. Moreover, he chose the titles of two of the books in the Geneva Bible, Susanna and Judith, for the names of his daughters, and was obviously closely acquainted with the books in question.[2]

Had Shakespeare any tendency towards Puritanism

[1] P. 3.   [2] See *Merchant of Venice*, IV. 1. 223.

he would have joined the ranks of nonconformity long before embarking upon his career as actor and dramatist. But there is no evidence that there was anything Puritan about him; no record of any fines for absenting himself from church; no tradition that he shared his father's recalcitrant attitude. It is impossible to believe that any man who had the smallest regard for Puritan ideals would join a profession which, in their eyes, was all that was unholy and reprehensible.

Possibly it was John Shakespeare's move towards the extreme wing of Protestantism that caused him to proceed no further with his successful application for "the coveted coat-armour of 'gentlehood' "[1] in 1576. Sir Sidney Lee says that, according to Guillim's "Display of Heraldrie" (1610), the Puritans regarded coat-armour with abhorrence. The strictest among them, it is true, condemned all worldly honours and distinctions, but it must be admitted that some well-known Puritans retained their coats-of-arms and used them freely. The revival of the Shakespeare application in 1596 was at the suggestion of William, whose anxiety to attain the rank of gentleman had nothing Puritan about it. He seems to have won his father's consent on the point, but the old man would not give way to the extent of impaling the arms of the Catholic Ardens of Park Hall. That William wished to do this reveals his distance from the Puritan outlook.

Whatever Calvinistic influences may have touched Shakespeare's early life, they had not made sufficient impression to deter him from seeking fame and fortune in the theatre. By taking this step he ranged himself

[1] *Shakespeare Studies*, Fripp, p. 88.

definitely with the opponents of Puritanism, whose attitude towards actors and acting was one of unrelenting hostility.

The Puritans were not content to wage war on the drama by preaching and writing only. They believed in active interference, and scored many a success in their fanatical campaign. Commencing with the conviction that plays, masques, interludes, dancing, maypoles, revels, gay clothing, and all forms of art were wiles of the devil for the damnation of the soul, they worked feverishly to suppress wherever they could any such frivolity and wickedness. Their attacks continued with unabated fury; and, but for the royal patronage and support of the Privy Council, the theatre must have fallen before the onslaught, as eventually it did fall in the next century.

The Puritans won some success even in Elizabeth's day. In 1583, before Shakespeare's career opened—perhaps before he had seen London at all—they had contrived to put an end to Sunday performances of secular plays. These performances were then held in the inn-yards; and the objectors maintained that they provided a counter-attraction to the religious service. Further, they urged, that servants and employees were enticed from their duties, that accidents from falling scaffolding and the like happened too frequently, and—most importantly—that the mixing of young men and girls on these occasions was a danger to morality.

A greater Puritan success than the suppression of Sunday plays was the banishment of the players from the inn-yards altogether. By gaining a majority on the governing councils they refused to grant the licence without which no play could be performed.

In this way they hoped to kill the drama, for it was in the inn-yards that it had become established and grown to its present dimensions and popularity. Probably the plot would have succeeded if it had not been for one fortunate circumstance. By the time Puritanism had become so influential the first theatres had been constructed. The opposition of the local councils and the refusal of the licence merely drove the actors' companies into homes of their own, where they were secure from interference and could act away without molestation. The Puritans, however, did not give up the struggle. The councillors had no power to close the theatres, which were outside their jurisdiction, but they had recourse to pen and pulpit to bring the stage into discredit, and used their powers of persuasion to decrease the size of the audiences.

The heavy guns of Calvinist ascetic criticism were also turned upon the lives and morals of the actors. The old argument, of which we have heard so much, that members of the profession are exposed to exceptional temptations, was advanced. To this was added a condemnation of their prodigality and extravagance. It was claimed that actors aped the rich and aristocratic classes, wore their elegant and fashionable clothes, copied their foibles, and pursued a shameful hedonism—all of which roused the anger of the austere killjoys. Although the Puritans exaggerated, carried away by their zeal, it is true there were grounds for their censure. Many of the actors were loose livers, and the comic interludes in the drama too frequently descended to the obscene. Many of the jokes and incidents, even in Shakespeare, are offensive to our ears. They were written, of course, to amuse

o

the theatre-going public, which was overwhelmingly anti-Puritan and could digest pretty strong stuff in its entertainment.

To the argument that the play should be a reflection of real life, that the dramatist should hold "a mirror up to nature," the Puritan turned a deaf ear. He replied that sin, weakness, and folly should be repented of and prayed over at home, not paraded in the theatre for all the world to laugh at. "What could people holding such views make of a Falstaff?" asks Professor Creizenach.[1] To which I would add, "How could any author who had the smallest sympathy with such views create a Falstaff?"

In their search for the most opprobrious terms in which to describe the art of acting, Puritans called it "Popery." When desirous of insulting the actors grossly, they called them "Papists." We have seen that this was the probable origin of the old rumour that Shakespeare died a Catholic. The actors, however, gave as good as they received; and even the Popery charge failed to shake their popularity with the masses.

In view of the bitterness of the Puritan attack, it is not surprising to find that most of Shakespeare's fellow-dramatists were strongly anti-Puritan. In the early days of the onslaught upon their profession, actors and playwrights as a body were slow to feel resentment, and hoped to win their opponents over by patience and forbearance. But brotherly love met with little response from the Puritans, so intensely did they feel upon the matter. When, therefore, the dramatists saw their policy of goodwill had failed and the threat to their livelihood becoming ever more

[1] *The English Drama in the Age of Shakespeare*, p. 104.

menacing, they fell back on retaliation. They caricatured the Puritan on the stage; and perhaps we can hardly condemn them if they overdid it. They satirized him for his sanctimoniousness and hypocrisy; they derided him for his narrow-mindedness and his sackcloth and ashes. They depicted him piously turning his eyes to heaven yet never allowing an opportunity for self-advantage to escape him. His words were saintly, but his deeds often deserved the description of sharp practice. In more than one play a Puritan is shown decrying personal decoration and adornment, yet carrying on a flourishing and lucrative trade in the feathers used for this very purpose. The extreme Calvinists were covered with ridicule, treated with contempt, exposed as humbugs, and shown up in the most repulsive light.

We should expect Shakespeare to share the antagonism towards Puritanism which found such bitter expression in his brother-dramatists. There is plenty of evidence that he understood and sympathized with their irritation and resentment against those who worked with tireless energy to deprive them of their means of livelihood. But we never find in Shakespeare that pitiless censure and offensive mocking of the Puritan which formed such a favourite theme with, for example, Middleton. He did not storm against their bigotry and intolerance and cover their supposed cant and hypocrisy with derision. He treated them to gentle banter, laughed at them, and not unkindly, and partook but mildly of the indignation of his confrères.

Some people have professed to see in this restraint of Shakespeare towards the enemies of the theatre a sneaking sympathy with the Puritan doctrine. There are, however, so many mentions of Puritanism in the plays to contradict such an inference that another explanation of his moderation must be sought. It is quickly found when we pause to consider the humanity of Shakespeare, his complete want of bias or prejudice, his readiness to adopt a long-suffering, patient attitude towards the follies of mankind, and his ability for seeing the other person's point of view. Our greatest poet was too great a man to condemn another for his opinions when they did not happen to coincide with his own, even when those opinions were actively detrimental to his own business interests. This good-will towards men which animated him, this philo-sophic broad-mindedness, were the very influences that held him to his central position of orthodox Protestantism and caused him to favour compromise rather than to fly to either of the warring extremes of Puritanism or Roman Catholicism.

The temperate and harmless nature of Shakespeare's anti-Puritan banter is well illustrated in the delightful comedy of *Twelfth Night*. There is first the scene in which Maria speaks of Malvolio to Sir Toby Belch and Sir Andrew Aguecheek (II. 3. 150–165):

Sir Toby . . . tell us something of him.
Maria Marry, sir, sometimes he is a kind of puritan.
Sir Andrew O, if I thought that, I 'ld beat him like a dog!
Sir Toby What, for being a puritan? Thy exquisite reason, dear knight?
Sir Andrew I have no exquisite reason for 't, but I have reason good enough.
Maria The devil a puritan that he is, or any thing constantly, but a time-pleaser; an affectioned ass, that cons state without book and utters it by great swarths: the best persuaded of himself, so crammed, as he thinks, with excellencies, that it is his grounds of faith that all that look on him love him.

The words of the pleasure-loving knights would raise a laugh at the Puritan's expense and doubtless expressed more or less the popular attitude—certainly the attitude of the average theatre audience. Maria's description of Malvolio pictured that smug, self-satisfied, gloomy, pseudo-pious air, which so many Puritans seemed to adopt. It was this pose of the Puritans that Shakespeare laughed at, not their religious beliefs. He respected the faith of all earnest people, and hated religious persecution, as he showed when he wrote in *The Winter's Tale* (II. 3. 115–116): "It is an heretic that makes the fire, Not she which burns in 't."

In Malvolio, Shakespeare drew a type of Puritan with which the public were familiar enough. He was detected as a killjoy and suspected to be a hypocrite. He was against all forms of pleasure. Malvolio is true to type when he reproves Olivia's uncle, Sir Toby, for making merry with his bibulous friends at a late hour (II. 3. 93–99):

Have you no wit, manners, nor honesty, but to gabble like tinkers at this time of night? Do ye make an alehouse of my lady's house, that ye squeak out your coziers' catches without any mitigation or remorse of voice? Is there no respect of place, persons, nor time in you?

Sir Toby makes the characteristic anti-Puritan remark in reply (123–125): "Dost thou think, because thou art virtuous, there shall be no more cakes and ale?"

Shakespeare knew that many of those who appeared to be actuated by a burning religious zeal very often were far from feeling inwardly all they professed. They deceived others and not infrequently themselves as well. Malvolio in speech, manner, and pretences has all the Puritan frailties, and is mocked and tricked by the other characters, cheated of love, and left with rankling feelings of hate against those who have befooled him. The pompous, self-important steward is heaped with ridicule, but it is not the kind of ridicule which leaves permanent resentment behind it. Malvolio was created some years before the dramatists attacked the Puritans with their sharpened prongs of slander, mockery, and insult. Shakespeare's digs by the side of the invective of Middleton and others are the buzzings of the harmless fly to the sting of the wasp. *Twelfth Night* was written in a gay and happy mood, but the later abuse of the Puritans was in the vein of the most deadly retaliation.

Before leaving *Twelfth Night* we must notice another shaft loosed at the Puritans' condemnation of the theatre. One of their loudest criticisms concerned the practice of the young boy actors of wearing female apparel. They claimed that it was expressly forbidden by verse 5 of chapter xxii of the Book of Deuteronomy:

The woman shall not wear that which pertaineth unto a man, neither shall a man put on a woman's garment: for all that do so are abomination unto the Lord thy God.

In *Twelfth Night* Viola assumes a male disguise, and in so doing wins the love of Olivia. She declares she now sees how dangerous such a device may prove, since it gives opportunity to the enemy, the Devil, to harm an innocent soul (II. 2. 28–29):

> Disguise, I see, thou art a wickedness,
> Wherein the pregnant enemy does much.

In *All's Well that Ends Well* there is an interesting passage in which Papist and Puritan are contrasted (I. 3. 54–59):

If men could be contented to be what they are, there were no fear in marriage; for young Charbon the puritan and old Poysam the papist howsome'er their hearts are severed in religion, their heads are both one; they may joul horns together, like any deer i' the herd.

From this we gather that Shakespeare had little real sympathy with the extremist section either of the old or the new religion. His deep insight into human nature enabled him to look beneath the superficial differences of religious persuasion and find the instincts and impulses which all mankind, Protestant, Puritan, and Papist, shared in common. (As regards the names used in the above quotation, it has been suggested that "Charbon" stands for "Chair-bonne" and "Poysam" for "Poisson," the respective lenten fares of Puritan and Papist.)[1]

Another passage in *All's Well that Ends Well* refers to the wearing of the surplice in the Reformed Church, a practice which Puritans condemned as a relic of Popery (I. 3. 97–100):

Clown Though honesty be no puritan, yet it will do no hurt; it will wear the surplice of humility over the black gown of a big heart.

The interpretation of this passage has proved so difficult as to cause commentators to suspect the accuracy of the text. Bishop Wordsworth gives the following paraphrase[2]: "An honest man will not be troubled with unnecessary scruples, especially in a case where his obedience is required to a lawful command, however the command may be distasteful to himself. He will put on the surplice—to which the

[1] *The Temple Shakespeare*, p. 148.
[2] *Shakespeare's Knowledge and Use of the Bible*, p. 226.

Puritans objected. But still when he has done so, though so far not a Puritan, this is no security that he may not all the while *intus et in cute*, as bad as if he were—having as proud a heart as if he wore a black gown." The Bishop considers that the Clown's speech implies some distrust and dislike of the Puritanical character, but that Shakespeare, nevertheless, wants them to have fair play and objects to hearing them criticized by people who in worth and disposition are inferior to them. This interpretation is in keeping with what we know of his freedom from religious prejudice and his love for all mankind.

In *The Winter's Tale* occurs another instance of what may be termed Shakespeare's anti-Puritan quips. The Clown remarks (IV. 3. 43–47):

She hath made me four-and-twenty nosegays for the shearers, three-man song-men all, and very good ones; but they are most of them means and bases; but one puritan amongst them, and he sings psalms to hornpipes.

On this passage Thomas Carter, who claims Shakespeare as a Puritan, writes[1]: "If anything, this is a stingless satire on the fondness of the Puritans and Calvinists for Marot's Psalm tunes, but it can hardly be said to be discourteous or to convey any personal feeling." Certainly no one detects any strong feeling or prejudice in the Clown's remark. Bishop Wordsworth says[2]: "The utmost offence which appears to be committed in these words is, that the Clown playfully satirizes the objectional practice which the Puritans introduced . . . of singing sacred songs to *jiggish* tunes." To me the quotation appears typical

[1] *Shakespeare and Holy Scripture*, p. 24.
[2] *Shakespeare's Knowledge and Use of the Bible*, p. 227.

of the light-hearted, half-amused attitude which Shakespeare adopted towards the Calvinist, an attitude that contained nothing of hate, bitterness, or religious bias.

If anything could prove Shakespeare's anti-Puritanism, it is the creation of that old rascal Falstaff—liar, thief, drunkard, rake, and coward. Such a conception would be impossible in a Puritan. His deception and hypocrisy are the Puritan faults as seen by their enemies. He is glib in his quotation of Scripture, and apes the very language of those who claimed to have a monopoly of "the narrow way." A typical instance occurs in the scene in the Prince's apartment in London. Referring to Poins and the Prince, he says to Poins (*1 Henry IV*, I. 2. 170–174):

Well, *God give thee the spirit of persuasian and him* the ears of profiting, that what thou speakest may move and what he hears may be believed, that the true prince may, for recreation sake, prove a false thief.

The old boaster, pretending to be what he patently was not, laying claim to virtues which all the world knew he lacked, would remind the audience of the insincere, canting humbugs who were the worst feature of the Puritan movement. Against such hypocrites it was legitimate to indulge in satire; and a dramatist could do so without reflecting on the really earnest religionists.

Other passages there are where Shakespeare does not mention the Puritans by name, but appears to have them in mind. Bishop Warburton called attention to such a case in *Timon of Athens*. Sempronius, speaking of one of Timon's fair-weather friends, says (III. 3. 31–34):

How fairly this lord strives to appear foul! takes virtuous copies to be wicked; like those that under hot ardent zeal would set whole realms on fire.

In the same category are the lines from *Hamlet*, where Polonius is probably thinking of the Puritans when he says (III. 1. 46–49):

> We are oft to blame in this—
> 'Tis too much proved—that with devotion's visage
> And pious action we do sugar o'er
> The devil himself.

The Puritan is again named in *Pericles*, but in this case the lines were not written by Shakespeare. It may, however, be as well to quote them:

Bawd . . . she has me her quirks, her reasons, her master reasons, her prayers, her knees; that she would make a puritan of the devil, if he should cheapen a kiss of her.

(IV. 6. 7–10.)

Our final instance of Shakespeare's antipathy to Puritanism is in the character of Angelo. There are critics who profess to see something akin to sectarian bitterness in' the fall of this self-righteous, sanctimonious hypocrite. But it is patent that *Measure for Measure*, a play of deep thought, is more than a simple exposure of revolting cant. It is a sermon on the battle between chastity and sexual temptation. There is, however, in Angelo's fall an object lesson to those worst of Puritans who adopted the attitude of "God, I thank thee that I am not as other men."

Surveying the data before him, Sir Sidney Lee wrote: "With Puritans and Puritanism Shakespeare was not in sympathy. Shakespeare's references to Puritans in the plays of his middle life are so uniformly discourteous that they must be judged to reflect his personal feelings." Dr. Brandes credited Shakespeare with a deeper hatred of the Puritans. He says,[1] "We catch a glimpse at this point of one of the subsidiary causes of Shakespeare's melancholy: as actor and playwright he stands in a more and more strained relation to the continually growing Free Church movement of the age, to Puritanism, which he comes to regard as nothing but narrow-mindedness and hypocrisy. It was the deadly enemy of his calling. From *Twelfth Night* an unremitting war against Puritanism conceived as hypocrisy is carried on through *Hamlet*, through the revised version of *All's Well that Ends Well*, and through *Measure for Measure*, in which his wrath rises to tempestuous pitch and creates a figure to which Molière's *Tartuffe* can alone supply a parallel."

In saying that Shakespeare's "wrath rises to tempestuous pitch," it seems to me that Dr. Brandes overstates the case. A calm consideration of the anti-Puritan passages shows quite clearly that Shakespeare had no love for the extreme Protestant wing, but his opposition is nowhere tinged with anger, bitterness, or bias. He laughs, teases, ridicules, burlesques, but there is none of that cruel, insulting, withering satire that was being poured upon the luckless Puritan heads by the dramatists at the time when *Measure for Measure* was written. Shakespeare was too great to stoop to religious bigotry and persecution. But we must not- mistake his restraint and moderation for lurking sympathy with the Puritans. They were the fruits of his humanity. He disliked the Puritans. He had nothing in common with them. They were a

[1] Vol. I. p. 281.

nuisance to him. But he could admire their good qualities as easily as he could laugh at their foibles, and he could place their religious peculiarities on one side and see them only as members of the human family.

The view is held by some scholars that while Shakespeare was anti-Puritan during his play-writing career, he was converted during his semi-retirement at Stratford. There were, apparently, strong Puritan influences in the town at the time. John Shakespeare had fallen under their spell, and Shakespeare's own daughter, Susanna, married a Puritan in Dr. John Hall. But there is no evidence that the Poet moved from the position of orthodox Protestant, which he had held for so long. There is a popular tradition that his last fatal illness was caused by a merry and not-too-wise meeting with Ben Jonson and Drayton. This, if true, would show that Shakespeare a short while before his death was no nearer Calvinism than he had been during his busy career in the theatres of London. Clever critics have been able to make out a case for almost any view of Shakespeare and his works, however bizarre and improbable. But the cleverest of them cannot make him a Puritan. All they can achieve is to show that his antagonism to Puritanism was less bitter and malicious than that of his fellow-dramatists.

XIV

SHAKESPEARE A CONFORMING PROTESTANT

No great author ever revealed so little of his own individuality as Shakespeare. He has vouchsafed us but glimpses of the man behind the masterpieces; and these glimpses are few and far between, and as brief as flashes of lightning which illumine a darkened countryside. His inmost thoughts are hidden behind a veil which is only occasionally, and very reluctantly, drawn aside. Shakespeare desired his audience to be interested in his characters. He was not at all anxious that they should be interested in the playwright. It was his characters' thoughts and feelings that he put before them, not his own. Even his friends and contemporaries appear to have known little of the real Shakespeare. He was a gay and cheerful companion, who entered wholeheartedly into any fun that was going, a man always ready with kindly help, tolerant, forgiving, slow to take offence. His happy, care-free demeanour did not suggest a mind concerned with deep philosophic problems; yet he would retire from the rowdy, jolly company at the tavern to the peace of his lodgings, and as the fruit of hours of quiet work would produce those profound tragedies like *Hamlet* and *Macbeth*, which continue, and always will continue, to stir the soul of man to its very depth.

Self-revelation, it would seem, was a literary luxury that Shakespeare sternly denied himself. For this reason his men and women almost have the distinction of historical personages, while he himself is but a shadowy figure in the background. Since

Shakespeare preferred to be so secretive about his inner life, it is not surprising to find he says little or nothing upon the subject on which the average person is most inclined to be reticent, namely, religion. His admirers have sought in vain for anything that might, even at a stretch, be interpreted as a confession of faith. There is nothing to guide the inquirer in the whole of his works. We have, therefore, to approach the subject from a different angle, and arrive at what he did believe by convincing ourselves first of what he obviously did *not* believe.

There are, we have seen, sufficient anti-Catholic passages in his plays—particularly the famous "No-Popery" speech in *King John*, which no Catholic would have dared to write—to be safe in concluding that he was no adherent of the old Faith. What we know of the circumstances of his life, his youth, and associations in London, confirm this view. Again, there is sufficient light banter directed against the Puritans, which, while it lacks the sting of the bitter attacks of other dramatists, leaves no doubt that he had little liking for Puritanism. Once more his life history, especially his connection with the theatre, anathema to the Puritans, supports the contention. By the process of elimination, then, we arrive at the conclusion that Shakespeare was a conforming Protestant. What positive evidence is there, external and internal, to convince us that this conclusion is the correct one?

No critic can do more than prove that Shakespeare was a conforming Protestant outwardly. His real religion, hidden behind a garment of orthodoxy, undoubtedly transcended creed and dogma, ritual and ceremony. But he discovered that loyalty to the

State Church was not only convenient, but approached most nearly to that tolerance, moderation, lack of fanaticism, and central-mindedness which seem to have coloured all his religious thinking.

In his life story, as we have it, there is nothing inconsistent with conforming Protestantism. He began well by being baptized according to the ritual in the new Prayer Book. His father, during his early years, was distinguished for his zeal for the Elizabethan church compromise and the obliteration of all that savoured of Popery. John Shakespeare was typical of Stratford's religious sensibilities in the fifteen-sixties and fifteen-seventies. While Shakespeare was growing to "years of discretion" there was no disturbing element in his life that would be likely to deflect him from obedience to the law ecclesiastical. There is no record that he ever came into conflict with the Church authorities as a young man, that he was ever fined for non-attendance at service, that he was suspected of a desire to rebel or, as his father in later life, that he interpreted conformity as persecution. Even when he had left Stratford and was making his way in London, Shakespeare appears to have gone to church every Sunday, an observance expected of a loyal subject and law-abiding citizen.

We do not know what Shakespeare was doing between 1584 and 1592. Rumour and tradition have provided him with a number of very different jobs, among them those of scrivener, dyer, printer, apothecary, soldier, and schoolmaster. The most popular tradition is that the master commenced his association with the theatre in the humble capacity of pageboy. However that may be, it is certain that most of those years were spent in making a position for himself in the theatrical world. He had succeeded sufficiently by 1592 to arouse the jealousy of such an established playwright as Greene. His name may not have been known to the public at large, but he was becoming increasingly respected as an author by the fellows of his company.

Something must have attracted Shakespeare to the Stage, for it was not a usual calling for a country-bred lad in those days. We know that during his father's periods of office the Queen's Players and the Earl of Worcester's Company visited Stratford. Shakespeare also seems to show, as J. J. Jusserand writes,[1] "a great familiarity with mystery plays and their noisy Herod, moralities and their facetious Vice, with ballad-singers, jugglers, and jesters." It is quite likely that he saw the pageant of the Queen's visit to Kenilworth when he was a boy of eleven. Whatever turned his thoughts to the theatre as a possible means of livelihood, it is interesting to note for the purposes of our study that he was not deterred by any religious scruples. No boy from a Puritan family could have pondered such a step for a moment. Very few Catholics are known to have entered the profession.

Mixing with his new colleagues, Shakespeare would find himself in an atmosphere of strong Protestant conformity. All the dramatists who had won a position for themselves were on the side of the Established Church. There were no Puritans among them, and only here and there a man with leanings towards Catholicism. The orthodoxy of the profession was understandable. The great public to whom they appealed were overwhelmingly Protestants of the Anglican Church. Only by the help of the Queen, the

[1] *A Literary History of the English People*, Vol. III. p. 157.

head of the Church, and her Privy Council were the actors able to withstand the fierce attack of the Puritans against their very existence. Players and playwrights won most applause after 1588 by their extreme patriotism; and as patriotism and Catholicism were then a contradiction of terms, there was little sympathy with Rome among the citizens of Shakespeare's new world.

The strong orthodox Protestantism of the actors and dramatists is most clearly seen in their attacks upon both Puritan and Papist. It is rare indeed to come across any passage that is in itself a clear, unambiguous declaration of faith and adherence to the Anglican doctrine. Professor Creizenach writes,[1] "The positive teachings of their Church were, however, not of a nature to permeate their works in the same manner as the Greek religion affected Attic drama, or Catholicism the Spanish." Membership of the central Church was the most satisfactory position from the dramatist's point of view, since he was not hindered by its dogma from formulating and expressing his own view of life and the universe. It is this very attitude that Shakespeare learned and adopted from his fellow-workers on the stage; and it explains his freedom from the dogmatic.

The Elizabethan stage advanced to the point where the religious element in drama was almost entirely eliminated. Whereas in the days of the mysteries and moralities religion was the beginning and end of all plays, the fashion so far reacted that by 1605 a Statute of James I went to the length of forbidding altogether the mention of the name of the Deity in the theatre. The attacks on the Catholics were inspired as much by

[1] *The English Drama in the Age of Shakespeare*, p. 110.

P

patriotism and politics, and the attacks on the Puritans by commercialism, as by religion. Hence the preference of the dramatists for the middle path.

If Shakespeare's conscience quietly acquiesced in his choice of a career, it was equally complacent while he plunged into the Bohemian life led by those whom the theatre supported. To quote again from Jusserand's "Life of Shakespeare,"[1] "Whether from the influence of his surroundings, from temptations, personal inclination, or the part which must be allotted to the weaker sides of human nature, certain it is that the famous 'Will' did not, in London, set the example of domestic virtues." From scraps of information handed down to posterity by his contemporaries and acquaintances we build up a picture of a jolly fellow, real good company, who might be met with in the inns and taverns, greeting his friends, and engaging in discussion and argument. Sometimes he would bandy words with the scholarly Ben Jonson, described by Fuller as 'like a Spanish great gallion . . . solid but slow in his performances,' while he himself was an 'English man of war, lesser in bulk, but lighter in sailing, could turn with all tides, tack about, and take advantage of all winds, by the quickness of his wit and invention.' "[2]

That he was very familiar with taverns, and not always the most respectable at that, is clear enough from such scenes as the Boar's Head in *Henry IV* and the Garter Inn at Windsor in the *Merry Wives*. The very character of Falstaff, with his gluttony and shamelessness, was drawn from Shakespeare's own observations in the haunts of the loose-living, free-

---

[1] *A Literary History of the English People*, Vol. III. p. 225.

[2] Fuller's *History of the Worthies of England—Warwickshire*.

drinking actors. That he could hold his own with any man, that he could drink as well as most, and that he was not out of sympathy with the extravagance and worldliness of his friends and colleagues, is vouched for by a hundred passages in the plays. He was not averse to adventures in love, as we know from the entry in John Manningham's diary (March 13th, 1602)[1] which tells how he supplanted his friend Burbage at a tryst with the wife of a London citizen. Nor was he a stranger to more sordid experiences to judge from his self-disgust in Sonnet CXXIX and certain of the speeches and lewd characters in *Measure for Measure*. There was nothing of the Puritan in this mode of life, but it was typical of the acting fraternity against whom the Puritans railed and stormed.

In another direction, too, Shakespeare's conduct would incense the Puritan. We know that poets were compelled to depend for their existence on the favours of a rich patron; and Shakespeare only did what all poets of the day had to do, when he flattered and fawned upon the wealthy, elegant, gilded young nobleman, the Earl of Southampton. His art brought him in contact with the cultured and educated class, those who swaggered in rich and fashionable clothes, who lived careless and prodigal lives, and, while containing a smattering of Catholics, were in the main Protestants of the centre party. The glamour and glitter of the Court dazzled the eyes of the Poet, beside which the strict asceticism of the Puritans seemed sombre indeed. The noble patrons of the arts were not interested in self-discipline and self-denial, and expected from those they patronized risky and often indecent verse to tickle their sensual fancy. This

---

[1] See Halliwell-Phillipps, *Outlines*, II. 82.

vogue was dictated to Shakespeare by circumstances and was not necessarily his own choice. He does not appear, however, to have had any scruples about adopting it; and his thorough treatment in *Venus and Adonis* and *Lucrece* could not have emanated from one of Puritan susceptibilities.

From all we know of his life in London, of his actor friends and associates, his royal and noble patrons at Court, it is clear that he mixed almost the whole of his time with orthodox Protestants. His professional and business interests placed an impassable gulf between him and the Puritans. The Catholics were a dwindling minority, small in numbers and influence, considered unpatriotic by most Englishmen, and only worth the notice of the established playwright as a means of rousing the intense nationalism of his audience.

From a bundle of old law papers found in the Record Office by Professor Wallace in 1910,[1] we learn that for some years Shakespeare lodged, when in town, with a French Huguenot named Christopher Mountjoy, at his house in Silver Street. A Roman Catholic would certainly have chosen a more congenial atmosphere in which to live, while a strict Puritan would never have been comfortable in a house whose head was engaged in the frivolous and vain occupation of making head-dresses for women, which happened to be Mountjoy's trade. But Shakespeare appears to have been on the most friendly terms with the Huguenot and his family, and to have been consulted on so intimate a matter as the daughter's dowry. The

---

[1] The papers related to a minor law case in which Shakespeare figured as witness. See *The Genuine in Shakespeare*, J. M. Robertson, p. 155.

law papers do not tell us much, but that little confirms our impression of a happy, good-tempered, kindly individual, free of cant and bitterness, and sympathetic to all his fellows.

While it is true that Shakespeare shared the Bohemianism of his brother actors and business colleagues, and thereby proved how much he was out of sympathy with the Puritan element, it must be recorded on his behalf that he never plunged into the wildness and excess of which many of the theatrical crowd were guilty. He never endangered his reputation at home, for he had always in mind that eventual return to Stratford, when he would settle down as an honoured and respected country gentleman.

All the reliable biographical details that we possess, then, confirm the theory that Shakespeare was a conforming Protestant. Turning from a consideration of external to that of internal evidence, we find nothing in conflict with that theory, and further proof in its support. One indubitable sign of his Anglican mind is his staunch loyalty to the Queen, the head of the Established Church. Granted that flattery of the most powerful patron of the theatre was to be expected, there are still no grounds for doubting Shakespeare's sincere admiration of Elizabeth. When considering the famous anti-papal speech of *King John*, we noted how eloquently he stated the case for English independence of Rome and laughed at the harmless retaliatory weapon of excommunication. We saw how unlikely such a speech would be in a monarch of John's period and how well it suited his own age. This is one of the occasions on which the dramatist puts a speech into the mouth of one of his characters which is not in harmony with the times in which that character lived; and it is from such passages that we learn the prevalent thought of his own day and his own concurrence in it.

Shakespeare fully subscribed to the doctrine of the divine right of kings, and by so doing accepted the Act of Supremacy as receiving the sanction of Heaven and being consequently inviolable. The following few lines from *King John* describe exactly the view of the royal supremacy held by the orthodox Protestant (III. 1. 153–158):

> . . . no Italian priest
> Shall tithe or toll in our dominions;
> But as we, under heaven, are supreme head,
> So under Him that great supremacy,
> Where we do reign, we will alone uphold,
> Without the assistance of a mortal hand.

Compliments to royalty abound throughout the plays; and special compliments to the Queen, similar to that in *Midsummer Night's Dream* (II. 1. 148–169), are sufficiently numerous for us to realize that Elizabeth had in the Poet one of her most humble, obedient, and loyal subjects. It is true that Shakespeare did not contribute to the chorus of praise and lamentation which burst from the poets on the death of the great Queen. The explanation is, perhaps, Shakespeare's inborn distaste and avoidance of the obvious. It is difficult to credit his silence with any religious significance.

Consistent with an orthodox Protestantism was the deep feeling of patriotism which stirred the heart of Shakespeare. The finest poetry ever inspired by the love of England came from his pen. In this he was a true son of his age, for the English claim to a place in the New World, the denial of that claim by mighty

Spain, the impudent challenge of little England in reply, and the actual defeat of the powerful rival, had given the Elizabethans a self-confidence and feeling of security which the country had never previously possessed. The English people had found themselves and were exulting in the discovery.

After the fiasco of the Armada, 1588, pride and patriotism received their fullest expression in all branches of the national life. The theatre added its contribution in that long series of plays chronicling English history, which won enormous popularity. When his country was so miraculously and gloriously delivered from the threat of a Spanish invasion, Shakespeare was an ardent and enthusiastic young man of twenty-four. As we perceive how strongly less imaginative minds were moved by these great events, we can form some estimate of the deep and lasting impression they must have made upon the greatest of our poets. Very naturally, then, his first incursions into dramatic authorship was his handling of the historical play; and so well did he succeed that he aroused the jealousy of those who had shown him the way, and made it an impossible task for any to follow him.

Patriotism is not to-day the monopoly of any religious sect; but at the time of the Armada patriotism was not consistent with Catholicism, since a victory for Philip II of Spain was to have been followed by a return of England to allegiance to the Pope. Hence the writers of the Chronicle Plays, Shakespeare in particular, were fiercely anti-Catholic, not so much on religious as on political grounds. Such an attitude was mainly responsible for the much-quoted passage from *King John*—the most definite sectarian pronouncement to be found in the whole of Shakespeare.

Not only environment, loyalty, and patriotism made Shakespeare a conforming Protestant. Careful study of his works reveals another influence—the influence of the Renaissance mind.

After Shakespeare came to London from Stratford, he entered a social circle of literary and philosophic bent, whose ideas were drawn from the Renaissance. The Renaissance mind was Protestant in sympathy in so far as it can be said to have had any religious sympathies at all. R. M. Alden writes[1]: "The Renaissance, as we know, had reacted from the domination of the religious element in the thought and art of the Middle Age, and substituted for it—sometimes deliberately, sometimes unconsciously—a more than pagan spirit of secularity, concerned frankly with this present world." With this point of view Shakespeare undoubtedly identified himself. He was wholly interested in problems and experiences of this present world and devoted his genius to the dissection of the human heart and mind without much thought of the spiritualized existence in the hereafter. Many critics have been impressed by what is described as "his great want of other worldliness"; and not a few have been rather unpleasantly surprised that even in his death scenes the characters seem to cling to the mundane and are unable to turn their minds to a contemplation of the life beyond the grave. Not that the Renaissance mind was definitely anti-religious. On the contrary, it could be (quoting Alden again) "entirely compatible with a reserved minimum of fairly orthodox belief." This,

[1] *Shakespeare*, p. 350.

I think there is no doubt, was Shakespeare's religious position.

That Shakespeare did ponder, and frequently, on the deep mysteries of existence, the great tragedies of thought, particularly *Hamlet*, are more than ample proof. But such meditation is more accurately described as philosophic than religious. Of pure religion the plays provide us with little, and that little is orthodox Christianity. In the majority of them, religious motives and ideas play no part at all. In others their part is a minor one. A close study of the early plays from this angle suggests an acceptance without doubt or difficulty of the creed of the Reformed Church. That this impression of Protestantism should be conveyed, however indistinctly, is significant, since the periods are all pre-Reformation, and there are no Protestant heroes. In no lines of Shakespeare is there anything against Protestantism to be compared with the anti-papal outburst in *King John*.

Comparatively speaking, religious allusions are few in Shakespeare, and those that do exist must be treated with reserve. Few of them can be relied upon as self-revelations. Most often it is the character speaking, and the confessions are consistent with that character's nature and circumstances. As the Rev. George Gilfillan says,[1] "Cæsar and Antony talk like heathens. Isabella in *Measure for Measure* speaks like a Christian. Cardinal Wolsey is a Catholic. Prospero is a philosopher."

The poems confirm the evidence of the plays. They are frankly worldly and sensual. *Venus and Adonis* and *Lucrece* deal with the unbeautiful side of human love and were written to appeal to a luxurious, reckless,

[1] *The Life and Poetry of William Shakespeare*, p. xvi.

extravagant, voluptuous nobleman—a type of the class against whom the Puritans raved, but on whose patronage the poets depended for their very existence. There is nothing in the poems inconsistent with the orthodox Protestantism professed by the Court of Elizabeth. On the other hand, their lack of sectarian controversies and their frank secularity would appeal to the taste and discrimination of the orthodox arbiters of literature and art. The problem of the Sonnets is ever with us. Some critics, it is true, would give them a spiritual interpretation; but the majority do not believe that they have a higher than human meaning; and this view coincides with the statement of the first editor that they are "seren, cleere, and eligantly plain" with "no intricate or cloudy stuffe" to trouble and perplex the intellect.

There is little *positive* evidence of Shakespeare's conformity to the State Church to be extracted from the plays. It will be as well to note, however, that he appears to have subscribed to the doctrine of Baptismal Grace, which every orthodox Protestant would be taught in the Church of England. Henry V, speaking to the Archbishop of Canterbury, says (I. 2. 30–32):

> For we will hear, note and believe in heart
> That what you speak is in your conscience wash'd
> As pure as sin with baptism.

In *Othello* Iago suggests that Desdemona has such influence over her husband that she could, if so inclined:

> . . . win the Moor, were 't to renounce his baptism,
> All seals and symbols of redeemed sin.
>
> (II. 3. 349–350.)

Bishop Wordsworth, in addition to noting the above

point, finds further evidence of Shakespeare's Church loyalty in his familiar use of the response "Amen." It occurs in the plays more than sixty times, and according to the Bishop "may alone be regarded as sufficient indication to that effect."[1] He quotes two instances. The first, which strikes him as singularly solemn and impressive, is taken from *Henry V* (v. 2. 395–396):

> That English may as French, French Englishmen,
> Receive each other. God speak this Amen!

The second instance occurs in *Richard III*. Richmond after his final victory declares (v. 5. 8):

> Great God of heaven, say amen to all!

About the great festivals of the Church, ignored by the Puritans, Shakespeare has little to say; but the lines on Christmas in *Hamlet* reveal the reverence for that sacred commemoration of a true member of the Anglican community (1. 1. 158–164):

> Some say that ever 'gainst that season comes
> Wherein our Saviour's birth is celebrated,
> This bird of dawning singeth all night long:
> And then, they say, no spirit dares stir abroad,
> The nights are wholesome, then no planets strikes,
> No fairy takes nor witch hath power to charm,
> So hallow'd and so gracious is the time.

Shakespeare's other references to Christmas, like his meagre references to Whitsun and Easter, deal with the jollification and old pagan customs associated with the seasons, the very reason why the Puritans, when they acquired the power, banned them altogether.

[1] *Shakespeare's Knowledge and Use of the Bible*, p. 228.

We can make no religious capital out of the Poet's references to Sunday. There is a passage in *Much Ado About Nothing* (I. I. 204) where the words "sigh away Sundays" are interpreted by some critics as a dislike of the strict manner in which the Puritans kept the Lord's Day. But his chief interest in Sunday was its popularity for wedding celebrations.

Coming at the last to Shakespeare's Will, we find him professing sincerely his belief in God and trusting in the merits of Christ for the salvation of his soul. This is the most direct confession of faith that we have from him; and so much was the language that of orthodox Protestantism that some enthusiast, over-eager to prove him a Catholic, was constrained to forge a new Will to strengthen the Roman case.

An impartial review of the whole evidence, external and internal, leads to the only possible inference that Shakespeare steered a course of religious moderation between the extremes of Catholicism and Puritanism. As a broad-minded, tolerant, human individual, he found his natural place with the central Church. Fanaticism was impossible in him: abuse and persecution were revolting. He had little interest in creed and dogma. Ritual and ceremony attracted him only as a stage spectacle. Fripp writes,[1] "It is sometimes said that 'Shakespeare was not a Christian.' It depends on what we mean by a Christian. He was of the broad kind . . . with the Lord's Prayer as its central symbol rather than a creed. See *Modern Churchman*, May 1929." John Bailey describes him as[2] "the centrally-minded man with his eye fixed on realities and essentials." "It is not easy," he says, "to think of him as definitely a Churchman of any Church or creed." The same

[1] *Shakespeare Haunts*, p. 60, note.　　　[2] *Shakespeare*, pp. 22, 23.

writer adds, he was "indifferent to the niceties of dogma and the shibboleths of ecclesiastical parties." These quotations summarize the truth of Shakespeare's religion, which we might epitomize in the sentence: "Outwardly a conforming Protestant: inwardly a Christian philosopher unfettered by creed."

XV

THE POET AND CHRISTIAN DOCTRINE

EXAMINING Shakespeare's attitude towards Christian
dogma, we commence by observing that no play is
concerned primarily with a doctrinal theme. Some of
the dramas have a strong religious strain running
through them, such as *Hamlet* and *Measure for Measure*;
but in no single instance can it be said that the main
interest is theological. Nevertheless, the Poet's references to dogma are very numerous indeed; and from
them we can form an accurate opinion of his feelings
towards the teachings of Christianity. There is, of
course, the difficulty which is ever-present in Shakespearean criticism—the difficulty of distinguishing his
own points of view from those which he attributes
to his characters. Selections from the numerous
passages bearing upon profound doctrinal propositions must, therefore, be made with the utmost care,
if we are to have any confidence that we are repre-
senting fairly the convictions of the Poet. It is not so
difficult, perhaps, to find Shakespeare himself in the
references to Christian doctrine, as it is when he
speaks on some other important subjects—aristocracy
versus people, for example. Many of the religious
allusions are not essential to the dialogue. They are
often supererogatory and parenthetical. They do
not advance the action, nor materially aid the
characterization. They could be omitted without
dramatic loss. This does not apply to *all* such passages,
naturally. (In the case of Shylock religious comments
help us to understand him. The religiously-minded

Henry VI must speak in pious phrases.) But it applies to a good many of them; and we are justified in thinking that Shakespeare would not have included these if he had not believed in their truth himself and known that the majority of his audience believed in it also.

It will be as well to explain more clearly the specific scope and purpose of this chapter. By "Christian doctrine" is meant Christian dogma as opposed to Christian ethics. Matthew Arnold gives the following definition,[1] "*Dogma* means, not necessarily a true doctrine, but merely a doctrine or system of doctrine determined, decreed, received." According to W. G. T. Shedd,[2] "Dogmatic theology, properly constructed, presents *dogmas* in the first sense; namely, as propositions formulated from inspired data." A dictionary[3] defines dogma as "doctrine asserted and adopted on authority, as distinguished from that which is the result of one's own reasoning or experience." Ethics, on the other hand, are defined by the same authority[4] as, "The science or doctrine of the sources, principles, sanctions, and ideals of human conduct and character; the science of morally right."

Bearing these definitions in mind, our immediate purpose, then, is to determine Shakespeare's mental attitude toward the teachings of the Christian Church on such doctrinal points as the Person and attributes of God, the Atonement, the Immortality of the Soul, the Day of Judgment, Satan, Hell, and the like. We are not concerned for the moment with his estimate

---

[1] *Literature and Dogma*, p. 164 (O. & Co., 1873).
[2] *Dogmatic Theology*, Intro., p. 11 (S. 1889).
[3] Funk and Wagnall's *New Standard Dictionary*, p. 742.
[4] *Ibid.*, p. 856.

of right and wrong, his ideals of conduct, and his moral philosophy as a whole. This will be treated in a later chapter of its own. There is a difference of a striking character in the position adopted by Shakespeare on these two important questions. In the case of Christian dogma he accepts without question what his spiritual advisers have taught him. As to Christian ethics, he has very decided ideas of his own on what is good and what is evil in word, thought, and deed.

Studiously orthodox on points of Christian dogma, Shakespeare even uses the orthodox language of Christianity when he puts pious and devout speeches into the mouths of his characters. There is no doubt that he reverenced the doctrine of the Church. He experienced no intellectual difficulty in accepting it. He did not find that it conflicted either with his reason or conscience. As R. M. Alden writes,[1] he "repeatedly refers to the subject-matter of Christianity with an air of reverent acceptance, especially where it is associated with the national tradition, as in the utterances of Henry the Fourth and Henry the Fifth." Hamlet, who a majority of critics are strong in affirming is nearest to the Poet himself of all his creations, reveals in his grand soliloquies the influence upon his thinking of religious teaching.

While accepting the creed of his own Protestant Church of England, Shakespeare had no bitterness or prejudice against those who worshipped differently. Our study of his religion failed to reveal anything of sectarian narrowness. He was conventional in his day, but we do not know how deep his convictions went. Perhaps his tolerance and humanity were born

[1] *Shakespeare*, p. 350.

of the suspicion that no one church had a monopoly of truth. Paul Gibson writes,[1] "As transition was the key-note of Shakespeare's age, especially transition in religious thought, we notice that the writer for all time has been particularly careful to refrain from giving too important a place to what might eventually prove to be but a one-sided view of truth." This broad-mindedness in a time of religious controversy is the most remarkable and outstanding fact of Shakespeare's Christianity.

To re-state the Poet's position, we can say with some confidence that as regards the spiritual life, the things which are unseen, he accepted the explanations of Christian dogma and repeated them reverently. As regards ethics, the manner in which a Christian should think and behave in this present world, Shakespeare relied upon his own observations and was not afraid to voice his own opinions. In the one case he was a listening pupil: in the other, he assumed the rôle of preacher.

Shakespeare's orthodoxy both in thought and language touching Christian doctrine is well illustrated in his reference to the Deity. He accepts fully the Christian concept of God. In the plays written up to 1605, he alludes to Him with extraordinary frequency; but we find that in the plays written after the Statute of James I had forbidden in that year the mention of the Persons of the Holy Trinity on the stage, the dramatist, conforming, as was his wont, to the laws spiritual and temporal, rarely uses the word "god" except in a pagan sense. The only play to which this does not apply is *Henry VIII*, written in collaboration with Fletcher; and it is interesting to

[1] *Shakespeare's Use of the Supernatural*, p. 44.

note that some critics believe that this drama of pageantry, though not performed until 1613, was commenced at the end of Elizabeth's reign or the beginning of the reign of her successor, that is, before the Statute referred to came into force.

I do not propose to indulge in a plethora of quotation illustrative of the various aspects of Shakespeare's thought of God. Anything like a classification of his allusions to our heavenly Father would not only be tedious, but of little value to our study, since it is the Poet's own view-point, and not that of his characters, which we wish to investigate. It will be best to confine ourselves to a careful selection of passages which seem best to elucidate his own conceptions.

Shakespeare accepts the Christian teaching that God is the Creator of all things, but he is most impressed by the revelation that He is the Creator, or Father, of men. Man as the image and likeness of God is among the most exalted ideas of Christian theology, and one that is ever-present in the Poet's mind. Queen Margaret speaks of the villainous Richard III as "that foul defacer of God's handiwork" (IV. 4. 51); and, in lighter vein, Beatrice is made to say that she will not marry "till God make men of some other metal than earth" (*Much Ado About Nothing*, II. 1. 62). The most striking passage, however, comes from the lips of Hamlet (II. 2. 315–320):

What a piece of work is man! how noble in reason! how infinite in faculty! in form and moving how express and admirable! in action how like an angel! in apprehension how like a god! the beauty of the world! the paragon of animals!

The recognition of men and women as the highest creation of God is linked to the belief that He controls

the destiny of His children. Hamlet says, later on, to
Horatio (v. 2. 10–11):

> There's a divinity that shapes our ends,
> Rough-hew them how we will.

The play of *Hamlet* is interesting from a spiritual
point of view, for it reveals the mind of a philosopher
dissatisfied with the temporal and visible world and
all its inexplicable sin and pain, and reaching out
towards religious supernaturalism in an endeavour
to find the answer to its baffling mysteries. But the
human mind cannot penetrate beyond the veil, and
Hamlet can do no more than accept the dogmatic
explanations of the Church and content himself with
the conclusion, "There are more things in heaven
and earth than are dreamt of in your philosophy"
(i. 5. 167–168).

Faith in a divine Providence, which guards and
guides humanity, is strong in Shakespeare. He makes
even the guilty Macbeth declare: "In the great hand
of God I stand" (ii. 3. 136); and in *2 Henry VI* the
devout king to say, "God shall be my hope, my stay,
my guide and lantern to my feet" (ii. 3. 24–25).
Many passages reiterate this belief in a benign Providence overshadowing all.

God as the giver of all good things to man, including
food, shelter, and clothing, is a teaching of the Old
and New Testaments which finds a ready acceptance
with Shakespeare. No better lines could be selected
in this connection than those spoken by Old Adam
in *As You Like It*, when he gives Orlando his savings,
amounting to five hundred crowns (ii. 3. 43–45):

> Take that, and He that doth the ravens feed,
> Yea, providently caters for the sparrow,
> Be comfort to my age.

There can be no doubt that, as he wrote this, the Poet remembered verse 9 of Psalm cxlvii, He feedeth the young ravens that call upon Him, and the twenty-sixth verse of chapter vi of St. Matthew's Gospel, "Behold the fowls of the air: for they sow not, neither do they reap, nor gather into barns, yet your heavenly Father feedeth them." Additional importance is lent to this passage by the fact that Shakespeare wrote it for himself to speak on the stage, Old Adam being one of his own acting parts.

Shakespeare's concept of the Person of the Deity seems to have been the one, now growing daily less acceptable to religious thinkers, of a magnified mortal, a mighty potentate, seated on a golden throne in the heavens. This was the conventional view of his day, and even the Renaissance mind had done little to shake it. The Bishop of Winchester uses this description of God as found in the Prayer Book, when referring to the deceased king, Henry V: "He was a king bless'd of the King of kings" (*1 Henry VI*, 1. 1. 28). Earthly kings were only viceroys of the One Omnipotent and drew their authority from Him. In that famous chamber scene in Westminster Palace, when the dying Henry IV surprises Prince Harry trying on the Crown, the chastened and ashamed heir hands back the emblem of sovereignty to his father, saying (*2 Henry IV*, IV. 5. 143–155):

> There is your crown;
> And He that wears the crown immortally
> Long guard it yours!

This divine right of kings was fully accepted by all loyal subjects in Tudor times. Not until the next century was it challenged and discarded. The strength of Shakespeare's conviction is expressed through the person of Richard II (III. 2. 54–57):

> Not all the water in the rough rude sea
> Can wash the balm off from an anointed king;
> The breath of worldly men cannot depose
> The deputy elected by the Lord.

And further on in the same play (III. 3. 74–81):

> . . . we thought ourself thy lawful king:
> And if we be, how dare thy joints forget
> To pay their awful duty to our presence?
> If we be not, show us the hand of God
> That hath dismiss'd us from our stewardship;
> For well we know, no hand of blood and bone
> Can gripe the sacred handle of our sceptre,
> Unless he do profane, steal, or usurp.

Not only as a King was God represented by orthodox Christianity, but also as the righteous Judge of all mankind. The deeply religious sovereign, Henry VI, from whom many pious and sincere, if conventional, observations and assertions fall from time to time, remarks in the second play of the trilogy (III. 2. 136, 139–40):

> O Thou that judgest all things, stay my thoughts!
>
> .   .   .   .   .
>
> If my suspect be false, forgive me, God;
> For judgement only doth belong to Thee.

The acknowledgment that divine justice is infallible, unerring, impartial, and relentless is made by the Buckingham of *Richard III* as he stands before the "block of shame." In King Edward's time the Duke had prayed to heaven that doom might fall upon him if he were ever disloyal to the King or his heirs.

Ambition has led him to that very disloyalty, and he accepts his punishment with bowed head (v. 1. 20–22):

> That high All-seer that I dallied with
> Hath turn'd my feigned prayer on my head,
> And given in earnest what I begg'd in jest.

Closely connected with the conception of God as the Supreme Judge, who even in this world rewarded and punished mortals according to their deserts, was the apprehensive expectation of that terrible ordeal which lay beyond human life, the Day of Judgment. The Church taught that after death would come an intermediate state to be followed by the most awful of all experiences, the appearance before the judgment seat of God. Here those who had sinned would have to make open confession, bearing witness against themselves, and trusting to the divine mercy for the saving of their souls from Hell. No excuses or concealments would avail there, but pure justice would be done to all. Such thoughts as these trouble the guilty Claudius in *Hamlet*, when he prays to God to forgive him the murder of his brother, albeit with the inner conviction that no pardon can be his while he clings to the fruits of his sin. He observes very truly (III. 3. 57–64);

> In the corrupted currents of this world
> Offence's gilded hand may shove by justice,
> And oft 'tis seen the wicked prize itself
> Buys out the law: but 'tis not so above;
> There is no shuffling, there the action lies
> In his true nature, and we ourselves compell'd
> Even to the teeth and forehead of our faults,
> To give in evidence.

Shakespeare reverently attributes to God all the qualities with which the Bible endows Him. His wisdom, patience, love, justice are fully acknowledged. He is declared to be almighty, omniscient, "Him that all things knows" (*All's Well*, II. 1. 152). While just in punishing sin He is always ready with mercy and forgiveness for the penitent heart. It will be remembered how Portia in her famous speech in the trial scene of the *Merchant of Venice* says of mercy (IV. 1. 195-197):

> It is an attribute of God himself;
> And earthly power doth then show likest God's
> When mercy seasons justice.

Without further dwelling on the point, it is clear that Shakespeare's God was the God of the orthodox Christianity of his day.

If Shakespeare's idea of God commended itself to the orthodox, his declaration of man's duty towards his Maker must in equal degree have won clerical approval. Once again he followed closely the teaching of the Church. Exhortations to praise God are too numerous to need special quotation. The advice to trust Him—"leave it all to God" (*Richard III*, II. 3. 45) —is also repeated again and again. Submission to the will of God is seen in the devout—"To whom God will, there be the victory!" says Henry VI (*3 Henry VI*, II. 5. 15). Gratitude to God, with a becoming modesty as to one's own achievements, was the mark of a true Christian; and we find that Shakespeare's ideal Englishman, Henry V, is particularly careful of this godly requirement. After the battle of Agincourt the victor declares: "Praised be God, and not our strength for it!" (IV. 7. 90); and later on issues very definite orders to guide the conduct of his soldiers (IV. 8. 119–121):

> And be it death proclaimed through our host
> To boast of this or take that praise from God
> Which is his only.

The same king remarks that "nothing so becomes a man as modest stillness and humility" (III. 1. 4), though the demeanour is recommended only for the piping times of peace. Before a battle the righteous man often invokes God's blessing upon his arms, while the wicked is troubled by his misdeeds, and sometimes makes an eleventh-hour confession in a desperate effort to escape retribution. But though "By penitence the Eternal's wrath's appeased" (*Two Gentlemen of Verona*, v. 4. 81), that penitence must be sincere if past sins are to be cancelled.

Acknowledgment of God as the supreme Ruler of the universe, eternal, all-powerful, all-knowing, all-seeing, is genuine and frank in Shakespeare; and men are counselled to submit, obey, serve, trust, and praise, if they would attain the happiness of heaven.

There is nothing original, questioning, nor dissenting in Shakespeare's idea of God. It does not depart from the doctrine of the Church in any particular. In the speeches of Henry VI, who was, according to historical evidence, a deeply religious man, we should expect to find the very words of Christian theology. A careful dramatist would see to this; and we should not conclude therefrom that the sentiments expressed were necessarily his own. But the case of Hamlet is different. Hamlet was a meditative philosopher, reflecting, in all probability, much of Shakespeare's own individuality. When Hamlet also uses the orthodox language of Christianity, and the dogma of the Church is grafted on to a heathen story, often with an effect of incongruity, then we are entitled to assume that the Poet is voicing his religious convictions and telling us that those convictions were conventional.

Just as he borrowed freely the language of the Prayer Book in which to speak of God, so Shakespeare borrows it again in his references to Jesus Christ. He mentions very few of the biographical facts of Our Saviour's life antecedent to the supreme and final sacrifice on the Cross. He refers to the birth of Jesus in *Hamlet* (I. I. 159) and the name of the Virgin Mary (*Richard II*, II. I. 56); but he has nothing to say of His ministry, His gospel, and His miracles of healing. He alludes to the betrayal by Judas in several plays; but the whole of the Poet's reverent interest in Our Lord appears to be concentrated on that great purpose of His life, the Atonement.

The Atonement is one of the most perplexing mysteries in theology, and is as difficult to understand as to explain. Shakespeare, apparently, did not attempt to probe the problem for himself. He was content to accept the interpretation of his spiritual pastors. This involved the dogmas of the fall of Adam, original sin, and vicarious redemption by the agony of the Cross. Our Poet did not question any of them. Falstaff observes, "In the state of innocency Adam fell" (*I Henry IV*, III. 3. 185); and in *Henry V* the Archbishop of Canterbury, speaking of the sudden reformation of the young king on his accession, says to the Bishop of Ely (I. I. 28–31);

> Consideration like an angel came
> And whipp'd the offending Adam out of him,
> Leaving his body as a paradise,
> To envelop and contain celestial spirits.

The passages dealing with the Atonement are numerous and interesting. Shakespeare leaves us in no uncertainty as to his full concurrence in the teaching of the Church. There is no doubt that he believed in the efficacy of Jesus' sacrifice, and as a Christian, conscious of his own shortcomings, was full of the gratitude that fills the hearts of all true followers of the Nazarene. In *Measure for Measure* Isabella is brutally told by Angelo that her brother is a forfeit of the law. She cries out (II. 2. 72–75):

> Alas, alas!
> Why, all the souls that were, were forfeit once;
> And He that might the vantage best have took
> Found out the remedy.

John of Gaunt, in his famous speech on England in *Richard II*, speaks of the reputation of the English Kings in the Crusades (II. 1. 53–56):

> Renowned for their deeds as far from home,
> For Christian service and true chivalry,
> As is the sepulchre in stubborn Jewry
> Of the world's ransom, blessed Mary's Son.

When Henry IV was firmly established on the throne in place of his cousin Richard, he purposed leading an English expedition to the Holy Land (*1 Henry IV*, I. 1. 24–27):

> To chase these pagans in those holy fields
> Over whose acres walk'd those blessed feet,
> Which fourteen hundred years ago were nail'd
> For our advantage on the bitter cross.

One further extract from the plays citing the Atonement may be given. It occurs in *Richard III* where the imprisoned Clarence is visited in the Tower by the two murderers hired by the Crookback. Realizing their fell intention, Clarence addresses them (I. 4. 194–196):

> I charge you, as you hope to have redemption
> By Christ's dear blood shed for our grievous sins,
> That you depart, and lay no hands on me.

The above selections from his writings on the mission of Jesus and its fulfilment are corroborated by the direct statement of Shakespeare as contained in his Will. The first provision of the document reads: "I commend my soul into the hands of God my Creator, hoping and assuredly believing, through the only merits of Jesus Christ my Saviour, to be made partaker of life everlasting."

These words of the Will affirm Shakespeare's belief in the immortality of the soul—a belief that is reiterated in numerous passages in his works. Balthasar, informing Romeo of Juliet's supposed death, says, "Her immortal part with angels lives" (v. 1. 19). Cleopatra, about to commit suicide, declares, "I have immortal longings in me" (v. 2. 283). In *Measure for Measure* Claudio hears of the time of his execution in these words of the Provost: "By eight to-morrow Thou must be made immortal" (IV. 2. 67–68). In the romantic, moonlit garden of Belmont the poetic Lorenzo whispers into the ears of Jessica of the beauty of the stars and the music of the spheres (*Merchant of Venice*, v. 1. 63–65):

> Such harmony is in immortal souls;
> But while this muddy vesture of decay
> Doth grossly close it in, we cannot hear it.

When Hamlet prepares to follow the beckoning hand

of his father's ghost, Horatio is fearful for his safety and would restrain him. The Prince will not listen (I. 4. 64–67):

> Why, what should be the fear?
> I do not set my life at a pin's fee;
> And for my soul, what can it do to that,
> Being a thing immortal as itself?

It is impossible to omit Shakespeare's wonderful lines on the temporal nature of the body and the eternal quality of the soul, which are not put into the mouth of a dramatic figure, but are a direct pronouncement of the Poet in Sonnet CXLVI.

> Poor soul, the centre of my sinful earth,
> . . . these rebel powers that thee array,
> Why dost thou pine within and suffer dearth,
> Painting thy outward walls so costly gay?
> Why so large cost, having so short a lease,
> Dost thou upon thy fading mansion spend?
> Shall worms, inheritors of this excess,
> Eat up thy charge? is this thy body's end?
> Then, soul, live thou upon thy servant's loss,
> And let that pine to aggravate thy store;
> Buy terms divine in selling hours of dross;
> Within be fed, without be rich no more:
> So shalt thou feed on Death, that feeds on men,
> And, Death once dead, there's no more dying then.

Seeing that Shakespeare accepted fully the teaching of the Church on immortality, it is surprising to find, as we have previously remarked, that his death scenes have so little thought to give to life beyond the grave. His characters often seem to cling desperately to temporalities and keep their dying eyes fixed on earth instead of lifting them to their spiritual destiny.

In his views of Heaven, Shakespeare does not desert

his conventional standpoint. He uses the word frequently as a synonym for God, particularly in the Chronicle Plays; but there is a sufficiency of passages to reveal his orthodox concept of Heaven as an abode of bliss for the souls of the righteous, situated geographically above the clouds. The bereaved Constance, seeking spiritual consolation for the death of her son, Arthur, says to Cardinal Pandulph (*King John*, III. 4. 76–77):

> And, father cardinal, I have heard you say
> That we shall see and know our friends in heaven.

Shakespeare held the view, now somewhat old-fashioned, of a personal devil, called Satan, or Lucifer, and a hell-fire in which the damned were imprisoned in everlasting torment. His ideas of the underworld seem to be inextricably mixed with current superstition as to witches, devils, ghosts, and the evil eye. It may be stated again that there are few references to the Popish purgatory—evidence, we saw, of his anti-papal convictions.

Shakespeare subscribes to the orthodox idea of the good and evil angels, who were supposed to be continuously whispering their exhortations and temptations into the consciousness of every man and woman. The most striking use of this figure occurs in Sonnet CXLIV:

> Two loves I have of comfort and despair,
> Which like two spirits do suggest me still:
> The better angel is a man right fair,
> The worser spirit a woman colour'd ill.
> To win me soon to hell, my female evil
> Tempteth my better angel from my side,
> And would corrupt my saint to be a devil,
> Wooing his purity with her foul pride.

And whether that my angel be turn'd fiend
Suspect I may, yet not directly tell;
But, being both from me, both to each friend,
I guess one angel in another's hell:
  Yet this shall I ne'er know, but live in doubt,
  Till my bad angel fire my good one out.

Shakespeare's eschatological ideas were drawn from the Bible. Isa. li. 6 reads, "Lift up your eyes to the heavens, and look upon the earth beneath: for the heavens shall vanish away like smoke, and the earth shall wax old like a garment, and they that dwell therein shall die in like manner. . . ." This may be compared with Prospero's speech in *The Tempest* (IV. I. 148–156):

                      These our actors,
As I foretold you, were all spirits, and
Are melted into air, into thin air:
And, like the baseless fabric of this vision,
The cloud capp'd towers, the gorgeous palaces,
The solemn temples, the great globe itself,
Yea, all which it inherit, shall dissolve,
And, like this insubstantial pageant faded,
Leave not a rack behind.

Research brings us to one conclusion: that in matters of religious supernaturalism Shakespeare accepted the dogma of the Church, even repeating the orthodox language of Christianity, and left us no evidence that his reason was offended or his conscience troubled by the teachings of his spiritual pastors and masters.

XVI

CHURCH RITUAL AND OBSERVANCES

WE have seen that towards creed and dogma Shakespeare maintained an attitude of reverent acceptance, although he recognized that religion had to be translated into terms of everyday living if it was to be more than a superficial interest. His attitude towards church ritual was of much the same character. He was careful to observe all the forms and ceremonies laid down by the Prayer Book, but he did not mistake these outward signs and symbols for the regenerating and uplifting truth which lay behind them. He realized that ritual was helpful as a means of explaining the spiritual and abstract to unimaginative minds. He knew that solemnities aided worshippers to expel all mundane thoughts and concentrate on the sacred matters before them. He did not believe, however, that ritual possessed any efficacy of its own. It was only a means to an end.

There is no doubt that Shakespeare was interested in ritual. If he had no need of it himself in his religious life, he was tolerant enough not to criticize others who did need it. His own interest was probably limited to its attraction as a colourful spectacle, and a spectacle that could be used with great effect in the theatre. In other words, his interest was professional rather than religious.

Throughout his works, particularly in the Chronicle Plays and those in which friars and monks are introduced, Shakespeare reveals a close acquaintance with the rubric of the Roman Catholic Church.

Some have advanced this fact as evidence of his Catholicism. But he uses the Popish ritual as a dramatist and historian, writing of times prior to the Reformation, when England was still beneath the supremacy of the Pope, and all the Cardinals, Legates, Archbishops, and Bishops were servants of His Holiness. Nothing less could be expected of a playwright who did his work efficiently.

The great men of the Church were introduced in their gorgeous robes of office and were often attended by a considerable train, carrying, as we learn from the stage directions of *Henry VIII*, silver crosses and other insignia. The Bishops in their white vestments were valuable to an Elizabethan producer, compelled in the absence of scenery to depend for colour and contrast on costume. We frequently discover a hint in the dialogue as to how these ecclesiastics were robed. For example, in *2 Henry IV*, the Earl of Westmorland addresses the Archbishop of York (IV. I. 41, 45–46):

> You, Lord Archbishop,
>
> .   .   .   .   .
>
> Whose white investments figure innocence,
> The dove and very blessed spirit of peace.

The Poet was familiar with the rite of administering the sacrament to the dying, and honours the custom of paying all respects to the dead. Many corpses are brought on to the stage in Shakespearean drama, attended by guards, mourners, and holy men. One instance occurs early in *Richard III*, where the Lady Anne, following the bier of King Henry VI, is horrified at the sacrilegious action of Gloucester in interrupting the solemn funeral procession. Another rite mentioned in several instances by the Poet is that of confession. Juljet, wishing to consult Friar Laurence in secret as to her predicament, makes the following excuse through the Nurse (III. 5. 231–233):

> Go in, and tell my lady I am gone,
> Having displeased my father, to Laurence' cell,
> To make confession and to be absolved.

The Church is recognized as the channel of communication between God and man. In *2 Henry IV*, Prince John of Lancaster says to Scroop, Archbishop of York (IV. 2. 16–22):

> Who hath not heard it spoken,
> How deep you were within the books of God?
> To us, the speaker in his parliament;
> To us, the imagined voice of God himself;
> The very opener and intellingencer
> Between the grace, the sanctities of heaven,
> And our dull workings.

The Prince proceeds to castigate the Archbishop for misusing the reverence of his place and stirring up rebellion against his father, King Henry IV, "under the counterfeited zeal of God."

It was the custom of monarchs to consult the heads of the Church before embarking on some great enterprise in order to obtain a verdict on the righteousness and justice of their cause. Thus Henry V, before going "with his forces into France," consults the Archbishop of Canterbury on the validity of his claim to the French Crown. Sometimes, of course, when the Church's ruling did not coincide with the wishes of the king, it was disregarded. Bolingbroke is a case in point, when he ignored the protest of the Bishop of Carlisle against his usurpation of Richard II's throne.

Henry VIII, of course, went to the length of changing the whole national religion.

In *Richard III* another interesting rite is noticed. The Queen-Mother, Elizabeth, realizing the danger that threatens herself and her young sons at the hands of the Dukes of Gloucester and Buckingham, flies with the younger, the little Duke of York, to the sanctuary at Westminster. Buckingham is anxious to lay hands upon the Prince and requests Cardinal Bourchier to persuade his mother to release him. If she refuses, he purposes "from her jealous arms" to "pluck him perforce" (III. i. 36). The Cardinal replies (37–43):

> My Lord of Buckingham, if my weak oratory
> Can from his mother win the Duke of York,
> Anon expect him here; but if she be obdurate
> To mild entreaties, God in heaven forbid
> We should infringe the holy privilege
> Of blessed sanctuary! Not for all this land
> Would I be guilty of so deep a sin.

But Buckingham replies:

> You are too senseless-obstinate, my lord,
> Too ceremonious and traditional . . .

and by clever argument overrides the Cardinal's scruples.

As a conforming Protestant, Shakespeare was careful about all Church observances required of him. We have not been able to discover any record of disobedience on his part. He was never in conflict with the ecclesiastical authorities for defiance of the law. Prudence characterized his every religious action and speech.

The observance of Sunday and attendance at divine service were not left to individual preference, but were the law of the land, which imposed heavy penalties for infringement. The mark of a loyal and virtuous subject of the Queen was a regular appearance at Church. Moreover, the Bishops were not slack in enforcing the law and would compel churchwardens to give evidence against their own friends before magistrates, who were, however, not less kindly disposed towards the recusants. As in the case of John Shakespeare, the offenders were often let off on the feeblest of excuses, only to be "presented" again, if they continued to absent themselves from the Parish Church. An example of a docile Protestant is Mistress Page in the *Merry Wives of Windsor*, who, according to Mistress Quickly, is "as fartuous (virtuous) a civil modest wife, and one, I tell you, that will not miss you morning nor evening prayer, as any is in Windsor" (II. 2. 100–103). No doubt many of the Elizabethans were coaxed to Church by fear of the law rather than by spiritual enthusiasm.

From Benedick's remark, "Sigh away Sundays," in *Much Ado About Nothing* (I. 1. 204), it would seem that Shakespeare realized that to some people, at any rate, if not to himself, Sunday was often a dull day. Some critics see in the passage a dig at the gloomy way in which the Puritans passed the Day of Rest. Before Shakespeare had entered upon his theatrical career, they had succeeded in stopping the performance of Sunday plays, and made inroad into the actor's profits. Even when Sunday performances were allowed, they were not permitted to begin until after the times fixed for divine service. Then the Puritans asserted that people were induced to miss church in order that they might get to the theatre early and obtain a good seat.

Sunday as a day of rest is noticed in *Hamlet*, where Marcellus, commenting upon the warlike preparations in Denmark, complains that the "sore task does not divide the Sunday from the week" (i. i. 75–76), but proceeds with "sweaty haste" night and day. In *1 Henry IV* (iii. i. 261) we find an allusion to "Sunday-citizens," Shakespeare's way of describing people dressed up in their Sunday best.

From *The Taming of the Shrew* we learn that Sunday was a popular day for weddings. Baptista asks Petruchio how he has progressed in the wooing of his daughter, Katharina, and receives the reply, (ii. i. 299–300):

> . . . we have 'greed so well together,
> That upon Sunday is the wedding day.

Although Katharina retorts, "I'll see thee hang'd on Sunday first," Petruchio persuades them to accept his version of the matter. Baptista is pleased to consent, and decides that his younger daughter, Bianca, shall be married "on the Sunday following" (397). The action of the third act of *Othello* takes place on a Sunday, but Shakespeare's purpose in this is not very clear. Perhaps he wished to point a contrast between the Christian attitude towards Sunday and that of the free-thinking Moor.

One of the most striking features of the new religion was the introduction of the sermon. All parsons were obliged by statute to preach; but it was found in practice that many of the country priests were too ignorant to undertake the duty, while others were not sufficiently reliable in the holding of orthodox views. Until they satisfied their superiors on both these points, they were forbidden to compose their own sermons, but required to read the "homilies already set out, or other such necessary doctrine as is or shall be prescribed for the quiet instruction and edification of the people."[1]

Shakespeare has little to tell us of his own views on the sermon, though he does not appear to have had much taste for the long preaching of the Puritans. Timon of Athens replies somewhat impatiently to Flavius, "Come, sermon me no further (II. 2. 181). The Poet, to judge from the well-known lines from *As You Like It* (II. 1. 16–17), found the most appealing sermons in the beauties of nature:

> . . . tongues in trees, books in the running brooks,
> Sermons in stones, and good in everything.

A bone of contention between the orthodox Protestants and the Puritans was the wearing of the surplice, which the latter condemned as a relic of Popery. Shakespeare's only allusion occurs in *All's Well* (I. 3. 97–100), which we have quoted in our Puritan chapter. Its exact meaning is somewhat obscure.

> Though honesty be no puritan, yet it will do no hurt; it will wear the surplice of humility over the black gown of a big heart.

As to the ceremony of baptism, we have already noted that Shakespeare seems to have accepted the doctrine of Baptismal Grace as taught in the Church of England.[2] This, we argued, was additional proof of his religious conventionality. Two passages appear

---

[1] *Parker's Advertisements*, 1565–1566; Prother, *Select Statutes*, p. 191.
[2] See *Shakespeare's Knowledge and Use of the Bible*, Bishop Wordsworth, p. 231.

to support the Anglican point of view. Henry V, seeking confirmation of the validity of his French claims from the Archbishop of Canterbury, says to His Grace (I. 2. 30–32):

> For we will hear, note and believe in heart
> That what you speak is in your conscience wash'd
> As pure as sin with baptism.

In *Othello* Iago says Desdemona's influence over her husband is such that she could

> . . . win the Moor, were 't to renounce his baptism,
> All seals and symbols of redeemed sin.
>
> (II. 3. 349–350.)

Juliet, bewailing the fact that her lover, Romeo, bears the name of Montague, hateful to the Capulets, begs him to doff his name and take herself in payment. Romeo declares with enthusiasm (II. 2. 49–50):

> I take thee at thy word:
> Call me but love, and I'll be new baptized.

The Poet has few references to baptism in his works, but we know from the registers that his first child, Susanna, was baptized at the Parish Church on Trinity Sunday, 1583, according to the ceremony in the Prayer Book. Two years later his twins, Judith and Hamnet, were likewise baptized in the same church and according to the same rites.

Shakespeare was clearly interested deeply in the matter of Christian burial. He alludes to it more often than to any other rite of the Church. Numerous references are scattered throughout the plays, while his own last words pronounced a curse upon any that should disturb his bones.[1]

---

[1] The Lines on the Grave.

The dramatist emphasized the necessity of paying all respect to the dead. Victorious soldiers invariably accord due funeral rites to their conquered and slain enemy. Even murderers and usurpers are unwilling to deprive their victims of this final solemnity. According to the importance of the deceased in life, so were his obsequies. After Marc Antony's eulogy of the fallen Brutus at the end of *Julius Cæsar*, Octavius says (v. 5. 76–79):

> According to his virtue let us use him,
> With all respect and rites of burial.
> Within my tent his bones to-night shall lie,
> Most like a soldier, order'd honourably.

Sir William Lucy in *1 Henry VI* begs the bodies of the fallen English nobles from the victorious French (iv. 7. 85–86):

> . . . that I may bear them hence
> And give them burial as beseems their worth.

In *Romeo and Juliet* Shakespeare touches upon the different customs that attended a funeral in his day. Arrangements have been made for Juliet's wedding to Paris; and when the news of her sad and tragic death is brought, Capulet says (iv. 5. 84–90):

> All things that we ordained festival,
> Turn from their office to black funeral:
> Our instruments to melancholy bells;
> Our wedding cheer to a sad burial feast;
> Our solemn hymns to sullen dirges change;
> Our bridal flowers serve for a buried corse,
> And all things change them to the contrary.

Another reference to the funeral feast occurs in *Hamlet*, when the Prince, stung to bitterness at the thought of his mother's hasty remarriage, says to Horatio, "The funeral baked-meats Did coldly furnish forth the marriage tables" (I. 2. 180–181).

The custom of tolling the bell at funerals is referred to again in *Titus Andronicus* (v. 3. 197): but lines more certainly from Shakespeare's hand occur in Sonnet LXXI:

> No longer mourn for me when I am dead
> Than you shall hear the surly sullen bell
> Give warning to the world that I am fled
> From this vile world, with vilest worms to dwell:
> Nay, if you read this line, remember not
> The hand that writ it.

In *Cymbeline* the custom of strewing the grave with flowers is mentioned. Over the body of Fidele, Arviragus says (IV. 2. 218–220):

> With fairest flowers,
> Whilst summer lasts, and I live here, Fidele,
> I'll sweeten thy sad grave.

In the same play we have a notice of the usage of the Church of laying the dead looking to the East. Guiderius, still concerned with the interment of Fidele, says (255–256): "We must lay his head to the east; My father hath a reason for 't." As *Cymbeline* is concerned with pagan times, the Christian reason for so burying the dead is not given. It is done because "that is the attitude of prayer, and because at the last trump they will hurry eastwards."[1]

It is no easy matter to sift the Shakespearean wheat from the other writers' chaff in *Titus Andronicus*; and in selecting passages from that early play, we cannot be confident that we are quoting Shakespeare.

---

[1] *Encyclopædia Britannica*, 13th Ed., XI. 331.

It will be as well to note, however, that the desirability of burial among one's ancestors is touched upon in two passages (I. I. 84 and v. 3. 192).

Quite the most interesting of the poet's references to the rite of Christian burial occurs in the grave-diggers scene of *Hamlet*. The question in this case is whether Ophelia has committed suicide and so deprived herself of the right to the full obsequies and interment in consecrated ground. The two grave-diggers argue the point and get thoroughly entangled in the legal reasoning, mixing up justifiable homicide in self-defence with *felo-de-se* to the great amusement of the intelligent audience. (It may be remarked, parenthetically, that the dramatist shows himself quite familiar with the law of burial and coroners' inquests. Fripp[1] calls attention to the fact that the case of the suicide of Katharine Hamlet startled Stratford when Shakespeare was fifteen. He believes that the Poet was then a clerk in an attorney's office, and makes the interesting suggestion that many of the details of Ophelia's end were drawn from the real-life tragedy of Katharine Hamlet.)

The Coroner's inquest found that Ophelia had thrown herself into the water, but was not at the time fully responsible for her actions. It was decreed that she was entitled to Christian burial, though the grave-diggers believe the finding would have been different if she had not been a gentlewoman. The Church is not wholly convinced by the Coroner's verdict and does not see its way to accord full rites to Ophelia. Hamlet, surprised by the arrival of the cortège at the churchyard, says (v. I. 241–244):

[1] *Shakespeare Studies*, pp. 132–133.

> The queen, the courtiers: who is this they follow?
> And with such maimed rites? This doth betoken
> The corse they follow did with desperate hand
> Fordo its own life: 'twas of some estate.

Laertes, Ophelia's brother, is indignant at the curtailed solemnities. "What ceremony else?" he inquires of the head Priest, and receives the answer (249–257):

> Her obsequies have been as far enlarged
> As we have warranty: her death was doubtful;
> And, but that great command o'ersways the order,
> She should in ground unsanctified have lodged
> Till the last trumpet; for charitable prayers,
> Shards, flints, and pebbles should be thrown on her:
> Yet here she is allow'd her virgin crants [garlands],
> Her maiden strewments and the bringing home
> Of bell and burial.

Laertes still asks, "Must there no more be done?" and the Priest remains firm (258–261):

> No more be done:
> We should profane the service of the dead
> To sing a requiem and such rest to her
> As to peace-parted souls.

Laertes is furious, and prophesies that his sister shall be "a ministering angel" when "the churlish priest" "lies howling."

The law, which Shakespeare knew so well and criticized so effectively in *Hamlet*, forbade the burial of suicides with religious rites and in consecrated ground until the Burial Laws Amendment Act, 1880, modified the harshness of its decree.

A passage from *Titus Andronicus* states the case of that wretched and unfortunate sinner who is denied all final solemnities. It refers to the villainous Queen of the Goths (v. 3. 195–200):

> As for that heinous tiger, Tamora,
> No funeral rite, nor man in mourning weeds,
> No mournful bell shall ring her burial;
> But throw her forth to beasts and birds of prey:
> Her life was beastly and devoid of pity,
> And, being so, shall have like want of pity.

On holy matrimony Shakespeare has much to say. We are not concerned at the moment with his ethical view of marriage except to observe that he considered it a sacred, blessed, and happy state, which all should idealize. He strongly upheld the sanctity of the marriage vow, as Hamlet's disgust at his mother's conduct fully verifies. He also refers in *Henry V* to "God, the best maker of all marriages" (v. 2. 387).

The marriage customs of Shakespeare's time were rather different to those prevailing to-day. The betrothed couple were first united by a civil contract, which was followed, sometimes at a considerable interval, by the religious ceremony. Men and women cohabited between the two ceremonies, and any children born were legitimate, but the wife could not claim her dowry until the Church had added its blessing. An exact circumstance of this nature is described in *Measure for Measure*, where Claudio says (I. 2. 149–155):

> Thus stands it with me: upon a true contract
> I got possession of Julietta's bed:
> You know the lady; she is fast my wife,
> Save that we do the denunciation lack
> Of outward order: this we came not to,
> Only for propagation of a dower
> Remaining in the coffer of her friends.

Juliet is with child; and the Puritan deputy of the Duke, Angelo, censures Claudio for the omission of the Church rites and promises to take extreme measures against him.

Angelo represents the Puritan point of view in regard to the double marriage ceremony; and in this case there was a growing body of public opinion, which was ready to advise young couples: "To the church; take the priest, clerk, and some sufficient honest witnesses" (*Taming of the Shrew*, IV. 4. 94). At the time of writing *Measure for Measure* Shakespeare sympathized with Claudio, whose case was apparently a repetition of his own. Towards the end of his life, however, he seems to have seen the defects and dangers of the system, and, like many of his contemporaries, adopted the Puritan demand. On giving his consent to the betrothal of Miranda and Ferdinand in *The Tempest*, Prospero warns the young man (IV. 1. 15-19):

> If thou does break her virgin-knot before
> All sanctimonious ceremonies may
> With full and holy rite be minister'd,
> No sweet aspersion shall the heavens let fall
> To make this contract grow.

A Christian observance on which Shakespeare eloquently insists is that of Prayer. The Elizabethan Church was in the habit of calling the people to prayer in times of national danger, in the flush of victory, and during those terrible seasons of plague. It was natural, then, for Shakespeare to give a prominent place in his drama to appeals to the Almighty, and wonderful prayers are put in the mouths of some of his hero characters. A famous example is that of Richmond on the eve of the battle of Bosworth (*Richard III*, v. 3. 108-117):

O Thou, whose captain I account myself,
Look on my forces with a gracious eye;
Put in their hands thy bruising irons of wrath,
That they may crush down with a heavy fall
The usurping helmets of our adversaries!
Make us thy ministers of chastisement,
That we may praise thee in the victory!
To thee I do commend my watchful soul,
Ere I let fall the windows of mine eyes:
Sleeping and waking, O, defend me still!

With this may be compared Henry V's prayer before Agincourt (IV. 1. 306–312; 319–322):

O God of battles! steel my soldiers' hearts;
Possess them not with fear; take from them now
The sense of reckoning, if the opposed numbers
Pluck their hearts from them. Not to-day, O Lord,
O, not to-day, think not upon the fault
My father made in compassing the crown!
I Richard's body have interred new:

.   .   .   .   .

. . . More will I do,
Though all that I can do is nothing worth,
Since that my penitence comes after all,
Imploring pardon.

The prayer of thanksgiving is strongly advocated by the Poet; while the prayer of pity is begged from the multitude by those who, as the Duke of Buckingham in *Henry VIII*, are led away to execution.

One of the most striking scenes in *Hamlet* is the refusal of the Prince, now certain of Claudius's guilt, to slay him when he surprises him at prayer. The words of Claudius himself are a homily on the necessity of sincerity in prayer. He knows he can expect no response from God to his petition to be forgiven his fault while tightly grasping the worldly gains for which that fault was committed. At the end he gives up the attempt and rises from his knees, saying (III. 3. 97–98):

> My words fly up, my thoughts remain below:
> Words without thoughts never to heaven go.

Imogen had a beautiful idea of the duty and efficacy of prayer, when she prayed three times daily for her absent lover, Posthumus, and would have appealed to him to do the same for her, had not her father hindered their leave-taking (*Cymbeline*, I. 3. 30–33). She tells Pisanio she would

> . . . have charged him [Posthumus]
> At the sixth hour of morn, at noon, at midnight,
> To encounter me with orisons, for then
> I am in heaven for him.

The value of prayer is further expounded in the Epilogue of *The Tempest*.

> And my ending is despair,
> Unless I be relieved by prayer,
> Which pierces so, that it assaults
> Mercy itself, and frees all faults.

The Christian duty to pray for others, particularly for one's enemies, is urged by Shakespeare. The following lines are from *Richard III* (I. 3. 316–317):

> A virtuous and a Christian-like conclusion,
> To pray for them that have done scathe to us.

Menecrates in *Antony and Cleopatra* reminds us that our prayers are often unanswered because we ask for things contrary to our highest interests (II. 1. 5–8):

> We, ignorant of ourselves,
> Beg often our own harms, which the wise powers
> Deny us for our good: so find we profit
> By losing of our prayers.

Shakespeare was, without doubt, a prayerful man, who never overlooked this important religious duty, and urged it upon his fellows.

Another observance, now somewhat gravely neglected, is that of saying grace before meals. In Shakespeare's day people were generally careful to perform this rite, to judge from the devotional manuals of Edward VI and Elizabeth. Shakespeare himself referred to the custom in a number of plays. In *The Taming of the Shrew* Petruchio and Katharina sit down to supper in Petruchio's country house. The former says, "Will you give thanks, sweet Kate; or else shall I?" (IV. 1. 162). Even when his scene is set in pagan times, the Poet introduces the subject of grace; and in his defence we must recall the heathen practice of pouring out a libation to the gods before commencing a banquet. The following lines of *Coriolanus* were obviously written by a man accustomed to return thanks for good things received. The scene is a camp at a small distance from Rome, and the speakers are Aufidius, the Volscian general, and his Lieutenant (IV. 7. 1–6):

> *Auf.* Do they still fly to the Roman [Coriolanus]?
> *Lieu.* I do not know what witchcraft's in him, but
> Your soldiers use him as the grace 'fore meat,
> Their talk at table and their thanks at end;
> And you are darken'd in this action, sir,
> Even by your own.

The most striking grace in Shakespeare is that spoken by Timon of Athens, heathen though he is. It begins (III. 6. 79–85):

You great benefactors, sprinkle our society with thankfulness.
For your own gifts, make yourselves praised: but reserve still to

give, lest your deities be despised. Lend to each man enough, that one need not lend to another; for, were your godheads to borrow of men, men would forsake the gods. . . .

Another grace, of a somewhat different character, appears in the same play, and is spoken by Apemantus (I. 2. 63–72). The line preceding the grace itself reads, "Feasts are too proud to give thanks to the gods," which is interpreted by some critics as a protest by the Poet against the omission of grace at public banquets.

It will be remembered that in the *Merchant of Venice* Bassanio is diffident about allowing his rather wild companion, Gratiano, to accompany him to Belmont. He consents, when Gratiano promises to be most circumspect in his behaviour, even undertaking "while grace is saying," to "hood mine eyes thus with my hat, and sigh, and say 'amen' " (II. 2. 202). This was probably another of Shakespeare's sly digs at the Puritans.

Another interesting passage occurs in the conversation between Lucio and Two Gentlemen in *Measure for Measure* (I. 2. 14–27):

First Gent. There's not a soldier of us all that, in the thanksgiving before meat, do relish the petition well that prays for peace.

Sec. Gent. I never heard any soldier dislike it.

Lucio I believe thee; for I think thou never wast where grace was said.

Sec. Gent. No? a dozen times at least.

First Gent. What, in metre?

Lucio In any proportion or in any language.

First Gent. I think, or in any religion.

Lucio. Ay, why not? Grace is grace, despite of all controversy: as, for example, thou thyself art a wicked villain, despite of all grace.

(Bishop Wordsworth[1] explains the word "proportion" as "prose or verse, chant or hymn.")

Lucio's "graceless" pun had already been used by Shakespeare in *1 Henry IV* (I. 2. 18–22), which may conclude our quotations on this subject.

Falstaff God save thy grace—majesty, I should say, for grace
    thou wilt have none—
Prince What, none?
Falstaff No, by my troth, not so much as will serve to be prologue
    to an egg and butter.

Falstaff humorously suggests that the more meagre the fare the shorter the grace.

The only Shakespearean reference to the great festivals of the Church which has any religious significance is the passage in *Hamlet* on Christmas (I. I. 158–164):

> Some say that ever 'gainst that season comes
> Wherein our Saviour's birth is celebrated,
> This bird of dawning singeth all night long:
> And then, they say, no spirit dare stir abroad,
> The nights are wholesome, then no planets strike,
> No fairy takes nor witch hath power to charm,
> So hallow'd and so gracious is the time.

The other allusions to Christmas touch upon its lighter side. We hear of "a Christmas comedy" in *Love's Labour's Lost* (V. 2. 462) and "a Christmas gambold" in *The Taming of the Shrew* (Induction II. 140). The only mention of Easter describes it as a time when new doublets are worn. (*Romeo and Juliet*, III. I. 30): and as to Whitsuntide we hear of its pastorals (*The Winter's Tale*, IV. 4. 134), its morris dances

[1] *Shakespeare's Knowledge and Use of the Bible*, p. 153.

(*Henry V*, II. 4. 25), and its "pageants of delight" (*Two Gentlemen of Verona*, IV. 4. 163).

Private feasting and a public fast are contrasted in *Lucrece* (891). The only other reference to fasting occurs in *Pericles*: "fish for fasting-days" (II. 1. 86). It is interesting that the Wednesday fast was inaugurated by Elizabeth, not so much to advance piety, as to help the English fishing industry.

Shakespeare's attitude towards all religious observances was consistent with his ready acceptance of Christian doctrine. He was orthodox, a conforming Protestant of the central school of thought. He accepted the Church's explanations of things that transcended mortal vision and was obedient in taking the necessary earthly steps for his ultimate salvation.

XVII

SHAKESPEARE AND THE SCRIPTURES

THE manner in which the most penetrating and respected of critics can find themselves in honest disagreement on Shakespearean matters of first importance is revealed in a study of the Poet's knowledge and use of Holy Scripture. One school of thought agrees with Dr. Furnivall that "he is saturated with the Bible story," and with Bishop Wordsworth, who describes him as "in a more than ordinary degree, a diligent, and a devout reader of the Word of God."[1] Another school of thought supports Sir Sidney Lee, who does not consider that Shakespeare's Bible knowledge was greater than a clever boy would acquire at school or in church on Sundays; and J. J. Jusserand, who says: "His biblical allusions are numerous, but commonplace, most of them, and they do not denote any exceptional knowledge of the Scriptures."[2]

To reach our own conclusions, we must examine Shakespeare's indebtedness to the Bible from three angles. Firstly, we must consider his wealth of reference to the facts, history, characters, and parable stories of the Old and New Testaments; when we shall, I think, decide that the Poet knew his Bible a great deal better than most people do to-day. We must not forget, however, that in Good Queen Bess's reign the Bible was the one book that was familiar to all Englishmen, and was very useful to a popular dramatist in consequence. Secondly, we must try to measure

[1] *Shakespeare's Knowledge and Use of the Bible*, p. 2.
[2] *A Literary History of the English People*, III. 170.

the Poet's obligation to Holy Writ for language, expression, poetic imagery, elucidation, and simile. And in this connection we must remember how compulsory attendance at Church to hear the Bible read had made the people so well acquainted with the very diction of the English translations that everyday speech and conversation were largely influenced by it. Nevertheless, we shall, I believe, find that Shakespeare's literary borrowings are more than could be expected from incidental or listless attendance at divine service. Thirdly, we must determine how far his own ethical philosophy was derived from the teaching of Scripture, particularly the Gospel. We have seen that in regard to matters which are beyond the range of the mortal senses, Shakespeare accepted, without questioning, the Christian doctrine. We shall be able to satisfy ourselves that in the sphere of human experience also the Bible influenced his ethical attitude.

Hitherto I have spoken of the Bible as if there were only one version extant to which Shakespeare could have referred. There were, of course, numerous English translations available to him; and now that we have, as it were, cleared the decks for our discussion, it will be well to describe them. This is all the more necessary, since no small controversy has raged over the question of the version used by the Poet.

The first complete translation of the Scriptures into English was made in the fourteenth century and is known as the Wycliffite Bible. The first time any part of the Scriptures was *printed* in English was in 1525, when William Tyndale, in the face of bitter opposition and stupendous difficulties, produced his version of the New Testament. Between 1536 and

1540 numerous editions of this work were issued. Tyndale was also responsible for a translation of the Pentateuch.

The earliest complete English Bible to appear in print was the work of Miles Coverdale, issued in 1535, and licensed by the King in 1537. In the same year another Bible, the work of John Rogers, was published in folio and printed in black-letter or old English lettering. This was known as Matthew's Bible (Rogers used Thomas Matthew as a *nom de plume*) and was also licensed. Printers were quick to see that the publication of Bibles was a profitable business; and in 1539 a further edition, edited by Richard Taverner, appeared.

All the foregoing translations of the Scriptures were the work of private individuals; and before the publishers could circulate them it was necessary to obtain a royal licence. In 1539, however, these early versions were superseded by the issue of the first authorized version, known as the Great Bible. It enjoyed the warranty of Cranmer, Archbishop of Canterbury, and Thomas Cromwell, the chief Secretary of State. Coverdale was the editor, and Richard Grafton and Edward Whitchurch the printers. Its name was suggested by its folio format. The *Encyclopædia Britannica* says,[1] "The title-page represents Henry VIII giving the 'Word of God' to Cromwell and Cranmer, who, in their order, distribute it to laymen and clerics, and describes the volume as 'truly translated after the veryte of the Hebreue and Greke texts by ye dylygent studye of dyverse excellent learned men, expert in the forsayde tongues.'"

Cromwell ordered a copy of the Great Bible to be set up in every church of the land, where all parish-

[1] Vol. III. p. 900 (13th ed.).

ioners could read it. The people required little encouragement and willingly gathered to listen whenever some accomplished reader would officiate for their benefit. The number of books required to carry out Cromwell's order was 11,000; and seven editions of the Great Bible were therefore called for in the space of two years. In the second (1540) edition a long preface by the Archbishop of Canterbury was added, with the notice, "This is the Byble apoynted to the vse in churches," on the title-page. This edition became known as "Cranmer's Bible."

Tyndale's New Testament and Pentateuch were forbidden in 1543, and Coverdale's version in 1546. Other proscriptions suppressed all but the Great Bible itself. There followed also a reversal of religious policy, which, instead of giving all and sundry access to the Scriptures, confined their reading to the upper and educated classes. After the death of Henry VIII, however, the ban was lifted, and the common people were permitted once more to enjoy the guidance and comfort of Holy Writ. The result was a great revival of biblical study.

In the first Prayer Book of Edward VI, the psalms, epistles, and gospels were taken from the Great Bible. During Mary's reign all translations of Scripture were rigorously suppressed in accordance with the inveterate opposition of the Roman Church to the Bible in the vernacular. With the accession of Elizabeth the Great Bible regained its liberty, and the Elizabethan Prayer Book retained its gospels, epistles, and psalms intact. Indeed, the old version of the psalms was still preferred when the Bishops' Bible had superseded the Great Bible as the authorised version of Elizabeth's reign.

When, however, the Great Bible was restored after the death of Catholic Mary, it found itself in competition with a serious rival. Many of the staunch Protestant party had fled from the Roman persecution in England to the sanctuary of Geneva, the headquarters of the Calvinists and the home of their great leader, Calvin. Coverdale himself was among the refugees; and he and others employed their time on a new and better translation of the Scriptures. Firstly, they completed the New Testament; and, despite the vigilance of Catholic enemies, were able to smuggle some copies into England in 1557, where they made considerable impression. Besides Coverdale, William Whittingham, Anthony Gilby, Thomas Sampson, and probably John Knox as well, were busily employed on the new translation, and had completed the whole book from Genesis to Revelation, including the Apocrypha, by 1560.

At this date there was no religious or legal obstacle to the sale of the new version in England; and, becoming known as the Genevan Bible, it quickly won a remarkable popularity. Its success was thoroughly deserved. Not only was the translation a great improvement on its predecessors, but the book was issued in convenient quarto form and printed in Roman type, which was so much more easily read than the Old English of the Great Bible. For the first time the text was divided into chapter and verse; and italics were used to denote words which were not represented in the original Hebrew or Greek. There were pictures, maps, and explanatory marginal notes; and the price was within the purse of multitudes who could never hope to purchase the authorized version. The sale of the Genevan Bible was enormous;

and, although it was forbidden to read from it in churches, it became the Bible of the people and the Bible of the home. Nearly two hundred editions were issued between 1560 and the Civil War; and the Great Bible was almost eclipsed by its more useful, cheaper, and up-to-date rival.

The influence of the Genevan Bible grew so rapidly during the first decade of Elizabeth's reign that the Bishops of the Established Church took steps to counter it. To this end they produced in 1568 what became known as the Bishops' Bible, which owed its existence to the energy of Archbishop Parker. It superseded the Great Bible as the authorized version of the time, and legal enactments compelled its use in churches. But it was a large and expensive volume, and consequently could not compete with the Genevan version as the Bible of the household. It is, indeed, doubtful if even the strong measures by which its public reading was enforced succeeded in keeping the Genevan Bible wholly out of the churches. Even scholars were not satisfied that the translations of the new Bible were an improvement on its forerunner; while the public generally found it ill-adapted to its requirements. The Bishops' Bible lasted about forty years, the latest date on any copy being 1606. It was superseded by the King James version, now famous the world over.

The Roman party had regarded the different versions of the Bible in the vulgar tongue with unrelenting hostility. The old Church would have liked to retain their practice of denying the laity direct access to Holy Writ and keeping them dependent upon the interpretation of the priest. But the advent of the New Learning had made this position untenable. The Catholics were driven to the disagreeable necessity either of issuing a version of their own or allowing the Catholic influence to wane while the people imbibed their scriptural knowledge at Protestant wells. The translations of the Roman Church were late in the field. The New Testament was printed at Rheims in 1582; but not until 1609-1610 was the entire Bible published at Douai. The Rheims and Douai version, as it was called, was not a success. The translation from the Latin vulgate was much too literal. When the English was not stilted it was ambiguous, and not infrequently altogether unintelligible. It could not hope to hold its own with the popular Bible of Geneva.

At a conference of the High Church and Low Church parties at Hampton Court in 1604, James I inaugurated a revision of the Bishops' Bible, which was completed and published in 1611. This, our much beloved Authorized Version, is recognized among all English-speaking peoples as the real English Bible. So well did the scholars employed do their work that no official effort to improve their rendering was made until the Revised Version was undertaken in the latter half of the nineteenth century.

We are now able to revert to the question: Which Bible did Shakespeare use? A profitable beginning can be made be eliminating the versions he certainly did not use. King James's Authorized Version was issued in 1611, the year in which the dramatist was engaged upon his last play, *The Tempest*. Only his contributions to the pageant of *Henry VIII* followed; and it is therefore obvious that the Poet owed nothing to this translation. It is, however, not unlikely that the translation owed much to Shakespeare in the field of language and expression. Again, the Douai Bible of the Roman Catholic party, published in 1609–1610, when the Poet's career was almost at an end, could not possibly have had any influence on his style. All the very early printed translations of Scripture were proscribed in the reign of Henry VIII. There remain as possible sources, therefore, the Great Bible, the Genevan Bible, the Bishops' Bible, and the Rheims translation of the New Testament. All these were available to the Poet. When he was a boy, the Great Bible was by no means obsolete. Although it was superseded for reading in Churches by the Bishops' Bible in 1568, yet the gospels, epistles, and psalms from this version were retained in the Prayer Book. Attending Church as a conforming Protestant, Shakespeare would receive much of his Bible knowledge in the language of the Great Bible by way of the Prayer Book. The direct readings of Scripture would be in the words of the Bishops' Bible. His home instruction and private reading would probably be from the popular, handy, and cheap Genevan version.

Reading the plays of Shakespeare with this purpose in mind, and comparing his biblical references with the different renderings in the Bibles available to him, we find echoes of all three versions. Mr. Thomas Carter in *Shakespeare and Holy Scripture: with the version he used* gives quotations from all the 37 plays, *Venus and Adonis, Lucrece,* and the Sonnets, and compares them with the rendering in the Genevan Bible. The study proves without any doubt that the Poet was familiar with the Calvinist version; and probably, like most of his contemporaries, his own private copy was Genevan. The citation of these parallels does not, however, prove that this was the *only* version of the

Bible to which he referred and with which he was familiar. If we take a wider aspect and survey the question in the manner of Mr. H. R. D. Anders in his *Shakespeare's Books*,[1] we are able to recognize the renderings of the Bishops' Bible and the Great Bible in numerous instances in the plays. The Poet's retentive memory stored up phrase and simile that appealed to him on reading or hearing them; and it would not be surprising to learn that, when he came to use them in his work, he could not give off-hand the version from which they were borrowed.

In examining Shakespearean plays for parallels to Bible renderings, care must be exercised to make as certain as possible that the passage in question was actually written by Shakespeare. We know that he worked upon old plays to a large extent and often retained considerable portions of the old writer's dialogue. Biblical allusions occurring in such portions are obviously not Shakespearean and prove nothing. Neglect to take this circumstance into account has misled people into thinking that there are echoes of the New Testament of the Catholics in Shakespeare. There are indeed passages which are undoubtedly derived from the Rheims text; but these passages appear in the old versions of the plays before Shakespeare touched them. There is nothing in the genuine Shakespearean portions that recall the Rheims version, from which we conclude that Shakespeare was unacquainted with that version and could not for that reason have been a Roman Catholic.

Another difficulty in estimating Shakespeare's relation to Scripture is the fact that the Bible translations and Shakespeare's works are literary products of the

[1] See *Shakespeare's England*, I. 76.

same age. As we should expect to find in contemporary writings, the same words, phrases, and expressions are used, not because one party was influenced by the other, but because these words and phrases were then commonly current. Because many such are either no longer used or have taken on a new meaning, we are apt to be the more struck by these resemblances and to suspect borrowing and imitation. For these various reasons I do not think I am justified in giving space here to extended quotations side by side with their Biblical parallels. This task has been performed by other writers, who have been able to show to most people's satisfaction that Shakespeare's knowledge of the versions of the Bible was extensive and his use prolific.

To set out to try to prove that Shakespeare was solely indebted to one particular version of the Bible is, in my view, to attempt to prove the impossible and untrue. I have no doubt that he was instructed himself from the Genevan Bible, that he chose the names for his daughters from two of its books, that he reared his children on it, and that he used it for his own private study and reading. We have satisfied ourselves that he was a conforming Protestant and would, therefore, hear the Bishops' version read to him in church every Sunday. Direct access to the Great Bible he did not have, but its psalms, gospels, and epistles were preserved for him in the Prayer Book. Remembering the Poet's wonderful gifts of acquiring and retaining all that he heard, saw, or read, we should expect to find the influence of all three versions in his works. This is the case; and all that critical study could ever prove is that he was more familiar with one version than another.

Dismissing the matter of the particular version, it is now possible to examine the Poet's knowledge and use of the Bible generally in his dramatic art. As the Rev. Ronald Bayne writes,[1] his handling of the Book of books "was in no sense professional or theological." He took full advantage of it as a man of letters and a dramatist. He availed himself of the people's close acquaintance with its teaching, history, and language; and he found in it a storehouse of literary treasure, familiar to, and understood by, his audience.

Firstly, we promised ourselves to consider how numerous and apt are the Poet's references to the history and characters of the Scriptures. If we follow in chronological order the important events and personages of the Bible noted by Shakespeare, we shall be able to dismiss at once the suggestion that his scriptural knowledge was meagre. He mentions, in various connections, the Creation, Adam, the Fall of Man, the death of Abel, the curse of Cain, Noah, his three sons who re-people the Earth, the descent of Europe from Japhet, Abraham, Jacob, and Laban, Pharaoh's dream of the lean kine, the Plagues of darkness and the death of the first-born, the law in the Book of Numbers, Deborah, Jephthah, David and Goliath, the Queen of Sheba's visit to Solomon, Job, Nebuchadnezzar, and Daniel of the Book of Susannah in the Apocrypha; and this list is by no means complete. Turning to the New Testament, we have already noted Shakespeare's frequent thought of Jesus and, in particular, his gratitude for the culminating act of His ministry, the Atonement. We find allusions also to the slaughter of the innocents by

[1] See *Shakespeare's England*, I. 76.

Herod, the twelve Apostles, the treachery of Judas, the washing of his hands by Pilate, the Crucifixion, and St. Paul. These references to the Bible story are direct; but the indirect references are more numerous, though not so easily recognized. For example: in *2 Henry VI*, Eleanor, Duchess of Gloucester, is condemned for treason; and her husband, Duke Humphrey, thus addresses himself (II. 3. 17–19):

> Mine eyes are full of tears, my heart of grief.
> Ah, Humphrey, this dishonour in thine age
> Will bring thy head with sorrow to the ground.

Shakespeare was thinking of the words of Jacob in Genesis (xlii. 38), when his sons wished to take Benjamin, the youngest, with them on their return to Egypt: "If mischief befall him by the way in the which ye go, then shall ye bring down my gray hairs with sorrow to the grave." Indirect references to persons and events of the New Testament can also be discerned. In *Hamlet* we have the following dialogue (I. 1. 147–150):

> *Bernardo* It was about to speak, when the cock crew.
> *Horatio* And then it started like a guilty thing
> Upon a fearful summons.

We may compare the experience of Peter as recorded in St. Matthew (xxvi. 74–75): "Then he began to curse and to swear, saying, I know not the man. And immediately the cock crew. And Peter remembered the word of Jesus, which said unto him, Before the cock crow, thou shalt deny me thrice. And he went out, and wept bitterly." Mr. G. Wilson Knight, in an essay on *Measure for Measure* and the Gospels,[1] has shown how the parables of Jesus are recalled by the

---

[1] *The Wheel of Life*, pp. 80–160.

theme and dialogue of this play. It is true, as regards the New Testament, that the traces of Bible influence on Shakespeare's work refer less to people and happenings than to the thought and teaching of the Master and his followers.

Perhaps the play which reveals the Poet's knowledge of the Old Testament in its most interesting light is the *Merchant of Venice*. In the character of Shylock the Jew, one of the dramatist's most masterly creations, he has astonished the world by presenting a member of the persecuted race which all nations recognize as true to type. He has achieved this perfection by building Shylock's culture upon the law and prophets. As I have written in my study of the comedy,[1] Shylock "substantiates his statements, justifies his acts, and explains his point of view by quotations from Jewish history and literature." He refers to Laban, Jacob, Barrabas, Hagar, and Daniel; and Antonio drily remarks, "The devil can cite Scripture for his purpose." Without exceptional biblical knowledge such a wonderful piece of characterization would have been impossible to Shakespeare, for in his day Jews were excluded from England, and had been for hundreds of years. He could not, therefore, draw his materials from personal observation, and was dependent upon what literature, and first and foremost the Bible, taught him.

Another of the Poet's remarkable achievements in characterization, Falstaff, has a connection of a somewhat different kind with Bible incident. The fat knight quotes volubly from Scripture, though his attitude is, as we should expect, careless and irreverent. His glib allusions recall the Fall of Adam, Dives who lived

[1] *A Study of the "Merchant of Venice,"* p. 91.

in purple, the ragged Lazarus, Pharaoh and his lean kine, the counsels of Achitophel, the sorrows of Job, the legions of angels, and several other characters and incidents. The creator of so ready a user of biblical testimony must necessarily have been more than usually familiar with the Canon himself.

The second great use that Shakespeare made of the Bible was to draw upon its almost limitless treasure of poetic expression and imagery. As a writer, he had the advantage of an audience so familiar with scriptural language, that they would at once recognize and appreciate his allusions whenever he made use of them for metaphor and simile. In many other lines the biblical inspiration is not so apparent to the casual listener, though the student can detect it in both diction and sentiment. It will be sufficient in this connection to make a selection of a few of the more interesting passages and compare them with the Bible original.

In *King John* (v. 2. 154–158) occur the lines:

> Ladies and pale-visaged maids
> Like Amazons come tripping after drums;
> Their thimbles into armed gauntlets change,
> Their needles to lances, and their gentle hearts
> To fierce and bloody inclination.

Scholars agree that the above was probably inspired by Isaiah's words, "They shall beat their swords into plowshares, and their spears into pruning-hooks" (II. 4); or, as given in the Genevan version, the version which Shakespeare most probably referred to: "They shall breake their swords also into mattocks and their speares into siethes." The same metaphor occurs in Mic. iv. 3; and again, though in this instance reversed, in Joel iii. 10.

In his magnificent funeral oration over the assassinated Cæsar, Marc Antony, cleverly depreciating his
own gifts and influence, tells the excited citizens that
if he were the orator that Brutus was,

> . . . there were an Antony
> Would ruffle up your spirits, and put a tongue
> In every wound of Cæsar, that should move
> The stones of Rome to rise and mutiny.
>
> (III. 2. 231–234.)

Shakespeare was thinking of Jesus' words (see St.
Luke xix. 40): "I tell you that, if these should hold
their peace, the stones would immediately cry out."

Another particularly interesting parallel occurs
between a speech of Constance in *King John* and
the complaints of Job—a parallel noted by Bishop
Wordsworth, Mr. Thomas Carter, and others. King
John of England and King Philip of France have
made a treaty whereby the Dauphin is to marry
Lady Blanch, the English sovereign's niece, while
Constance's son, Arthur, is excluded from succession
to the throne. The French King suggests that the
happy day of reconciliation should always be kept
as a holiday; but Constance cries out in her anger
and disappointment (III. 1. 83–91):

> A wicked day, and not a holy day!
> What hath this day deserved? what hath it done,
> That it in golden letters should be set
> Among the high tides in the calendar?
> Nay, rather turn this day out of the week,
> This day of shame, oppression, perjury:
> Or, if it must stand still, let wives with child
> Pray that their burthens may not fall this day,
> Lest that their hopes prodigiously be cross'd.

The verses in Chapter iii of the Book of Job read

T

(Genevan version) "Let the day perish wherein I was borne. Let that daye be darknesse, let not God regarde it from above, neither let the light shine upon it. Let darknesse possesse that night, let it not be joyned unto the dayes of the yeere, nor let it come into the count of moneths—neither let it see the dawning of the day."

It would be possible to multiply these parallels many times over, but I would refer those who wish to examine Shakespeare's phraseological obligation to Scripture more particularly to the books devoted wholly to that study—Bishop Wordsworth's *Shakespeare's Knowledge and Use of the Bible*, Mr. Thomas Carter's *Shakespeare and Holy Scripture*, and the Rev. T. R. Eaton's *Shakespeare and the Bible*. If my own quotations have been inadequate, these books will convince them that there can be no question of the extent and magnitude of Shakespeare's debt to Holy Writ.

The third direction in which Shakespeare was beholden to the Bible was in the influence of the moral teachings of the Old and New Testaments, more especially the New, on his own ethical philosophy. This is too large a matter to be dealt with properly in the space of a few paragraphs, since it involves his whole attitude towards right and wrong and his true inward religion as opposed to his passive acceptance of dogma and obedient observance of ecclesiastical law. The following chapter is, therefore, devoted to an examination of this aspect of his spiritual selfhood.

XVIII

SHAKESPEARE'S OWN ETHICAL PHILOSOPHY

On questions of religious supernaturalism Shakespeare was content to accept the dogmas of the Church. The nature and attributes of the Deity, man's relation to Him, and the spiritual life beyond the grave, were profound theses on which he could form no judgment and reach no conclusion that could be tested by his purely human experiences. While admitting that there was an Almighty Power and a realm of spirit which transcended the material and finite, he could not comprehend them in terms of his own thinking, and was willing to leave their explanation to those who were "deep within the books of God". Shakespeare went further in his loyalty towards Christian doctrine. We have seen how he repeated the very language of orthodox belief, and always with the air of reverent acceptance. We have noted how careful he was to observe the forms and ceremonies which his spiritual pastors assured him were essential to soul-salvation.

But Shakespeare was too deep a thinker not to realize that easy acceptance of a creed and the mechanical performance of specified rites did not make a man religious. He knew that scholastic theology did not turn sinners into saints. True religion must be lived and made practical; and before it can be lived in daily life, it must win the allegiance of the heart. Kindness, purity, unselfishness, honesty, joy, and gratitude were the outpourings of a mind that was religious in the best sense. Here was a field in which the Poet was not compelled to accept, and accept without discussion, the word of priest and church. Such things came wholly within the range of his own personal experience. He could examine and prove them for himself. They were to be found in the lives and characters of the men and women who surrounded him: and he was fully conscious that his own insight into human nature was so penetrating that he need not rely on any but himself for true interpretation.

Some readers would doubtless prefer the description "ethical philosophy" rather than "religion" for this outlook upon life. "Religion" has now come to mean for many a particular form of service and particular articles of faith rather than a way of living. But the religion which Jesus of Nazareth taught was most surely a way of living, a philosophy of life. And, as I shall hope to show, Shakespeare's philosophy of life was essentially Christian and owed its origin and influence to the Gospel.

The Poet Laureate[1] is probably right when he says that the spiritual values of life did not mean very much to the Poet during the first ten years of his dramatic career. No one is born with his ethical philosophy intact. Ideas grow in the soil of experience. The interests and estimates of youth are transient. So we find in the early plays that Shakespeare, while never hostile or disrespectful towards religion, yet feels little enthusiasm for it. His real interest is held by the traditions and superstitions of the countryside, and his poet's eye is on the temporal beauties and attractions of a lovely world. What glimmers of deeper religious feeling occur in the happily written dramas

[1] *Shakespeare and Spiritual Life*, by John Masefield, pp, 9.10.

of his first period suggest an uncritical adherence to the doctrine of the Reformed Church. Although organized and orthodox religion counted for so little with him, yet we find nothing in the Shakespeare of the early fifteen-nineties which is in conflict with that unerring distinction between right and wrong, which he so fully developed later, and is the true religion of the Poet's heart—in other words, his ethical philosophy.

When Shakespeare came to London as a young man in his early twenties, he was brought into contact with a cultured and literary set, such as the Renaissance produced in every country where it obtained a footing. One of the outstanding characteristics of that great awakening was the freeing of thought from the guidance and domination of the Church. In the Middle Ages art, politics, sociology, and all intellectualism had been inevitably bound up with religion. Now they were free, and rejoicing in their freedom. The change was revolutionary; and as revolutionary ideas make their strongest appeal to youth, unsobered by experience and a sense of responsibility, it was natural that Shakespeare should glory in this opportunity to allow his imagination to roam unfettered. Nevertheless, we do not find in him that aggressive anti-Christianity which animated so many of those liberated from that drag on thought which doctrinal religion can be.

As he grew older and wiser in the hard school of life, the Poet made the very common discovery that worldly success, transient pleasures, and superficial beauty lack the quality of being eternally satisfying. The fairest rose droops and falls; wherefore unchanging loveliness must be pursued beyond the limits of the material. Oft-repeated joys satiate, and enduring contentment can only be found in spiritual treasure. Gone was that optimism and light-heartedness in which the first, gay comedies were written. Shakespeare's attitude towards the Supernatural was no longer the merry and careless attitude which found expression in the Fairies of *Midsummer Night's Dream.* His mind began to run on ghostly visitants from a preternatural world, and thence to black-hearted witches, the consecrated ministers of evil. Religion in its narrower sense is confined in these early works to orthodox enunciation of the dogmas of the Church, reverently repeated, it is true, but devoid of the fire of enthusiasm. Religion in its wider meaning, however —religion as a philosophy of life—is evidenced in Shakespeare's undeviating sense of right and wrong and his demand for a high standard of conduct. While religious factions were seeing Orthodox Protestants, Puritans, and Papists, Shakespeare was only seeing men and women with a common human nature.

At the beginning of the great tragic period, which he introduces with the magnificent Roman drama of *Julius Cæsar*, Shakespeare's philosophy begins to take on a more decided religious flavour. It has not become, and never was to become, a religious thought hedged in by the dogma of any particular church. Such a position for the tolerant, humane, understanding master of the human heart was unthinkable. It was rather a mental review of man's human circumstances, with an understanding of the high morality demanded of him before he could qualify for a sphere higher and better than his present one. It was questioning reflection on those mysteries which have baffled the inquiring mind of humanity through all time.

The references to the Deity and Christianity scattered through the earlier plays show that the Poet for all his intellectual freedom never disputed the teachings of the Church about God, Jesus Christ, Atonement, and Eternal Life. We have seen that as a young man he found them very remote from his present surroundings and occupation. But with the approach of middle age, he pondered on things moral and spiritual more earnestly and longingly, and seems to have attained some insight at least into the values of Truth divine. His revelation appears to have taught him that God is good and wills everything good for man. Experience, however, insisted that men by no means enjoyed uninterrupted good. On the other hand, in the lives of most of God's creatures evil was patently predominant. The feasible explanation was that men interrupted the beneficent divine intention by their own ignorance, sins, and self-will. Yet man cannot be deprived of his sovereign gift of free-will for all his mistakes. The warnings and promptings of conscience are vouchsafed him as guides to the spiritual goal. In cases of great importance these warnings may take a more obvious and terrifying form, as they do in the alarming storm, which presages the murder of Julius Cæsar. But man has still the power to go his own way, to interrupt the order of his life by his blindness and unheeding foolishness, and to choose the path of expiation by suffering, through which he learns that good is perpetual and unchanging, and that only his faults have separated him from peace and harmony.

If the foregoing is a correct analysis of the trend of Shakespeare's thought on spiritual life during the writing of *Julius Cæsar*, it is clear, as Mr. Masefield points out,[1] that in *Hamlet*, written a year or so later, he is already questioning the correctness of his vision. This was characteristic of the Renaissance mind. It liked to prove all things, and was often found ranging itself against long-accepted beliefs—an attitude that brought it into violent conflict with the Church. All scholars agree that there is deep thought in the mind of Hamlet; and many believe that the obscurity and complexity of the character are due to the fact that the Poet endowed him with all the philosophic doubts and religious questionings which were troubling himself. It is difficult to decide whether there is more religion than philosophy or more philosophy than religion in *Hamlet*. But it seems to me that the two are so inextricably mixed in Shakespeare that his real inward religion and his ethical philosophy are the same thing. We see Hamlet given to study and meditation, pondering on the riddle of life and death, existence beyond the grave, the meaning and purpose of the fleeting and temporal with all its sin and suffering, and the nature of spiritual reality. Hamlet is intellectual, reflective, and reverent in thought, but his attitude is critical. He desires to examine, dissect, and analyse, and, if possible, satisfy himself with proof. He accepts the fact that "there are more things in heaven and earth than are dreamt of in your philosophy";[2] and comes to the advanced conclusion that "there is nothing either good or bad, but thinking makes it so."[3]

Writing of Hamlet's moral philosophy, Louis H. Victory says,[4] "No philosopher, moralist, preacher, or divine ever expounded doctrines more sublime or

---

[1] *Shakespeare and Spiritual Life*, p. 21.   [2] *Hamlet*, I. 5. 166–167.
[3] *Ibid.*, II. 2. 255.   [4] *The Higher Teaching of Shakespeare*, p. 119.

more ennobling." It is true, for the reason that Shakespeare was expressing himself through Hamlet and
showing, not only that his ethical creed was taking
definite shape in his mind, but that it was decidedly
and unmistakably of the highest Christian standards
as derived from the teachings of the Bible, free of
dogmatic trappings. The assertion that Shakespeare
produced a second Bible for his nation is no hyperbolic
outburst on the part of those whose enthusiasm for
his powers has outrun responsible judgment. His
consistent endorsement of all that is inspiring and
elevating in Holy Writ supports the contention, by
no means confined to the British, that he was "the
greatest moral genius of history."

In *Hamlet* we learn of Shakespeare's high,
almost idealistic, views on marriage—that in the
purity and sanctity of the marriage bond alone could
true love find its full expression. His standard of
wedded conduct was vastly higher than his contemporaries', as it is higher than our modern standards.
He would countenance no anticipation of the rites
and privileges of marriage, and makes Prospero
threaten Ferdinand that his union with Miranda
will not be blessed unless first "all sanctimonious
ceremonies may With full and holy rite be minister'd."[1]
It is true that Shakespeare made dramatic use of love
other than that which had the sanction of religion
and society. He handles with masterly skill the illicit
passion of Antony and Cleopatra and shows us the
tragedy to which it leads. He portrays in *Measure for
Measure* the fall of the self-righteous, self-confident
Angelo, assailed by sexual temptation when opportunity made resistance difficult. He does not ignore

[1] *The Tempest*, IV. 1. 16–17.

the libertine, the bawd, and the harlot; but he never
fails to emphasize the suffering, disgust, and dis-
content that must accompany a theft of marital rights.
His own life had not been blameless in the matter of
obedience to the seventh commandment; but his
remorse is genuine and serves to elucidate his ideal.
The self-revelatory Sonnet CXXIX expresses an inward dissatisfaction that illumines his better self.

> The expense of spirit in a waste of shame
> Is lust in action; and till action, lust
> Is perjured, murderous, bloody, full of blame,
> Savage, extreme, rude, cruel, not to trust;
> Enjoy'd no sooner but despised straight;
> Past reason hunted; and no sooner had,
> Past reason hated, as a swallowed bait,
> On purpose laid to make the taker mad:
> Mad in pursuit, and in possession so;
> Had, having, and in quest to have, extreme;
> A bliss in proof, and proved, a very woe;
> Before, a joy proposed; behind, a dream.
>   All this the world well knows; yet none knows well
>   To shun the heaven that leads men to this hell.

Pure love, the true as opposed to the false love of lust,
is the theme of Sonnet CXVI, which should be compared with the above.

> Let me not to the marriage of true minds
> Admit impediments. Love is not love
> Which alters when it alteration finds,
> Or bends with the remover to remove:
> O, no! it is an ever-fixed mark,
> That looks on tempests and is never shaken;
> It is the star to every wandering bark,
> Whose worth's unknown, although his height be taken.
> Love's not Time's fool, though rosy lips and cheeks
> Within his bending sickle's compass come;
> Love alters not with his brief hours and weeks,
> But bears it out even to the edge of doom.

> If this be error, and upon me proved,
> I never writ, nor no man ever loved.

The cloud of melancholy had settled on Hamlet even before the visit of his father's Ghost. The loss of his father was not the only cause. The hasty remarriage of his mother with his uncle troubled him even more. It shocked his sense of decency and propriety and was in his eyes a degradation of love and marriage. When he knew the whole truth, Hamlet visited Gertrude in her closet and threatened to set up a glass where she might see the inmost part of her. When the startled Queen asked him what was her offence, he replied (III. 4. 40-51):

> Such an act
> That blurs the grace and blush of modesty,
> Calls virtue hypocrite, takes off the rose
> From the fair forehead of an innocent love,
> And sets a blister there; makes marriage vows
> As false as dicers' oaths: O, such a deed
> As from the body of contraction plucks
> The very soul, and sweet religion makes
> A rhapsody of words: heaven's face doth glow;
> Yea, this solidity and compound mass,
> With tristful visage, as against this doom,
> Is thought-sick at the act.

As the Poet Laureate expresses it,[1] sex ran in Shakespeare like a sea. Certainly its insistence caused him to make mistakes; and just as certainly he bitterly regretted them. His references to immorality are sometimes careless and non-censorious. Frequently he lacks reticence when speaking of the intimacies of marriage. The coarseness and vulgarity of his age were responsible for these lapses from good taste. But we cannot doubt that, to use Mr. John Bailey's

[1] *Shakespeare and Spiritual Life*, p. 10.

words,[1] "In the matter of sex and sexual morality he is as sane and healthy as some of his contemporaries, and many of ours, are the reverse." Mr. C. H. Herford in his essay on "The Normality of Shakespeare as illustrated in his treatment of Love and Marriage" has no difficulty in finding abundant evidence in the majority of the plays to show that in this the Poet was an idealist and accepted the commandment of the Pentateuch as explained and amplified by Christ Jesus and insisted upon by His disciples.

The sanctity of marriage, the only hallower of love, is but one branch of ethics in which Shakespeare's philosophy coincided with, and was influenced, perhaps unconsciously, by the Bible teaching. I have noted the reference to it in *Hamlet*, because that play was written at the beginning of the great tragic period, in the course of which his moral philosophy was developed and achieved its fullest expression. Throughout these years of masterly creation the dramatist was more interested in thought at the back of action than in the action itself. The plays that followed *Hamlet*, *Troilus and Cressida*, *Measure for Measure*, and *Othello*, are all plays of thought. Every one of the great dramas revolves round a problem of conduct. In *Hamlet* we have the meditative philosopher shrinking from an act of violence abhorrent to his righteous soul, though possessing the fullest human justification for it. *Troilus and Cressida* is an unfinished play, most of it being still in draft form. Shakespeare only completed a few of the scenes, but those scenes equal his best work and reveal the profound thinker. The theme is thus described by Hazlitt:[2] "Cressida is a giddy girl, an unpractised jilt, who falls in love with Troilus, as

[1] *Shakespeare*, p. 25.   [2] *Characters of Shakespeare's Plays*, p. 73.

she afterwards deserts him, from mere levity and thoughtlessness of temper." The setting is the Trojan war, embodying the story of Helen, the sulks of Achilles, and the fall of Troy. How Shakespeare would have finished it we do not know, but Mr. Masefield says,[1] "He seems to be defining what he loathed in life, in women and authority."

In the next play of thought, *Measure for Measure*, critics have found much that is difficult to understand. Yet this play, when closely studied, reveals how near was Shakespeare's ethical sense to what our Christianity designates as right and wrong, truth and error. In his recently issued work, *The Wheel of Life*, Mr. G. Wilson Knight has a chapter on *Measure for Measure* and the Gospels,[2] in which he examines the ethics of the play with the parallel teaching in the New Testament. He writes "In *Measure for Measure* we have a careful dramatic pattern, a studied explication of a central theme: the moral nature of man in relation to the crudity of man's justice, especially in the matter of sexual vice. There is, too, a clear relation existing between the play and the Gospels, for the play's theme is this:

Judge not, that ye be not judged. For with what judgment ye judge, ye shall be judged: and with what measure ye mete, it shall be measured to you again.

(Matt. vii. 1–2.)

"The ethical standards of the Gospels are rooted in the thought of *Measure for Measure*." Mr. Knight then proceeds to an analysis of the play with continual references to the New Testament, which reveal how the teachings of Jesus ran through the mind of Shake-

[1] *Shakespeare and Spiritual Life,* p. 23.
[2] Chap. V. pp. 80–106.

speare in this handling of sexual temptation and sin. But close though the Poet keeps to the Bible's guidance, we find as usual, his thinking concentrated on this life on earth and never lifted to the contemplation of the spiritual existence beyond. This is consistent with all we have learned of his religious thought, which required a criterion for right conduct here and now, and relegated the amaterialistic life to a future when it might be more comprehensible.

The next play, *Othello*, acknowledged one of the four supreme masterpieces, presents another problem of behaviour. It is in line with Shakespeare's highest conception of tragedy. His philosophy was not content with merely rewarding the virtuous and punishing the wicked. There was more in it than that. Experience had taught him that such simplicity was far from the truth. In certain of the less profound plays he does, it is true, take the obvious and straightforward course, but in his greatest tragedies it is often a man of fine and noble character that is ruined through some inherent weakness which the particular circumstances of the plot expose with disastrous effect. Shakespeare, on the other hand, never offends against the Aristotelian canon by leaving the wicked in power and triumph. Evil doing and evil thinking are always punished as they deserve; and it has been truly said that in no other writings in the world, with the single exception of the Scriptures, has the contrast between good and evil been pointed so vividly.

The particular problem of *Othello* is the sin of jealousy. In the first place it is jealousy in Iago, a jealousy springing from self-love, and directed against the man who has supplanted him and the employer who, he imagines, has wronged him. Working under a screen of satanic hypocrisy this jealousy arouses in Othello, a man of frank, generous, noble disposition, a jealousy of a different kind—a jealousy which has its roots in passionate love of another, in this case, his wife, Desdemona. But the Poet's ethical sense revealed to him that all jealousy was sin, and urged to its limits would result in crime and tragedy. So Iago's rival is wounded, Desdemona is murdered, Othello is ruined, and the villainous plotter himself, when seeming about to escape, is destroyed by the timely intervention of Fate in the person of Emilia.

After *Othello* Shakespeare wrote *Macbeth,* in the estimation of many the finest of all his unrivalled masterpieces. The thought is profound, the poetry magnificent. The tragedy is shrouded in an unrelieved gloom, which betrays the pessimism and mental darkness into which the Poet had lapsed. He seems to have reached the belief, happily only temporarily held, that the forces of evil are more powerful than the forces of good. There are outside powers, inimical and hostile to man, who try to interfere with his happiness and prosperity and involve him in disaster. But man has still free-will and ability to resist. Evil cannot command: it can only attack man at the most vulnerable point of his moral armour, and by deceptive, fair-seeming, hypocritical, and tempting argument lure him to self-destruction:

> . . . to win us to our harm,
> The instruments of darkness tell us truths,
> Win us with honest trifles, to betray 's
> In deepest consequence.
>
> (I. 3. 123–126.)

Macbeth is a man of noble character, brave, loyal,

and generous. But, in common with all Shakespeare's tragic heroes, he has one serious failing, which overmasters the good in him and brings him to his ruin. Macbeth's fault is ambition. Ambition of the right kind is commendable; but Macbeth is ambitious for the sweets of this world, for power, place and adulation. It is in this flaw in an otherwise virtuous disposition that the powers of darkness see their opportunity. They lie, cheat, and prophesy falsely, silencing their victim's fears and scruples, and tempting him beyond his powers of resistance, until all that was fine and admirable in him is killed, and his terrified conscience plunges him into one crime after another, leading inevitably to shame and death. It is a sublime moral lesson that Shakespeare teaches us in *Macbeth*. Man is endowed with feelings and instincts that are potential instruments of the highest good. Misused and abused, however, they lay their possessor open to the blandishments of evil. Ambition in itself is a God-given aspiration; but it should aspire towards that which is good, spiritual, and eternal. Macbeth's ambition was directed towards the world, the flesh, and the Devil. He forgot that God sees all the workings of the human heart and mind; and he made the tragic mistake of using evil to defend himself from the effects of evil.

In the same wonderful year in which Shakespeare finished *Macbeth*, he wrote *King Lear*. In this play, as mighty a work of genius as its predecessor, the Poet handles the sin of ingratitude. To strengthen his theme he makes it *filial* ingratitude, which afflicts to the point of defeating a foolish, selfish, parental love. And still the dramatist went from one failing to another in his exposure of the wickedness of the human heart. In *Antony and Cleopatra* he attacks lust; in *Coriolanus*, pride; in *Timon of Athens* (unfinished and only partly Shakespearean) he returns to the theme of ingratitude, besides condemning misanthropy and intemperance. When we see how one unlovely trait can compass the ruin of a character that possesses much that is fine and noble (the theme of all the great tragedies), we can summarize Shakespeare's ethical philosophy in the Bible terms with which it exactly coincides, "Be ye therefore perfect, even as your Father which is in heaven is perfect."

The mood of pessimism and darkness, which credited evil with real power over men, passed from Shakespeare at the end of the great tragic period. In his last plays, *Cymbeline*, *The Winter's Tale*, and *The Tempest*, the motive is not sin and punishment, but forgiveness and reconciliation. After the storm and terror comes a divine calm. By this date Shakespeare had practically retired from the turmoil of London theatrical life to the peace and comfort of his Stratford home. As was his physical progress, so was his mental. Superstition had been shed; fears of supernatural evil had been discarded. The real spiritual powers were seen to be of the mind. Man obedient to his Maker, a willing and humble servant of the Most High, could draw upon the infinite supply of good and make it his own. Working as God would have him work, following the teachings of Christianity and the Bible, man found that supernatural powers were his by the process of thinking rightly. There is nothing here of creed and dogma, scholastic theology, and ecclesiastical rites and ceremonies. But that it is none the less religion, its unerring distinction between right and wrong is proof. And there are many who believe that Shakespeare was at the last nearer the truth of all things than any priest, philosopher, or poet who has ever lived.

XIX

THE CLERICAL CHARACTERS

An appropriate conclusion to our study of Shakespeare and religion will be a review of his attitude towards the Priests and Clergy. Here again we shall be impressed by that wonderful humanity and tolerance which characterized all this thoughts and feelings, religious as well as secular, and which is the strongest evidence of his true greatness. His lack of bias and bitterness are all the more remarkable in view of the fierce controversies of his day, particularly as those were not controversies from which he could stand aloof, but such as to interfere materially with his business interests and social life.

If Shakespeare's contemplation of the various creeds from Popery to Calvinism was so fair and broadminded that the most careful reading of his life and works was necessary before his own preferences could be defined with confidence, we should expect to find his handling of Priest and Parson equally kind and gentle. He does not hesitate on occasions to be amusing at their expense, but there is nothing of that gross disrespect which we find too often in contemporary writers. His faculty for placing himself in another's mental position enabled him to appreciate the difficulties of the clergy, their battles with sin and temptation, not only in others but in themselves, and the very hard requirement of their calling to renounce the world in return for the vague, unseen, eventual joys of heaven. Nevertheless, Shakespeare believed that having undertaken a high spiritual mission, the

priest should live up to the demands of his office—
in other words, practise what he preaches. As Portia
says in the *Merchant of Venice* (I. 2. 15–16), "It is a good
divine that follows his own instructions." King
Henry VI voices the same thought when he remon-
strates with Cardinal Beaufort for his hesitation in
accepting the Duke of Gloucester's offer to compose
their quarrel (III. 1. 127–130. *1 Henry VI*):

> Fie, uncle Beaufort! I have heard you preach
> That malice was a great and grievous sin;
> And will not you maintain the thing you teach,
> But prove a chief offender in the same?

In *2 Henry IV* Prince John of Lancaster criticizes
the Archbishop of York for so far forgetting the duties
of his priestly office as to stir up armed rebellion
against his sovereign (IV. 2. 4–10):

> My Lord of York, it better show'd with you,
> When that your flock, assembled by the bell,
> Encircled you to hear with reverence
> Your exposition on the holy text,
> Than now to see you here an iron man,
> Cheering a rout of rebels with your drum,
> Turning the word to sword and life to death.

Proceeding, Lancaster is made to describe the Poet's
own idea of a priest who serves his Master truly
(16–22):

> Who hath not heard it spoken
> How deep thou were within the books of God?
> To us the speaker in his parliament;
> To us the imagined voice of God himself;
> The very opener and intelligencer
> Between the grace, the sanctities of heaven,
> And our dull workings.

But His Grace of York has most reprehensively abused his power and position (23–30):

> But you misuse the reverence of your place;
> Employ the countenance and grace of heaven,
> As a false favourite doth his prince's name,
> In deeds dishonourable. You have ta'en up,
> Under the counterfeited zeal of God,
> The subjects of his substitute, my father,
> And both against the peace of heaven and him
> Have here up-swarm'd them.

There were, we shall see, among the clerical characters of the Chronicle Plays many who held high office in the Church and used their opportunities for self-advancement and worldly power. In every case the dramatist makes the evil-doer pay heavily for this betrayal of sacred duties and responsibilities. The Poet's own condemnation of such malpractice is unequivocal, even when he is following the facts of history.

Shakespeare's ideal priest was a kindly, sympathetic, cultured, spiritually minded man, who encouraged, consoled, and comforted those who turned to God for help and peace. He had no use for the dogmatic cleric, who placed more store on rites and ceremonies than on Christian charity. We find an instance of such in *Hamlet*, where the red-tapism of the Church only allows poor Ophelia "maimed" burial rites, because it is believed that she committed suicide. The Poet's opinion is recorded in the indignant words of the grieved brother, Laertes (v. 1. 263–265):

> I tell thee, churlish priest,
> A ministering angel shall my sister be
> When thou liest howling.

The priestly characters in Shakespeare's works fall

into three main groups—the Cardinals and Bishops of the Chronicle Plays, the Friars and Monks of the old monastic orders, and the Parish Clergy of his own day.

The earliest class to be handled by the dramatist were the Cardinals and Bishops, who belong to the plays of his youth. As to their characters, he was, of course, guided and governed by what his authority, the Holinshed *Chronicles*, recorded of them. The English dramas from *King John* to *Richard III* deal with pre-Reformation times in which political power was still largely in the hands of the Princes of the Church. Although kings and nobles had throughout the Middle Ages acquired an increasing measure of that culture and authority which enabled them to challenge ecclesiastical supremacy, yet the process was by no means complete, and enormous wealth and influence still remained with the higher clergy. Nor did it escape either the notice or condemnation of the dramatist that the Cardinals and Bishops were more concerned with temporal power, political prefer-ment, and material riches than spiritual advancement. Those priests who are censured and punished in the early plays are not attacked because they are priests, but because they fail to live the life of self-denial expected of their order. The criticism was amply justified by historic fact.

In the Church of Rome the highest dignitaries after the Pope himself are the Cardinals. In the plays of Shakespeare five Cardinals appear—Pandulph, Beau-fort, Bourchier, Wolsey, and Campeius. Cardinal Pandulph, as Papal Legate, is the most powerful political influence in the play of *King John*. When the English king is on the point of coming to terms with his French enemy, King Philip, Pandulph intervenes and in high-handed manner demands of John why he "doth wilfully spurn" against the holy Church and exclude the Pope's nominee, Stephen Langton, from the See of Canterbury. As we have seen in a previous chapter, John rebels against papal domination and declares for his personal supremacy in his own kingdom—the political claim of Elizabethan England. Pandulph replies by excommunicating John, as Pope Pius V had excommunicated Elizabeth in 1570. But although Shakespeare was writing in patriotic strain and made the English king indignantly repudiate the dictation of the overbearing Pandulph, yet he could not alter history, and the Pope's representative spoils the peace plans of France and England, controls their military dispositions, and, in the end, triumphs over John and brings him to the papal heel. As J. A. Heraud writes,[1] Pandulph has all the "priest's crafty sophistry," and is a true type of the plotting, bullying statesmen of the days of the Church's temporal power.

A priest who reflects little credit on his calling is Cardinal Beaufort, Bishop of Winchester, in Parts I and II of *Henry VI*. As great-uncle of the king, whose rebuke of his malicious mind I have already quoted, Beaufort was engaged in the worst kind of political intrigue, which had self-advantage as its only aim. Shakespeare accepted Hall's estimate of his character,[2] "More noble of blood than notable in learning; haut in stomacke and hygh in countenance; ryche above measure of all men and to fewe liberal; disdainfull to his kynne and dreadfull to his louers; preferrynge money before friendshippe . . . his covetous insaciable,

[1] *Shakespeare: His Inner Life*, p. 156.   [2] Hall's *Chronicle*, p. 210.

and hope of long lyfe, made hym bothe to forget God, his Prynce, and hymself, in his latter daies." It will not be necessary to follow "impious Beaufort, that false priest" (*2 Henry VI*, II. 4. 53) through all the details of his career of deceit, treachery, and crime. The facts are well known to students of Shakespeare and of history. Among the warring nobles "the character of Cardinal Beaufort is," says Hazlitt,[1] "the most prominent in the group: the account of his death is one of our author's masterpieces." The scene (III. 3. of Part II) is terrible indeed. Mr. Masefield thus describes it:[2] "The Cardinal is discovered in bed 'raving and staring as if he were madde.' He has poisoned his old enemy, the Duke Humphrey. Now he is dying; the murder is on his soul, and nothing has been gained by it. The path is made clearer for his enemies perhaps. That is the only result. Now he is dying, the waste of mind is at an end, and the figure of the victim is at the foot of the bed." The religiously minded king exclaims (5–6):

> Ah, what a sign it is of evil life,
> Where death's approach is seen so terrible!

Wretched Beaufort cries (8–17):

> Bring me unto my trial when you will.
> Died he not in his bed? where should he die?
> Can I make men live, whether they will or no?
> O, torture me no more! I will confess.
> Alive again? then show me where he is:
> I'll give a thousand pound to look upon him.
> He hath no eyes, the dust hath blinded them:
> Comb down his hair; look, look! it stands upright,
> Like lime-twigs set to catch my winged soul.
> Give me some drink. . . .

[1] *Characters of Shakespeare's Plays*, p. 179.
[2] *William Shakespeare*, p. 58.

It is a relief to turn from the revolting character of Beaufort to the next of Shakespeare's Cardinals, Thomas Bourchier, Archbishop of Canterbury. Although an important figure in history—he crowned three kings, Edward IV, Richard III, and Henry VII—he plays a small part, the smallest part of all Shakespeare's political churchmen, in the tragedy of *Richard III*. His only appearance is in Scene I of Act III; and from the few lines given him to speak, we gather that he does not possess much strength of character. When urged by the Duke of Buckingham to force the young Duke of York from sanctuary, he says (III. 1. 40–43):

> God in heaven forbid
> We should infringe the holy privilege
> Of blessed sanctuary! not for all this land
> Would I be guilty of so deep a sin.

But Buckingham has little difficulty in getting rid of his scruples; and Bourchier obediently departs to Westminster, returning soon afterwards with the little Prince.

In *Henry VIII* we encounter the towering figure of Cardinal Wolsey, the greatest power in history of all the English Cardinals. Shakespeare was responsible for only part of this play; and the drawing of Wolsey's character was largely the work of Fletcher, with, perhaps, some assistance from Massinger. There is no doubt that the younger playwright received valuable hints from the master, for Fletcher, never again reaches the standard of his collaboration with Shakespeare, the great "Farewell speech" and Wolsey's fall having long been mistaken for the hand of the supreme genius himself. Wolsey is proud, ambitious, unscrupulous, brilliantly clever, coarse, luxurious. He sets no limit to the accumulation of material riches or the extension of his power and influence throughout the land. He aspires to the papal throne itself and lays the most ingenious plots to attain his end. He is typical of those high prelates who used their priestly office for wealth, position, and political advantage. Wolsey was Archbishop of York and Papal Legate, in addition to holding other ecclesiastical emoluments which brought his revenues almost level with those of the King himself. But Wolsey's ambition outruns his discretion, and his fall is swift and terrible, and not without pathos. It is a fine portrayal of character, even if it is not wholly Shakespearean.

Another Cardinal appears in *Henry VIII*—Campeius, the Campeggio of history. He is sent by the Pope to England to join with Wolsey in the "impartial judging" of the King's divorce. He finds the obstinacy of Queen Katharine a stumbling-block, but finally persuades her not to persist in her appeal to the Pope and to throw herself on her royal husband's mercy. According to Holinshed, Campeius was "a man of great wit and experience," but in the play he is given a somewhat tortuous, unreliable character, is spoken of as partner in Wolsey's secret plotting, and finally, when the situation becomes embarrassing, is reported as having "stolen away to Rome." Such a reading of Campeius is not historically exact, but suits the requirements of the drama.

Of the Archbishops whom Shakespeare brings on the stage and who are not included in the ranks of the Cardinals, the most important is Richard Scroop, His Grace of York, a prominent character in the two parts of *Henry IV*. From Holinshed we learn that "the gravitie of his age, his integritie of life, and incomparable learning, with the reverend aspect of his amiable personage, mooved all men to have him in no small estimation."[1] Shakespeare calls him "noble," "gentle," "well-beloved," one whose influence is such he "turns insurrection to religion: Supposed sincere and holy in his thoughts, He's followed both with body and with mind." (*2 Henry IV*, I. i. 201–203). But this sincere churchman forgets the command, "Love your enemies," and is so resentful over his brother's death at Bristol (a historical error of Shakespeare's: it was a distant relative of Scroop who lost his life), that he joins the Northumberland rebellion against Henry IV, the whilom Bolingbroke. After the disaster of Shrewsbury, involving the death of Hotspur, the Archbishop becomes one of the chief leaders of the rebels. To himself he is able to justify his act of revolt on the ground that Henry is a usurper who deposed England's rightful king, Richard II. In Gaultree Forest Scroop, Hastings, Mowbray, and others meet the royal army under Prince John of Lancaster and the Earl of Westmorland. I have quoted the passage above in which Prince John rebukes the Archbishop for taking up arms against his sovereign when he would be more suitably employed in carrying out his holy and solemn duties. York replies with a statement of the grievances of the rebels, who are deceived by the Prince and Westmorland into laying down their arms and throwing themselves on the king's clemency. The treachery of their enemies is not discovered until it is too late to retract, and the Archbishop and his supporters are "brought to the correction of the law" (*2 Henry IV*, IV. 4. 85.) In spite of his execution as a rebel, Scroop is

[1] *Chronicles*, III. 529.

the most sincere, genuine, admirable, honest, and noble of all Shakespeare's Bishops with the single exception of Carlisle in *Richard II*.

Another Archbishop of York, Thomas Rotherham, plays a minor rôle in *Richard III*. (In the reign of Edward IV he held the office of Chancellor, but after the death of his sovereign was deprived of it, and imprisoned for his support of the widowed Queen Elizabeth and her party). When he hears that the Queen's brother and son have been incarcerated in Pomfret by "the mighty dukes, Gloucester and Buckingham," he resigns his seal and conducts Elizabeth and the little Duke of York to the Sanctuary at Westminster (II. 4).

Shakespeare mentions three Archbishops of Canterbury—Henry Chicheley of *Henry V*, Thomas Bourchier of *Richard III* (already referred to among the Cardinals), and Cranmer of *Henry VIII*, with whom he had little to do. Chicheley appears in the opening scene of *Henry V*. The young king asks for a ruling from the Church on the validity of his claim to the French crown; and the Archbishop assures him of the justice of his cause and urges him to win his rights by war. But we learn that the Primate is not influenced in his decision by disinterested patriotism. A Bill for largely disendowing the Church was on point of passing when Henry IV died. To divert the new king's attention from the measure, the crafty Archbishop succeeds in persuading him to throw down the challenge to France. Thus Henry is not answered by the voice of divine justice but by that of political expediency. By this act the whole character of the Archbishop, as a wordly minded politician, is revealed.

It is not an easy matter in the play of *Henry VIII*

to decide which parts were written by Shakespeare and which by Fletcher. Both dramatists handled the figure of Cranmer, the first Protestant to fill the See of Canterbury. In the scenes generally attributed to Shakespeare, we have in a few lines of soliloquy from the King the first suggestion of the coming, mighty change known as the English Reformation. Henry is extremely dissatisfied with the handling of his divorce case by Wolsey and Campeius. He mutters (II. 4. 235–240):

> I may perceive
> These cardinals trifle with me: I abhor
> This dilatory sloth and tricks of Rome.
> My learn'd and well-beloved servant, Cranmer,
> Prithee, return; with thy approach, I know,
> My comfort comes along.

Henry's hopes are not disappointed, and Cranmer enjoys the royal favour and support throughout the reign. The Catholic party, led by Bishop Gardiner, wish to arraign Cranmer as a heretic, but the King's goodwill is sufficient defence against all his enemies. Henry believes Cranmer when he avers, "The good I stand on is my truth and honesty" (v. 1. 122); and his estimate of his Archbishop is reiterated by others, who speak of him as "a worthy fellow" and "virtuous," and one who has "taken much pains in the king's business." The Protestant feelings of the two dramatists would predispose them in Cranmer's favour.

Among the other high clergy in Shakespearean drama is Thomas Merke, Bishop of Carlisle in the reign of Richard II. A faithful supporter of his lawful king, he returns with him from Ireland and is in attendance at Flint Castle in Wales, when Richard submits to the power of Bolingbroke. As Bolingbroke is about to "ascend the regal throne," Carlisle, with magnificent courage, registers his protest, calling the usurpation "so heinous, black, obscene a deed" (IV. I. 131) that civil war must follow. For his pains he is committed to the custody of the Abbot of Westminster, who is, however, himself concerned in a plot against Bolingbroke. Carlisle is brought before the new king as a fellow-conspirator in the Abbot's plot, but even his enemy can appreciate his fine qualities and pardons him for the "high sparks of honour" he has seen in him.

Two Bishops of Ely appear in the plays. John Fordham associates himself with Chicheley, Archbishop of Canterbury, in urging Henry V to emulate the gallant deeds of his ancestors, thus diverting his mind from the disendowment of the Church. John Morton deserts Richard III for Henry, Earl of Richmond, a defection that causes the Crookback more anxiety even than that of Buckingham. Stephen Gardiner, the Bishop of Winchester of *Henry VIII*, is a stout supporter of Wolsey and the implacable opponent of Cranmer and the Protestant party. The handling of this crafty, bitter, fanatical, cruel prelate seems to have been largely the work of Fletcher.

Except for the Churchmen in *Henry VIII*, the Cardinals and Bishops belong to Shakespeare's first period. His pictures of them are naturally dictated to a great extent by historical fact as recorded by Hall and Holinshed. Nevertheless, his skill in dramatic characterization has thrown their good and bad points into sharp relief; and we have no difficulty in hearing his genuine condemnation of those who abused their holy office and subordinated the service of God to the pursuit of material power and riches.

In dealing with the friars and monks, Shakespeare found himself much less restricted by his dramatic material. In the Chronicle Plays he had, obviously, to abide by historical fact and draw his prelates as the unscrupulous politicians many of them were. Such treatment is no evidence of any dislike or antipathy towards priests as a class. In the stories in which the friars enter, however, the Poet enjoyed a much greater latitude, and was able to rely upon his own feelings and conceptions to a larger extent. Here his great humanity and tolerance came into play and led him to treat the friar with a gentleness and kindness that have led some to suspect a religious bias towards Catholicism. The truth is, however, as Dr. Creizenach puts it,[1] "We find in him a delicate appreciation for the poétic element in some Catholic institutions which perished under the régime of the Reformation. He takes particular delight in contrasting the turmoil and passion of the world with the life of the cloister, where men give themselves up to contemplation, but at the same time stretch out helping and healing hands to their fellows struggling in the battle of life." Shakespeare's beautiful mental picture of the peaceful, sheltered, yet useful, life of the monastery caused him to give more important and dignified parts to his friars and monks than to his parish priests. Whereas the priests are people of no importance and often rather ridiculous figures, Friar Laurence and Friar Francis are distinguished for their sympathy and kindly help. This predilection led him to omit an abbey-robbing scene and expunge passages reflecting on the morals of monks and nuns when revising the old play, *The Troublesome Raigne of John, King of*

[1] *The English Drama in the Age of Shakespeare*, p. 103.

England. But that his motive was poetic and not religious is proved by the strong anti-Catholicism of John's replies to Cardinal Pandulph, which we have quoted more than once.

Shakespeare's most famous friar is Laurence, the Franciscan, in *Romeo and Juliet*. The main source of the tragedy was Arthur Brooke's long poem on the same subject. In his preface Brooke expressly stated that the story should serve as a warning to those who have any temptation to imitate these "unfortunate lovers" in "conferring their principall counsels with drunken gossyppes and superstitious friers, the natural fitte instrumentes of unchastitie." In spite of his anti-monastic preface, Brooke draws a kindly, honourable portrait of Laurence in his poem, an impression received by Shakespeare and transmitted by him in his own famous tragedy. Brooke's kindly friar and the Poet's own approval of the consecrated life of service, and not any Catholic leanings, were responsible for the benevolent Shakespearean characterization. The advice, compassion, and help which Friar Laurence bestows on the distraught lovers, the well-intentioned, though unsuccessful, efforts on their behalf, the beautiful poetry of his speeches and their lofty ethics, all prove how firmly the Friar stood in the affection of the dramatist himself. Coleridge instances Laurence as an example of Shakespeare's reverence for the clergy as a whole, a reverence he extended towards all established ranks and professions—kings, nobles, physicians, and the like. Writing of the difference between Shakespeare's treatment of the priestly character and that of his contemporaries, he says,[1] "In Beaumont and Fletcher priests are represented as

[1] *Coleridge's Shakespearean Criticism* (Raysor), II. 145.

a vulgar mockery; and, as in others of their dramatic personages, the errors of a few are mistaken for the demeanour of the many: but in Shakespeare they always carry with them our love and respect. He made no injurious abstracts: he took no copies from the worst parts of our nature; and, like the rest, his characters of priests are truly drawn from the general body."

Friar John, Laurence's helper, another Franciscan, has a minor part to play in *Romeo and Juliet*. He is sent with a letter to Romeo, but fails to deliver it, with the result that the banished lover believes Juliet is really dead when she is only under the influence of Friar Laurence's sleeping potion. Romeo kills himself in an agony of grief, an action imitated by Juliet when she awakens and learns the ghastly truth.

Shakespeare's liking for friars and monks finds further expression in *Much Ado About Nothing*. The story of Bandello, on which the play is largely based, contains no monk; but the friendly figure of Friar Francis is introduced into the comedy, and is instrumental in clearing Hero of the vile charge of unchastity brought against her by the villainous Don John. There is nothing particularly pious and saintly in Friar Francis's words or actions; and considering him in conjunction with Friar Laurence, the Rev. Ronald Bayne writes,[1] "The two characters entitle us only to say that Shakespeare was not unwilling, when the exigencies of his art put pressure upon him, to draw friars whose kindness of heart, sound judgment, and delicacy of feeling would do honour to any religion. But in these creations Shakespeare approaches his characters on their human side;

[1] *Shakespeare's England*, I. 54.

they are not champions or even types of their own religion."

Shakespeare introduces another friar, not found in his original, in the play of *As You Like It*. According to Lodge's novel, *Rosalynde*, the exiled Duke regains his state from his usurping brother, Frederick, by force of arms. The Poet, however, imputes this happy consummation to the religious eloquence of a friar, whom Frederick chanced to meet when advancing in force against the exiles.

Jaques reports (v. 4. 165–171):

> And to the skirts of this wild wood he came;
> Where meeting with an old religious man,
> After some question with him, was converted
> Both from his enterprise and from the world;
> His crown bequeathing to his banish'd brother.
> And all their lands restored to them again
> That were with him exiled.

Another instance of Shakespeare's great interest in friars occurs in the *Merchant of Venice*. Stephano, Portio's servant, reporting his mistress's return to Belmont, says (v. 1. 30–32): "She doth stray about By holy crosses, where she kneels and prays For happy wedlock hours." When Lorenzo asks, "Who comes with her?" Stephano answers, "None but a holy hermit and her maid." There is no dramatic purpose whatsoever served by this "holy hermit," who does not actually appear; and critics have been much puzzled by him. Possibly Shakespeare intended to allot yet another kindly action to a monk, but changed his mind when bringing his comedy to a speedy end.

Shakespeare is consistent with his treatment elsewhere when he makes the Duke Vincentio, the man who controls the action and judges the people of

Measure for Measure, assume the habit of a friar in order that he may the better see without being seen. The Duke visits a monastery and confers with the "holy father," Friar Thomas, explaining his reasons for disguise, begging a habit, and asking to be instructed, "How I may formally in person bear me Like a true friar" (I. 3. 47–48). We meet another Friar in *Measure for Measure*, Friar Peter, who Dr. Johnson suggested was really meant for the same person, previously called Friar Thomas. Friar Peter gives the Duke valuable help in his holy work of reform, receives his confidential instructions, and reports his calumniators.

In referring above to the imprisonment of the outspoken Bishop of Carlisle in *Richard II*, we saw him committed to the charge of the Abbot of Westminster. But this Abbot was not by any means one of Shakespeare's godly, peaceable, and friendly monks. He told his prisoner that he was himself concerned in a conspiracy against Henry IV. His treason was discovered; and when the king threatened him, we learn that "with clog of conscience and sour melancholy" he "yielded up his body to the grave" (v. 6. 20–21). The Abbot of Westminster was presented to the dramatist with the other historical material for his play, as was Peter of Pomfret, the hermit of *King John*, who prophesies that on the next Ascension Day the king will deliver up his crown. John orders the unwelcome prophet to be hanged, but since he was forced on that very day to yield his crown to Pandulph, he has to admit that in a sense Peter of Pomfret prophesied correctly.

We note that those references to monks which can be described as unfriendly are all historically justified by Holinshed and are not the free judgment of Shakespeare. In the same category is the story of the monk who poisoned King John at Swinstead Abbey, because, so the rumour goes, he threatened to make corn dearer. Hubert says, "The king, I fear, is poison'd by a monk" (v. 6. 23). The statement appears in Holinshed, also in the old play, *The Troublesome Raigne* . . . etc., where the name of the poisoner is given as Thomas.

There are a few scattered references to friars throughout the plays, which are worth quoting. In *Henry VIII* a certain Nicholas Henton (according to Holinshed, Nicholas Hopkins, "a monk of an house of the Chartreux order beside Bristow, called Henton") is reported as urging the Duke of Buckingham to treasonable thought and action by false prophecy. Cross-examined by the King, the resentful surveyor, who has been dismissed from the Duke's employ, gives evidence (i. 2. 146–150):

Surv.	He was brought to this
	By a vain prophecy of Nicholas Henton.
King	What was that Henton?
Surv.	Sir, a Chartreux friar,
	His confessor, who fed him every minute
	With words of sovereignty.

Confession to a friar is referred to again in *All's Well That Ends Well* (iv. 3. 124). In *The Taming of the Shrew* we have a reference to the English name of the Franciscans, the Grey Friars (iv. 1. 148–149):

> It was the friar of orders grey,
> As he forth walked on his way.

While recognizing that "all hoods make not monks"

(*Henry VIII* iii. 1. 23), Shakespeare was particularly well-disposed towards the members of the monastic and mendicant religious orders. He was equally tolerant and broad-minded in his attitude towards nuns and convents. No doubt the poetic element of the sheltered life in the women's case made a similar appeal to him. Certainly he treats them with every respect and admires their virtue and chastity.

Just as Shakespeare introduced into his plays friars who had no place in the originals, so in *The Comedy of Errors* he inserted the character of Æmilia, the abbess at Ephesus, who has no counterpart in the *Menaechmi* of Plautus. Æmilia refuses to surrender Antipholus of Syracuse, who has sought sanctuary in her abbey, until she has used all her means to restore him to his right mind. "It is," she says, "a branch and parcel of mine oath, A charitable duty of my order." (v. 1. 106–107). It transpires that the abbess is really the wife of Ægeon and the mother of the twin Antipholuses, who, after the loss of husband and sons at sea, sought, like so many women buffeted and broken by the world, the peace and balm of the cloistered life.

In *Measure for Measure* we have a true nun in Francisca, who explains the rules of the sisterhood of Saint Clare to Isabella, a novice desirous of entering the order. The following dialogue shows the Poet's acquaintance of the strict rules that bound the nun (i. 4. 1–15):

> *Isab.* And have you nuns no further privileges?
> *Fran.* Are not these large enough?
> *Isab.* Yes, truly: I speak not as desiring more;
> But rather wishing a more strict restraint
> Upon the sisterhood, the votarists of Saint Clare.

Lucio (*within*) : Ho! Peace be in this place!
Isab.   Who's that which calls?
Fran.   It is a man's voice. Gentle Isabella,
               Turn you the key, and know his business of him;
               You may, I may not; you are yet unsworn.
               When you have vow'd, you must not speak with men
               But in the presence of the prioress:
               Then, if you speak, you must not show your face;
               Or, if you show your face, you must not speak.

But the pure and saintly Isabella learns that there are more precious things in life even than lifelong chastity, and one of them is affection for one's fellow-beings. She never enters the nunnery, but becomes the wife of the Duke.

Shakespeare's other allusions to nuns are eloquent of his wonder at their self-denial and his admiration of their asceticism. When Hermia in *Midsummer Night's Dream* rejects the suitor chosen for her by her father, Duke Theseus warns her of the alternative (I. I. 67–68):

               . . . fair Hermia, question your desires;
               Know of your youth, examine well your blood,
               Whether, if you yield not to your father's choice,
               You can endure the livery of a nun;
               For aye to be in shady cloister mew'd,
               To live a barren sister all your life,
               Chanting faint hymns to the cold fruitless moon.
               Thrice-blessed they that master so their blood,
               To undergo such maiden pilgrimage;
               But earthlier happy is the rose distill'd,
               Than that which, withering on a virgin thorn,
               Grows, lives, and dies in single blessedness.

The above fairly represents Shakespeare's thoughts on nuns and convents. He speaks of a nun's kisses as having "the very ice of chastity" in them (*As you Like It*, III. 4. 18), and in the same meaning of "a nun's

lip to the friar's mouth" in *All's Well* (II. 2. 28). He
has, also, a reference or two to the retreat of women
to the convent in times of danger or sorrow. When
Friar Laurence sees that the waking Juliet must soon
learn that her Romeo is dead, he says to her, "Come,
I'll dispose of thee Among a sisterhood of holy nuns"
(v. 3. 157). Likewise the wretched Queen Elizabeth
of *Richard III*, having lost her princely sons, declares
that her daughters "shall be praying nuns, not weep-
ing queens" (IV. 4. 201). The only reference to nuns
in Shakespeare's works that could be construed at
a stretch as disparaging, occurs in that early poem,
A Lover's Complaint. There it is recorded of a gay Don
Juan that he has so enflamed the heart of "a sister
sanctified" that she would "the caged cloister fly"
and turn her back on religion. Although the passage
reveals an anti-Catholic strain in Shakespeare, it is
not a serious reflection on nuns as a class.

Turning from the consecrated men and women of
the Roman Catholic orders to the Protestant parish
clergy, we find a very different attitude on the part
of the Poet. This was not dictated by any religious
preference, but by the fact that, as regards monks
and friars, he was constrained to draw upon his
imagination, and was rather apt to idealize his conception; whereas for his portraits of the parish priest
he was able to rely upon his own observation.

The country clergy of Shakespeare's day were not,
it must be admitted, distinguished either for their
learning or their spiritual zeal. The rapid changes,
the miserable pay, the abuse of patronage, all tended
to drive the best type of man from the ministry. The
Reformation Party laid much store upon the sermon,
but many of the priests were so illiterate and in-

efficient that preaching was out of the question, and they could only be permitted to read what was set down for them in the manuals. To this class the title "Dominus," or "Sir," came to be applied, though originally given to those who had taken the first degree of Bachelor of Arts. When used in this connection, "Sir" was contrasted with "Master", which signified a priest or minister who had graduated at a university.

Shakespeare's parish priests are faithful reflections of those with whom he came in contact. He is mildly humorous at their expense, but never unkind nor malicious. He is careful to avoid coarseness, and always invites us to regard his Sir Hugh's with respect becoming their office. Sir Nathaniel, the curate of *Love's Labour's Lost* is desperately anxious to create an impression of learning and respectability. His flattery of the pedantic Holofernes, the schoolmaster, with his Latin interjections and heavy verbosity, reveals a simple soul who longs to be thought scholarly. He cannot bear to be laughed at. When he has made a terrible hash of the part of Alexander in the Masque of the Nine Worthies, Costard says of him (v. 2. 584–588):

There, an't shall please you; a foolish mild man; an honest man, look you, and soon dashed. He is a marvellous good neighbour faith, and a very good bowler: but, for Alisander—alas, you see how 'tis—a little o'erparted.

Sir Hugh Evans, the impulsive and choleric little Welshman of the *Merry Wives of Windsor* is a delightful sketch of the simple, unlearned country parson. His amusing Welshisms—"one that makes fritters of English," says Falstaff (v. 5. 151)—add to his comicality. Shakespeare means us to laugh at him, but not disrespectfully. He is kindly and earnest, sprinkles his conversation with such pious interjections as "Got deliver to a joyful resurrections!" (I. I. 53), and gravely pronounces such platitudes as, "I do despise a liar as I do despise one that is false, or as I despise one that is not true" (I. I. 69–71). He takes his profession very seriously and says to Shallow (I. I. 30–34):

> If Sir John Falstaff have committed disparagements unto you, I am of the church, and will be glad to do my benevolence to make atonements and compremises between you.

In the last scene, in Windsor Park, where the Fairies worry and pinch Falstaff, Sir Hugh says to the wicked old rascal, "Serve Got, and leave your desires, and fairies will not pinse you." (V. 5. 136).

Sir Hugh is delicious in his pedagogical rôle and betrays his laughable simplicity. He is always ready to take an interest in his neighbours' affairs, whether they ask for it or not, and by no means despises the pleasures of the table. His mock duel with the French physician, Doctor Caius, when he is "full of chollors" and "trempling of mind," with "great dispositions to cry" (III. I. 11 and 22) is Shakespeare in his best humorous vein. And while the dramatist means us to chuckle at Sir Hugh, his portrait is not at all unkind, slighting, or irreverent.

In *As You Like It* Shakespeare introduces another untutored parson, who is not quite so reputable as Sir Hugh and Sir Nathaniel. Sir Oliver Martext, "the vicar of the next village" (III. 3. 43), arrives in the forest to marry Touchstone and Audrey. He is a stickler for correct procedure—the woman "must be given, or the marriage is not lawful" (70). But Jacques, apparently, has grave suspicions of Martext's bona fide, for he advises Touchstone, "Have a good priest that can tell you what marriage is" (86). He prevents the ceremony; and Sir Oliver declares, "'Tis no matter: ne'er a fantastical knave of them all shall flout me of my calling" (108).

Martext is a Shakespearean skit on Martin Marprelate, a famous Puritan writer, who by means of fiery pamphlets attacked the Established Church. The Bishops were no literary match for Marprelate, and well-known writers like Lyly and Greene were commissioned to answer him. Marprelate was finally hanged; and Jacques's suspicion of Martext's order was probably suggested by Shakespeare's own anti-Puritan feeling.

In *Twelfth Night* Feste the Clown disguises himself as Sir Topas, the curate, and visits Malvolio, imprisoned on feigned suspicion of not being quite right in the head. Feste assumes the voice and character of the parson—"I am one of those gentle ones that will use the devil himself with courtesy" (IV. 2. 36) —and plays a cruel practical joke on the unhappy steward, stolidly refusing to accept his pleas of sanity. At the end of the play, when he learns how he has been tricked, Malvolio is furious and swears to be revenged.

Passing from Shakespeare's amused but kindly and respectful treatment of the parish clergy, we may consider the minor clerical characters, who make brief appearances on the stage in many of the plays. They are not sufficiently important to be included in the classifications considered above, but are added at the end to make our list of the dramatist's priests complete.

In considering *2 Henry VI*[1] we have already referred to two disreputable priestly characters in John Hume and John Southwell. They associate with Mother Jourdain, the witch, and Bolingbroke, the conjurer, in the practice of necromancy, and wickedly impose upon the unfortunate Duchess of Gloucester. In the midst of their ceremonies they are surprised by the Dukes of York and Buckingham, arrested, brought before the King, condemned and executed.

In *1 Henry IV* a certain Sir Michael appears (IV. 4), who is described as "a friend" of Scroop, Archbishop of York. The prefix "Sir" and the deliverance to him of confidential letters have led many to regard Sir Michael as the Archbishop's chaplain.

Sir Christopher Urswick, later chaplain to Henry VII, makes a brief appearance in *Richard III*, where he is sent to Richmond by Lord Derby, who hears from him the names of those nobles who are supporting the Earl against the Crookback. In the same play two Bishops appear, one each side of Richard, when he is assuming a piety that he believes will help him to the Crown. In Scene 2 of Act III there is yet another cleric, "good Sir John," who is apparently Lord Hastings' confessor. Finally, a priest is introduced into the last scene of *Twelfth Night* to testify to the betrothal of Olivia and Sebastian. His appearance is useful as confirming our views of Shakespeare's insistence on obedience to convention in the matter of true love. Note the Priest's evidence (v. 1. 159–164):

> A contract of eternal bond of love,
> Confirm'd by mutual joinder of your hands,
> Attested by the holy close of lips,

[1] Part I. pp. 139–41.

>Strengthen'd by interchangement of your rings;
>And all the ceremony of this compact
>Seal'd in my function, by my testimony.

In *Henry VIII* several of the higher clergy are introduced into the trial scene. John Longland, Bishop of Lincoln and confessor to the King, admits his part in counselling the divorce. The Bishops of Ely, St. Asaph, and Rochester appear, according to the stage directions, as counsel for the Queen, but take no part in the dialogue.

Shakespeare has no great use for pagan priests. In *Troilus and Cressida* we have Calchas, the Trojan priest, and Cassandra the prophetess; and in the Roman dramas soothsayers play a not unimportant rôle. For the most part the dramatist was guilty, as in *Hamlet*, of religious anachronisms, and introduced Christian priests, beliefs, and customs in scenes laid wholly in pagan times.

One final observation: In dramatizing history, Shakespeare often brought characters on the stage for no other reason than that they were mentioned in Holinshed or Plutarch. This accounts for the many appearances of priests in minor parts of no dramatic significance. It must be remembered, however, that the picturesque robes of the higher clergy often provided a welcome addition of colour to a stage devoid of scenery.

INDEX

Y